JOURNEY TO THE FIFTH DIMENSION—A DIVINE JOURNEY

NEPHELON GALAXY

Maria Zavou

BALBOA.
PRESS

A DIVISION OF HAY HOUSE

ISBN: 978-1-4525-4620-9 (sc)
ISBN: 978-1-4525-4621-6 (e)

Balboa Press books may be ordered through booksellers or by contacting:

Balboa Press
A Division of Hay House
1663 Liberty Drive
Bloomington, IN 47403
www.balboapress.com
1-(877) 407-4847

Because of the dynamic nature of the Internet, any web addresses or links contained in this book may have changed since publication and may no longer be valid. The views expressed in this work are solely those of the author and do not necessarily reflect the views of the publisher, and the publisher hereby disclaims any responsibility for them.

The author of this book does not dispense medical advice or prescribe the use of any technique as a form of treatment for physical, emotional, or medical problems without the advice of a physician, either directly or indirectly. The intent of the author is only to offer information of a general nature to help you in your quest for emotional and spiritual well-being. In the event you use any of the information in this book for yourself, which is your constitutional right, the author and the publisher assume no responsibility for your actions.

Any people depicted in stock imagery provided by Thinkstock are models, and such images are being used for illustrative purposes only.

Certain stock imagery © Thinkstock.

Printed in the United States of America

Balboa Press rev. date:2/22/2012

CONTENTS

MY HIGHER SELF "THE TRAINING"

THE AWAKENING

THE CONNECTION

THE ENLIGHTENMENT

THE PYRAMID AND ITS APPLICATION

A HIGHER COMMUNION WITH MY "SPIRITUAL COUNTERPART"

GODS AND DEMIGODS

THE HUMAN DOLPHINS

THE DISRUPTION OF EARTH'S MAGNETIC FIELD

COLLISION OF MATTER AND ANTI-MATTER

THE POLAR SHIFT

THE FALLEN SOULS

METATRON INITIATION

THE FOURTH JOURNEY

THE GENESIS AND THE FORMATION OF THE NEW ENERGY BODY

THE CODES OF IMMORTALITY

THE REGENERATING SYMBOLS

THE REVITALIZATION COMMANDS

ARCHANGEL ZAKCHIEL DURING THE INITIATION

SUBLIME COMMUNION WITH METATRON

THE FIFTH JOURNEY

KARMIC REMOVALS

GATE NUMBER NINE

THE RELEASE

KARMIC IMPRINTS

KARMIC CORDS

DNA CHANGE

NEW NERVE-CELL MORPHOLOGY

TRANSFORMATION OF THE MENTAL BODY

MUTATION OF THE HEART

THEY KEYS OF TRANSMUTATION

HIGH FREQUENCY VIBRATIONS. DIVINE BIOLOGY

THE SEAL OF IMMORTALITY

ALIGNMENTS

FOCALISATION SHIFT OF THE SEVEN CENTRES

UPGRADING CELLS OF A SUPERIOR FREQUENCY

MENTAL BODY

THE FIRST THREE CENTRES

ALIGNMENT OF THE EPIPHYSIS

ALIGNMENT OF THE HYPOPHISIS

ALIGNMENT OF THE THYROID GLAND

ALIGNMENT OF THE HEART

ALIGNMENT

SOLAR PLEXUS - GENITAL CENTRE

GENERAL ALIGNMENT

EXPERIENTIAL JOURNEY TO PLANET POSEIDON

THE NEW GENETIC CODE

THE NEW FORCE OF CREATION

LIGHT-EMITTING DISCS

THE JOURNEY TO THE RED PLANET

THE CHRISM OF THE LUMINOUS WARRIOR

THE PERSONAL WEAPON

TEACHING ON HANDLING THE WEAPON

THE INITIATION OF ARTEMIS

UPGRADING RELATIONSHIPS AND EMOTIONS.

INITIATION OF THE HOLY MARRIAGE

ATTRACTION OF SOUL MATES

THE GENETIC UNION

THE BIPOLAR COUPLE

PRE-INITIATION OF THE CHRISTIC VIBRATION

THE GOLDEN PLANET

THE JOURNEY

BEING BEAMED TO THE GOLDEN PLANET

HYPER FREQUENCIES OF THE SIXTH DIMENSION

THE UPGRADING SUBSTANCE

THE PRIMORDIAL STRUCTURE OF THE DIVINE CELL

NEW LIFE PLAN

CHRISTIC SOLAR VIBRATION

AWAKENED SOULS

ELOHIM NEPHELIM

MARIA ZAVOU

MARIA ZAVOU

Maria Zavou is a painter and hagiographer. She has studied at the School of Good Arts and the University of Saint Andrews at Chicago and has specialized in painting and hagiography. She is the author of the books: "The Awakening" and "The Return of the Angels".

She is a pioneer of spirituality and a channel of higher communication with spiritual masters and energies. She specializes in fields concerning superior consciousness and alternative energy therapy.

Through a continuous higher type of communication, specific information has been imparted to her, concerning man and the evolution of humanity, with the intention of assisting man to awaken his internal plan within his soul.

This specific wisdom which she has successfully developed, she conveys to the souls of those who are ready and prepared to follow their inspiration leaving behind obsolete ideas and beliefs and outmoded stereotypes.

Through constant self-improvement and meditation she has received the "gift" of intuitively perceiving and actually "seeing" the Higher Selves of people as well as the Archangels surrounding and supporting them. After many years of training she facilitates people to come into contact and to unify with the divine energies of their Higher Selves. The ways through which we can connect and be unified with them are taught at and presented at the seminars she holds.

Astral journeys to the Fifth dimension through channeling are carried out in her unique spiritual venue. Superior types of esoteric initiations are also performed there through which man transforms, mutates and reaches higher levels of evolution.

His karmic debts are dealt with and eliminated, and man manages to unite with his Higher Self through the initiation of the Holy Marriage. Her students manage, through proper training, to consciously access the Fifth dimension. The means through which all these are feasible are highly advanced and have been imparted to Maria Zavou. Moreover, these novel techniques manage to blend harmoniously and tie in with the new evolutionary frequencies of people.

Maria Zavou operates as a receiver and constitutes a channel of very powerful energies. Through the dynamics and the potential of her groups she manages to send and convey energies of a christic vibration to Earth. At the same time she also successfully provides her services to man by visually perceiving the karmic causes present in the bodies of various patients. Through her communication with the healer Archangels vital knowledge concerning applications of specific techniques have been imparted to her. It is through them that the angelic forces affect the bodies of people cleansing and purifying them of the dangerous toxins.

ZIRION

The escutcheon of the emerald world

INTRODUCTION

METATRON MY TEACHER
A PERSONAL MESSAGE RECEIVED
FROM A HIGHER COMMUNION

A CONCEPTUAL ANALYSIS

THE DIMENSIONS OF GOD
THE ANGELIC FORCES
THE MASTERS
Archangel METATRON
PELEUS – NEPHELE
MASTER ALVATAR
MASTERS ARION AND ARTEMIS
IRIAN
THE PYTHAGOREANS
JOHN THE BAPTIST THE FORERUNNER
MASTER MELCHISEDEK
MELCHIOR
SAINT CYPRIAN
MASTER AETHRA
THE HIGHER ANGELIC SELF
THE ENERGY BODIES
THE ENERGY CENTERS

Pyramids of genetic mutation

INTRODUCTION

I was thirty-two years old when for the first time I experienced a higher type of communion with the masters of Nephelon galaxy. It was then when the veil of illusion was lifted from my mind and soul. The teachers guided me and taught me how to understand myself and how to become aware of what caused my problems. They also made known to me that each and every one of us has to pay the price for everything he/she causes on his/her own. I came to the realization then that what is referred to as cosmic and universal perception remains untouched and unaffected by the influences of the various civilizations, societies, cultures and countries. Instead, it operates independently of the archives of each planet and beyond the galaxy.

In my first book "The Awakening" I describe my long esoteric journey and the training I had received from my Higher Self and the masters of the Fifth dimension residing in my homeland, the Emerald planet.

The trials and tribulations I underwent and had to endure broke my spirit, but the fire inside me that had lit in my soul urged me to keep going. I communicated with Archangelic orders and with my Higher Self.

These experiences of mine as well as the teachings I had received are all well documented in my second book "The Return of the Angels". The contact I had with the angels opened a path towards joy, happiness and optimism. That book was received with love because it activated people's love towards those creatures of God. People started receiving help and guidance and began finding solutions to their problems.

The most important thing in my life was when I came into contact with my Higher Self and the unification procedure began. Later on came the time for my teaching, the time when I would convey my knowledge.

The pictures of the future began to slowly unfold within me.

Since 1999 I have had the honor to be following the guiding light of master Metatron.

In order for somebody to reach the point of positive higher communication, dedication, practice, willingness and love for the spiritual world are the elements that are required. Only then is it possible for somebody to attract respective spiritual entities that will take it upon themselves to make proper adjustments rectifying problems in the chakras and rendering the person able to function as a pure receiver devoid of the drawbacks of his personality and the toxicity of his emotions. When man has worked much on his lower personality and has managed to come into contact with his angelic counterpart then he has also succeeded in attracting a superior teacher from the spiritual fields.

That's how I became a receiver and a channel of powerful energies intuitively confirming that all the rays passing through the Earth emit in frequencies of inconceivable speed and brightness. Following that, many regions and many souls come into tune with them acquiring thus the ability to evolve.

The third period of my life began after a broadening of my experiences that occurred through my astral journeys to the Fifth dimension. After many solitary intuitive journeys to its planets I was provided with the knowledge concerning the erasure of karmic debts, the knowledge of an intergalactic dialect as well as of the security codes that open the gates leading to the Fifth dimension.

The Fifth dimension is a dimension of action and it is located in the future. That is the place where all the discoveries are made and are later channeled to people who are compatible and open-minded here on Earth. The trainees in the Fifth dimension also become the transformers through whom novel ideas are later transferred to our planet. These ideas are then picked up by people possessing a higher type of intelligence. Thus, a great number of people materialize on a daily basis whatever advanced idea they conceptualize.

My groups and I travel just like time-travellers to Nephelon galaxy and become the recipients of primeval knowledge, transmutational procedures and the divine seed, so that we become capable of forming our lives in the way we see consider fit. The geneticists of the Fifth dimension, who are alchemists channel into the trainees divine protoplasm and divine seeds that activate mutations.

Through the mutational programmes the students acquire hyper-consciousness and hyper-intellect just by remembering that they are divine beings, while their higher frequencies alter and transform the morphogenetic fields of Earth.

It is through various initiations that the trainees align themselves with the divine cells of their genitors. As a result their DNA regains its divine attributes that it had been deprived of due to the Fall. Human matter becomes more refined and as the divine gifts start to emerge the students become more refined as well. With every journey to the Fifth dimension people enter and participate in even more advanced upgrading programmes and eventually they acquire the potential to change and they do change their future by designing it again from scratch.

Quality of life, harmony, and abundance are some elements characteristic of their future lives. The primeval nerve cells that they receive reinforce their immune systems. Their frequency becomes more etheric and their cells do not succumb to the earthly wear and tear.

The students are trained in ways to retain the life-giving energy of the Fifth dimension, which also opens up the road to longevity and immortality that the meta-humans will enjoy and experience.

Through a higher type of communion it was made known to me that the Earth during this specific age keeps continuously vibrating as it is completing the final cycle of its evolution. Its energy shift has begun and will be completed in about 2012-2015. Through this planetary motion, true knowledge will be unleashed, will become available to the wide public and will overturn and upset whatever we have taken for granted.

The truth concerning the origin of the Earth and life on it will be revealed while previous speculations will be dismissed. Simultaneously, a new age will dawn, a new evolutionary epoch for the planet will commence.

The time-travellers of the Fifth dimension operate as transformers of energies and assist Earth's soul to realize its transition in a milder manner.

This book contains mutational and transmutational codes that will activate the psychic archives of man.

As a result, whoever reads it will in a subliminal way pass through the various initiatory stages and will experience and undergo internal purification.

MARIA ZAVOU

METATRON
MY TEACHER

A PERSONAL MESSAGE RECEIVED
FROM A HIGHER COMMUNION

I will teach you the wisdom of primordial faith.

Entering the realm where ideas dwell you will have to confront a host of perceptions and beliefs that both new and old souls held dear and that have eventually and progressively been recorded on primeval scripts. The texts which you yourself have recorded through the ages await you now in a transcendental domain you yourself have created.

This realm constitutes a projection of your essence. By "recovering" this knowledge from your archive you have stabilized the central axis of communication with me.

This specific moment you should attempt to cast your eyes beyond the world of your spiritual projections.

Your teachers believe that you are ready, both psychically and spiritually, to pass through the gate that leads to enlightened thoughts of your own divine essence.

During the tutelage you will receive under the great masters many of your beliefs and perceptions will change. You are now on your personal road to Damascus. Your transition will be gradual, and as you pass certain trials parts of and various hidden aspects of your being will be enlightened. The codes responsible for the opening up of your soul appear to no one if one is not ready yet.

The plan concerning your teaching I have presented to your teachers, your guides and to the angels. They will all help you to succeed and progress while you are under my protection.

You will record many components that will be passed onto you as an overtone and will become evident in matter.

I am fully aware of your fears and your doubts but I reassure you that everything will be all right. Trust your spiritual counterpart, your Higher Self Mellenios. It knows the exact frequencies that will guide and progressively lead you to a new plan of knowledge.

A CONCEPTUAL ANALYSIS

THE DIMENSIONS OF GOD

God is an integrated entity that contains spirit, psyche (both the male and the female counterpart) and matter. That is, God constitutes a trihypostatic persona. The material substance of God is reflected throughout the Universe, the planets and human beings. Every planet and every star constitutes a living entity which moves and is contained by God, who simultaneously governs our Universe.

Using our contemporary means we have the potentiality to scan our galaxy. The immenseness of God's entity though we cannot see. Our brain is structured in such a way that it can perceive only whatever is substantial and whatever it can handle through the process of reasoning. All else is simply erased from man's memory just like hallucinations vanish. The male and the female counterpart are in a continuous connection. When these two higher parts of God are united within him, they give birth to smaller gods, the Higher Selves.

God is composed of ten dimensions. The spiritual part of God, the superior intellect, resides in the tenth dimension. This is the place where his thoughts are given birth to. In spite of this though, there are two more dimensions. These tend to define the zones which also constitute the gates through which the passage to other universes can be achieved.

The Higher Selves are born as small gods in the ninth dimension. Then, they dichotomize both their spiritual and their psychic essence in the eighth, the seventh and the Sixth dimensions. Christ and all the other great teachers are projected in the sixth. There we find the see of Michael the Archangel. This latter entity also constitutes a huge neural network that engulfs all the elements of the Universe.

The final active presence of the Higher Selves occurs in the Fifth dimension. From there they dichotomize again and send a part of their psyche to materialize in our dimension, the third. The fifth is the dimension in which the Higher Selves become active as conscious beings.

The fourth dimension is the astral one. It consists of interstellar matter in a fluidic state, and it displays height, breadth, and length as well as the relativity of time and it incorporates three levels, the higher, the middle and the lower one.

After death, souls enter the astral plane. There the souls experience a small interlude between their incarnations, that is, their descent into the third dimension in order to learn new lessons.

The third dimension is our dimension, the place where we live and we evolve. Here, the material manifestation of our Higher Selves is formulated and the material carrier (body) of our soul is laid to rest after natural death occurs. When the soul completes its training it returns to its real home which is the Fifth dimension. We, the people of planet Earth tend to operate within the properties defined by our three- dimensional world. We usually perceive only the dimensions of length, width and height. However, other parallel planes also exist that are called etheric.

Ether rejuvenates and supports the structure of the planet. It is an intermediary layer upon which the unconscious memory of the Earth and of all the people who have enjoyed a wealth of experience during all the evolutionary cycles of the planet are recorded. Many name this etheric dimension as the "Akashic archives" or "Akashic records". The history of the planet has been recorded therein, while the past, the present, and the future there become one. As far as the formation of the future is concerned facts can change in compliance with the intervention of man's drastic or concerted actions. Thus, the whole planet can collectively redefine its future and change it.

The etheric dimension, which also constitutes the electromagnetic field of the Earth, is inhabited by a plethora of elementals like gnomes, undines, sylphs and salamanders.

The second dimension is the dimension in which various multi-cellular organisms live and is located in the centre of the Earth, in contrast to the first dimension where unicellular organisms live.

The Angelic Forces

The Angelic forces are divided into three hierarchical types or spheres. Each hierarchical type is divided into two different branches, the forces of direction which are represented by the Elohim and the forces of action which are represented by the Nephelim. The first sphere further represents the archetypal world, the spiritual manifestation and emanation of God. The Seraphim, the Cherubim and the Thrones (also known as the Ophanim), from which love, harmony, and will, emanate respectively, are all choirs that constitute this type of hierarchy.

The second hierarchical type constitutes the psychic manifestation of God, the world of creation, the feminine side, the world of birth and death. It is composed of the Dominions (in Hellenic "Kyriotites", also known as Hasmallim), the Virtues (in Hellenic "Dynameis" also known as Malakim and Tarshishim), and the Powers (in Hellenic "Exousiai"), which represent wisdom, movement and form.

The third hierarchical type relates to the fourth and the Fifth dimensions and comprises the world of form that mediates between it and the higher forces. Within this final triad or sphere we find the principalities (in Hellenic "arches"), the Archangels and the angels, that represent time, fire, and the messengers. This is the world in which the Higher Selves of all people are also located. Right after this world comes the material world, the third dimension, where we all live, study and are taught together at the great school of earth.

The principalities are forces that form and structure the civilization and social fabrics of each country. The Archangels oversee the formation and development of the nations and in cooperation with the Higher Selves they direct the souls, whenever those descend for an incarnation, to one of the morphic levels of development. The power the Archangels possess is such that they can collectively be everywhere (be omnipresent), and be aware, at any given time, of which way an entire nation is moving towards. They are of a very acute and very high intelligence. Whole armies of angels exhibiting varying skills are trained by each Archangel.

Spiritual hierarchy constitutes a form of Higher Council of both the Archangelic and angelic powers. It is governed and supervised by the entity of Christ in collaboration with other great masters. Christ tends to be in a constant and direct connection with the divine essence and hence channels pure energy towards the celestial worlds. During this specific time and age, each one of the great masters is attuned to souls that have already chosen a corresponding frequency ray through which they are instructed by them. The forces of Nature together with the elemental realms of fire-air-water-and earth are controlled by the aforementioned principalities and the Archangels. If a slight disharmony occurs the angels intervene, however, if a considerable and more significant disharmony takes place then the principalities and the Archangels step in.

It is the union of divine light and divine thought (God's intellectual energy) that gives birth to the angelic entities. These entities are differently structured when compared to the Higher Selves, in that they are totally deprived of free will. However, they are governed by the divine laws. They materialize on respective fields and embark on their assigned missions, assisting God's creative task. They have no gender, and they are also deprived of the lower three energy centers (or chakras), namely the genital, the abdominal and the solar plexus chakras.

In many theosophical books, like the "Genesis", references are made to the fallen angels. It is a well known fact that some of them wanted to acquire the knowledge of dualism and of free will, possessed by the human soul. God did not deny them that knowledge. It may have even been within his plans to provide them with it. On account of this obsession, these angelic entities fell into the world of form and matter and their energy was condensed. Since the first day of their creation they had been structured to serve and assist God's plan. It was exactly because of this trait that by falling into much lower frequencies they totally forgot about their assignment and slowly but gradually mutated into non- positive entities. Since then, they are continuously trying to lure men's souls and to feed off their lower selves in order to survive.

Their fall eventually served the divine plan, because whenever the soul is reincarnated it bears within it the duality psyche-personality and free will. Thus, through many trials and tribulations and after having experienced both sides one learns and is trained. The soul is free to choose either the dark side or the bright one. The lesson that the soul needs to obtain has to do with internal balance and the upgrading of one's personality, which when aligned with the Higher Self will produce no karmic causality any more.

THE MASTERS

The masters and the Archangels are analytically presented in my book entitled "The return of the Angels", whereas in this book, I am only presenting information that I deem essential concerning them. Many divine couples whom in the planet's past we have called Gods are now operating in the Fifth dimension providing guidelines and directing the evolutionary programs through their apprentices here on earth. Some of these entities are Artemis (Diana), Athena (or Athene, or Minerva), Orpheus, Hermes, and John the Baptist (the Precursor or Forerunner). In addition, some healer Archangels that belong to higher orders, like the Archangels Vahiar, Eloim, and Zochriel also operate in that dimension, as do great teachers like Ilarion, Hyacinth, and Arion. In my book they are mentioned with the names they were known by when they first appeared on planet earth. Each one of these entities has a different name in the Fifth dimension. In the intuitive journeys however, they project their older vibration-name in order to be recognized by us. With the passage of time they have evolved and are now dwelling in the domains of the Fifth dimension. There, the masters work together with the geneticists and the healers aiming at the mutation and alignment of the human souls with their Higher Selves.

ARCHANGEL METATRON

Archangel Metatron is referred to in mystic books as Enoch and as being the only Archangel who has incarnated into many different distinguished and prominent figures in order to guide humanity. His work, just as a lot of information concerning his Archangelic and angelic realms, have all been recorded on papyri found at Qumran.

As a master he is aware of all the various levels of soul reformation. He has mutated genetically and is composed of an Archangel's cellular structure and that of a man's combined.

In that way he manages to maintain the attributes of an Archangel and the attributes of a human simultaneously. His human aspects have reached very high levels of evolution. He has an advanced neural network

and advanced abilities to project into various dimensions. He is able to project himself in an etheric form on Earth and on other planets simultaneously, whenever this is required, in order to boost the evolutionary process. He can also project himself through embryos (souls) that are born on the planet. This can be achieved through the process of bipartition, meaning that a part of his psyche is integrated in a chosen embryo, usually of crystalline structure. What is more, he is a great geneticist.

At this moment he is a teacher of the Fifth and Sixth dimensions and is in continuous contact with them. During the mutations he is responsible for the whole neural network and for the four cerebral lobes of the energy body.

PELEUS NEPHELE

This is the historic couple known as Theseus and Ariadne, which is now a bipolar deity couple of the Fifth dimension. They are the Archons of the Orange planet and they represent the perfect couple and love of all levels. When we beseech them to help us, we gradually open up the various levels of higher love and fulfillment consequently leading to the awakening of other humans.

MASTER ALVATAR

He is the Archon of Poseidon and considered to be the father of missions concerned with upgrading procedures. He has a multi-faceted crystal in his possession with which he manages to pass on equilibrating energies that mainly concern the human axis of balance, extending from the neck down to the coccyx, applying thus the required alignments along the way.

MASTERS ARION AND ARTEMIS

Many divine couples acting as genitors exist. Arion is the master who is responsible for training the students before receiving Archangel Michael's chrism. He is the representative teacher of defense and knowledge. With his assistance students manage to balance the lower part of their personalities with the brighter one and become capable of dealing with attacks, defending themselves like worthy warriors. Artemis cooperates very closely with Goddess Earth supporting her, as far as the impending departure of her soul is concerned.

IRIAN

Irian is a high hierarchy entity and the genitor of planet Zanar and its bipolar. He handles and deals with conduits, channeling cleansing and purificatory programs to planet Earth, being fully aware at all times of the exact size of the frequency needed to be channeled. On the therapeutic scale he manages to pinpoint specific recordings present in the nervous system, both the sympathetic and the parasympathetic ones, that have influenced our lives emotionally and mentally. He is solely responsible for directing and conducting their incineration, since he alone is aware of the particular frequency needed to burn these recordings. The novel elements she inserts into the nervous tissue of the energy bodies, transmit signals to the unconscious of planet Earth. Resultingly, these transmissions aid the planet's soul to relieve itself of all those toxic recordings with which it has been impregnated and assist it in peacefully returning to its motherland.

THE PYTHAGOREANS

The Pythagoreans and the Aristotelians had opened certain gateways in ancient Hellas. The information needed to complete that process had been handed down to them by Hermes Trismegistus on emerald plates. When they left they closed the gates behind them in order to avoid entities from the etheric plane and the centre of the earth escaping into our world and assuming control of it, which is what the latter wanted to achieve. In time, these despots were vanquished and overwhelmed anew when Jesus Christ appeared.

JOHN THE BAPTIST THE FORERUNNER

He is of the grand Master's caliber, just like Metatron. During baptism he touches with his scepter the epiphysis of the energy body and baptizes it. Later on, he seals the root center, ending thus the process of reincarnation, and then goes on to touch two hearts, first that of the Higher Self and second that of the energy body, uniting them with and linking them to the final gateway, that of the Fifth dimension. With that seal we are given the capability to determine the channel of return to our heavenly homeland.

MASTER MELCHISEDEK

A great teacher who tends to deal with alchemistic mutations. He belongs to the great sphere together with Archangel Metatron and other entities. He has projected himself as a teacher here on Earth. He works on the program having to do with the return of the souls together with Archangel Metatron and Christ forming with them a trinity. He is a master who, during some incarnations, has met with souls returning to their homeland.

MELCHIOR

He is the master of the christic ray, an alchemist of emotional mutation and transmutation of the astral vehicle. He knows how to dissolve the astral body and the way to assist the conscious transition to the Fifth dimension. During the initiations he administers the necessary primordial seeds that will later assist the pupil during the assumption process, the time of which will be at hand the moment his departure from Earth will have been decided upon.

SAINT CYPRIAN

In the fields of the Fifth dimension this master is the most prominent figure involved in the purification of incompatible energies, which we have received either during our current incarnation or in previous ones. He has been trained and educated at the highest level and currently he is mostly occupied with projecting himself in our dimension, trough various carriers functioning as transformers. He follows a strict and very specific program trying to purge as many attachments to or possessions of the human souls he can. He belongs to the Archangelic ray of Zakchiel.

MASTER AETHRA

She is quite knowledgeable concerning the various frequencies running through the galaxy and is adept in syntonising them. She is also fully aware of all the frequencies of creation in the galaxy. She teaches the higher type of materialization through frequencies of electro-magnetic currents. She is capable of either gathering and shaping them or materializing various forms and objects from them.

THE HIGHER ANGELIC SELF

The union between the spiritual and psychic parts of God gives birth to the Higher angelic Self. Thus, the Higher Selves are made in God's own image and likeness. These spiritual entities are all God's children. He has bestowed upon them the gift of free will, an element that is lacking in the abilities the angelic entities possess. The Higher Self sends its psychic projection, (meaning us) here on Earth, on the material plane to learn through experience and become worthy enough to be reunited once again with its spiritual counterpart.

After the Higher Self parts from the soul, it remains in the Fifth dimension and keeps monitoring the course its psychic projection embarks upon and follows throughout its life on Earth. Its attempts and efforts lie in the notion of some day becoming capable of attracting it and beginning with it the process of reunification. However, exactly because the soul lives through many lives during which it wanders into forgetfulness and focuses totally on material pleasures, it loses the awareness it once had of its spiritual hypostasis. It needs to learn many lessons and endure a lot of pain before it liberates itself from the restrictions of physical life. Tasting the positive and negative proclivities of material life is essential in order for it to become aware of the distinction between them so as to make better choices in the future.

The Higher Self is unique. Each different soul corresponds to one and only Higher Self by which it is accompanied during all its births and all its deaths. When the psyche has not yet completed its unification with the Higher Self, after physical death occurs it is accompanied by it to the respective energy field determined by its psychic and spiritual hypostases.

THE ENERGY BODIES

Energy bodies are formulated and born from the unification of the centers of the astral body with those of the Higher Self. This spiritual type of intercourse creates an embryo which constitutes the energy body and comprises the soul's higher and more refined means of transportation. It simultaneously activates the other half, which the Higher Self had lost after the Fall. Through this unification the Holy Marriage is achieved, which Socrates, Plato and many other subsequent scholars have referred to. The newly formed energy body constitutes the soul's vehicle, which will allow it to enter the realm of the Fifth dimension. The etheric and the astral vehicles burn the moment it returns to its homeland. That procedure should not alarm anyone since it is not death, but it signifies the entry to real life.

THE ENERGY CENTERS

The energy centers (chakras) or vortices constitute an entire network through which life-sustaining energy is transferred and channeled to all of man's subtle invisible bodies including the corporeal frame as well.

The invisible bodies are the following: the etheric, the mental and the spiritual.

Man's energy centers or Chakras are seven (7): the epiphysis, the hypophysis, the center of speech and of the thyroid, the center of the heart, the solar-plexus or stomach centre, the abdominal one and the genital one.

When these centers are not aligned with the divine source and are not purified, the energies that man receives tend to be of a very low vibration. It is then that he continuously experiences negative emotions that tend to sicken his cellular system. These influences somatize into the body and manifest themselves as "physical" problems by creating illnesses that afflict the physical organs of the material body.

In particular, the energy centers are focused on and attuned to differing astral levels. The entities that dwell there feed off the energy of the toxic thoughtforms that are emitted by people. As a result the corporeal frame ages and dies. Yet, when man manages to alter the focus of his energy centers he also becomes capable of prolonging his life.

At present, the geneticists of the Fifth dimension are helping men to change the focus of their centers so that they become capable of attuning themselves to higher vibrations, especially those synchronized with the Fifth dimension. With proper training (channeling) that takes place in my spiritual groups the centers alter their focus and become permanently aligned with the Higher Self. What is more, the energy centers are detached from their connections to the astral fields, which are responsible for the occurrences of rebirths. Man is relieved of the burden he had accumulated in his soul, he is freed and acquires the ability to materialize the power, the knowledge and the wisdom he has gained from his Higher Self.

KARMIC CAUSES

Karma is the law of moral causation. Karmic causes are the ones that we have ourselves created during our various incarnations which remain now as imprints in the various astral dimensions, and can only be canceled by the entities of the Fifth dimension.

THERAPIES

There are entities in the Fifth dimension that work as specialist doctors, who cure illnesses that have developed due to emotional intoxication and karmic causes. The form any illness can take is transferred into the energy body in the Fifth dimension after having been recorded on an etheric plate. That is where the diagnosis is made and the damage is restored. Small therapeutic spherules are infused into the plaque, which spread throughout the astral vehicle eliminating the causes of the various diseases. If the disease hasn't seriously spread to other parts of the physical body, then the therapy progressively restores any damage that may have ensued.

THE KARMIC CORDS

People not possessing the higher knowledge of spirituality lead their lives being actually trapped. They are encircled by cords of illusion and toxicity that create pseudo-realities around them. These virtual situations formulate the astral levels of the fourth dimension upon which the causes of their actions are recorded forming something like etheric imprints. These causes become animated as if playing in a theatre performance in each and every incarnation here on earth. The imprints of these recordings are projected from the astral realm onto man's energy centers.

The retroactive effect experienced by these imprints activates toxic behavior and toxic choices that determine a preordained course referred to by man as destiny. Destiny actually doesn't exist. When man is liberated from the astral cords, he himself creates his own destiny, as he comes into contact with the divine element in him, his divine counterpart.

For as long as he accepts the influences of those karmic imprints though, he continues to lack the realization of his own true nature. In that way, the toxic decisions he makes and the vices of the lower part of his personality governing him sustain themselves and are continuously nourished by the dark currents of the toxic entities. Consequently, without actually realizing it man adds more karmic causes to his personal spiritual archives. Under these circumstances he is driven to psychic conflicts and suffering. As a direct consequence of this toxicity to which he exposes himself, illnesses arise which in turn reach dreadful proportions that eventually overwhelm him. It is usually during this time that he turns to external sources to identify with and find the root and the causes of his suffering, instead of looking inside, so as to achieve self-realization. He tends to blame his immediate environment and is incapable of comprehending that the causes of his personal pain are actually the end result of his own personal choices.

Being aware of and being united with the Higher Self, provides an outlet and pulls man out of the lethargic state he finds himself in and reawakens his psyche. That is exactly the time when the path for true liberation actually opens. It (the Higher Self) trains man with compassion, understanding and love and leads him to the true dimension of life, which is the fifth. The entities that live there have completed the course of their life as well as the cycles of incarnation and have freed themselves from the bonds of pseudo-reality. They operate on different fields of evolution and have different types of expertise and specialties. In the Fifth dimension special doctors gradually and steadily detach man from his karmic cords, the moment no one here on Earth is given the power or has the right to perform such a task.

MUTATIONS OF THE PSYCHIC CELLS

Despite genetic heredity, there are imprints of previous incarnations in the DNA of the psychic cells. The psychographic profile of the soul (its plan) is encrypted within the central structures of these cells and the Higher Self takes this plan upon him and starts transforming it.

The transformation is carried out simultaneously not only on man but on the planet itself as well.

As these changes will be taking place earth will experience periods of unrest as well as political, religious, social, geological and climatological agitations.

Entire groups of souls will leave Earth at certain intervals. These will mostly be comprised of people who will have adjusted and have tuned themselves in with the new vibrations and have succeeded in constructing a strong energy body. They will be given the required protection offered by their Higher Self who will insert an etheric plate into the new psychographic profile of the soul that will be invulnerable to any type of low foreign energy vibration. This plate will be configured parallel to and in accordance with the course of the psyche's evolution. More and more people have already been participating and working hard in the spiritual groups and have been receiving powerful support from their Higher Selves and from the angelic entities of the Fifth dimension.

NEPHELON GALAXY

THE FIFTH DIMENSION

Nephelon galaxy belongs to the Fifth dimension and corresponds to our solar system. Each and every one of its planets stands for a planet of our solar system but in its five-dimensional form. The galaxy is governed by vibrating shades of color which give birth to action. It is this action that extends into our dimension on planet Earth and awakens the consciousness of all human souls as to their evolution.

The Fifth dimension is an intra-dimension into which the archetypes, the past, the present and the future all tend to converge. Its existence has already been accepted by certain astrophysicists. It is a real place, but in order to approach it a carrier compatible with the physical laws governing that dimension is required. That carrier is the energy body (or energy sheath) which is structured in my groups.

The Fifth dimension consists of the following forms: the dimension of dilating light, the dimension of super fast photons, the dimension of holograms and the dimension of the poly-morphic image.

This Fifth dimension is governed by frequencies of alternating color and sound vibrations. The sound vibrations tend to create five-dimensional musical notes which in turn vibrate the higher sentiments of its inhabitants.

They in turn experience these vibrations in each of their cells, a way through which they develop both in psyche and in spirit.

The genetic unification in the Fifth dimension takes place with the union of all the energy centers (chakras) through which exchange of information of the highest level ensues. During this union between the psyche and the Atman (the Higher Self) colored spheres are created which are complete cells. These constitute the nourishment, remedy, support of that plane and contain specific knowledge concerning it. Furthermore, they tend to just float around and vibrate in it.

If we wish to become recipients of this specific knowledge we only have to connect with those spheres through the pineal gland (or epiphysis). This union can also be realized through the connection between Higher Selves for the sole purpose of exchanging information.

On all the planets of the Fifth dimension exist some highly evolved couples which have been chosen. Upon uniting their centers they create explosions of energy. Then, these energies materialize and become little entities which are kept in matrices (energy machines). There they evolve with the purpose of descending to Earth, being sent there on an assignment. One of these delegations was formed by the twelve Olympian Gods. At every turning point of the history of this planet, entities that had been sent here taught the human race arts, technology and theurgy.

THE PLANETS OF THE FIFTH DIMENSION

The planets of the Fifth dimension are living organisms and some act as transformers sending energies to Earth. One of the dynamics of each planet is that it carries within it coordinative spheres that incorporate specific codes. Trough them the planet succeeds in communicating with other planets. The major planets which we travel to in order to enter our homecoming programs are: the Emerald planet Zirion, planet Poseidon, the Orange planet, The Mauve planet Zanar, the Red planet, and last but not least the Pink and the Blue planets.

The Pink planet, which corresponds to the constellation of Venus, is where entities of the Fifth dimension are trained so as to be assigned missions on Earth. That is the place where training concerning the alteration of the spiritual archives, beginning from the most primitive and ending at the most recent and newest ones, are held. Entities of the Fifth dimension as well travel to this beautiful planet, which is full of energy spheres and lakes, so as to filter their emotions.

The Red planet that corresponds to Mars is the planet of defense, where warriors are trained. Two of its most prominent genitors are Arion and Artemis. In the heart of the planet lies a purple pyramid which is the source of its dynamics and potential and the center of its defense.

The Mauve planet Zanar is also the place where the see of Archangel Zakchiel that of Archangel Iotheos and the seats of many other geneticists who regulate the recordings on the psychic cells, are found. It is surrounded by five rings that resemble rainbows. It is resplendent in various gradations of mauve, pink and gold, and is found next to the Orange planet with which it collaborates. Many particular psyche cleansing programs and therapies are performed there.

Poseidon is a silverfish-white iridescent planet whose satellites are Pan and Eros. For as long as the Lemurians and the Atlanteans inhabited Earth they kept receiving their guidance from Poseidon, the place where they were transferred later on. Poseidon cut off its contact with Atlantis the moment the Atlanteans came under other stellar influences. During that time entities came down to earth that tried to carry out mutations similar to those that we practice now. However, due to the stellar influences these pioneers had been receiving, the end results were not so encouraging and successful.

As a consequence that area gradually and steadily collapsed and many souls were plunged into "darkness" doomed and destined to enter channels of continuous incarnations. Remodeling of the cellular structure and memory of the archives as well as rejuvenation of the energy centers are performed on Poseidon.

The noetic archive of the planet is located within a central pyramid that tapers off in a rotating sphere.

On that planet there is an altar that resembles the "all-seeing eye" or "the Eye of Providence". It functions as an observer and transmits information to the Grand Council of the fifth hierarchy which in turn is responsible for the attunement and the diversification of spatial energy.

The Orange planet is the planet of cellular revitalization. Its biggest part consists of a liquid substance. During our travels there our body receives final cellular configuration.

The Blue planet corresponds to the planet we know in our world as Poseidon. It is regarded as Earth's brother and represents its unconscious knowledge. The esoteric knowledge imparted to us by all the sages that have come to Earth remains well documented on that planet.

The Blue planet lies on the borderline between the fifth and the Sixth dimension. It is inhabited by geneticists that work on mutations of the cognitive and neural systems. They collaborate extensively with Planet Zirion with which they have fraternized. The entities living on both planets occupy themselves with genetic programs. The Blue planet is the homeland of Archangels Iesmel, Alvaar, Achatios, and Uranios. The sky there is blue and corresponds to our sky. That planet is also considered the Higher Self of goddess Earth (Gaia).

The Gold planet Ilael is a planet of the Sixth dimension that is projected onto the fifth. It is the see of many other great teachers and of Christ who works on the program of attracting souls to their motherlands. Twelve rings run around it and it also has two gold satellites one on the right and the other on the left, that belong to the Fifth dimension and that play an equilibratory and transformatory role. The Golden planet sends out golden rays that travel via our Higher Selves. These energies travel through the energy body's cordlike connection. They are primarily transformed in the solar system of the trainees. Later on, they reach their astral, the etheric and material bodies.

Hereupon, they are channeled to the heart of the planet and we are placed in the position to come into contact with the Earth's heartbeats and to be able to syntonise with it so as to make the procedure of its soul's departure milder.

ZIRION THE EMERALD PLANET

Zirion represents Earth. It shares compatible frequencies with it, and is in a direct contact with it. It is the homeland of many entities that relate to Earth. That is the reason why most of the missions sent to our planet concerning reinstatement of the souls to the Fifth dimension have begun from there.

Discoveries pertaining to the evolution and development of Earth on all fields and levels are continuously channeled from the Emerald planet. It also constitutes the planet on which most of the mutations and karmic removals are performed, offering the souls the potential to gain immortality and achieve hyper-intellect.

It has five rings of defense around its etheric body. It possesses a broadcasting station through which it communicates with the constellation of Cassiopeia. This specific constellation functions as a transformer and as a broadcasting relay station through which the energies of the Fifth dimension pass. These comprise the configurational and reformational rays that assist in evolving our planet.

Zirion is a crystalline planet on which a certain crystalline structure resembling an emerald is found in abundance. The soft coloration of that crystal combined with a variety of other colors radiates at times mildly and at times powerfully.

Cities with enormous crystalline buildings exist on the planet. Their architecture is polymorphic and each of the facets taper off in a huge pyramid whose tip extends very high in the form of a crystalline antenna. These huge structures activate certain gateways that assist the arrival of entities coming from other planetary systems or dimensions. Within these buildings certain mutations, therapies, DNA modifications and detachments from karmic causes are performed.

There are also magnificent temples present there reminiscent of ancient Hellenic structures. The entities that live on Zirion feed off energies roaming around in parti-colored spheres. The constituents incorporated in these spheres nourish their cells and sustain these entities, not allowing them to wither.

There are also enormous chambers containing animated figurative representations acting as centers of knowledge. The knowledge is transferred into a huge rotating sphere located in the center of each chamber. All citizens have free access to those archives of knowledge, yet, they have to be accompanied by special teacher-guards who are familiar with the codes needed to activate the access control systems.

Students choose to enroll on specific courses during which projected rays enter their pineal and pituitary glands. In that fashion concrete and specific knowledge concerning specific majors and specializations is assimilated within fractions of a second.

The Emerald planet is ruled by a royal couple, Ziron and Moira. The couple is surrounded by many hierarchies of masters, Archangels, and angels and of other alternative dimensional beings that travel there to acquire knowledge and experiences.

A council of wise masters studies the evolutionary programs. They are entities that communicate with the hierarchy of the Sixth dimension which resides in the Gold planet.

The wise teachers select certain couples from which a new soul will be created. Their mating is accomplished by uniting all the energy centers. Aural energy is passed from one to the other. Between them a sphere is created that bears within it a pulsating spore. That is the divine spark composed of a structure similar to that of the primordial divine cell. In turn, it evolves kept in organic wombs until it develops a skeleton and a nervous system. The difference between its structure and that of a human one lies in the way information is structured.

When these entities develop they unite with others and what they produce is a divine couple. Some of those newly-born creatures however, when they are still in the form of a seed, are chosen to descend to Earth and enter a womb (gate) of an earthly woman so as to be born on Earth as crystal children. These children will eventually constitute the second delegation.

THE PORTALS

THE ENERGY GATEWAYS TO OTHER DIMENSIONS

Portals are gaps in the space-time continuum that lead to other dimensions. Acropolis, Delphi, and Mount Olympus constitute the central gateways of Hellas. Their opening process began in 1996. Following that the opening of subgates that united with the central ones took place. During that time several transformers all over the planet that had already been selected- among them me as well- created specific energy bases. Achieving that, meant, that energy from the Fifth dimension began entering our dimension assisting Earth to conclude its final cycle of evolution.

The energy field of the planet had been prepared to assist the transformers (time-travelers) to activate intermediary gateways leading to the Fifth dimension. For this objective various entities, guides, Archangelic navigators and specialized teachers were sent, who knew how to operate the gates. They trained human guides to assist them in making the required transformations and in using and operating the gates.

In my spiritual venue an etheric gateway has been opened defined and characterized by the presence of thousands of transfer rings. Upon its opening the rotation of four rings is activated. The commencement of this rotation propagates a fluidic network comprised of thousands of micro-crystal spheres. These spheres permeate the energy body, bringing into effect the first syntonization that is necessary for the travel.

I, as the guide of the fourth and Fifth dimensions, become attuned to the navigators of the fifth. This type of attunement takes place "verbally" using various key phrases that constitute secret codes given by the navigators of the fifth. The navigators unite with the group and they surround it with an energy rhombus.

The first gate concerns both the etheric and astral dimensions.

The second is the gate of the station that surrounds Nephelon galaxy and separates the fourth from the Fifth dimensions. The third gate is opened after utilizing the codes supplied by the navigators and those provided by the entities that are sent to accompany us. Through that gate we enter a peculiar vehicle that moves along all the relevant channels making its way towards one of the planets. The movement of the vehicles is achieved by means of superfast photon induced vortices. Each planet consists of five rings that protect it. Each ring that is approached by the vehicle sustains a gate. The vehicle's navigators provide the respective codes to open the five gates so that the vehicle can enter the planet's atmosphere.

THE GUIDES

THE GUARDIANS OF THE FIFTH DIMENSION

The guides are entities guardians of the Fifth dimension, that cooperate with the Higher Self in order to prepare man for this long journey. Some of the guardians have led a human life but their evolutionary course was such that allowed them to directly access the Fifth dimension.

The guides remain in the mutational chambers protecting the body's physical structure and its projected astral form from various types of interference usually pertaining to toxic substances that are emitted from the students' lower personality. These substances mainly concern emotions that manifest themselves as fear, anger or imbalance that tend to jam the umbilical-like connection cords. When these cords are blocked the experiential experience is terminated.

That is the time when the guides assume the crucial role of syntonization. They burn the toxic substances and they restore a smooth flow within the umbilical cord-like connections. Two guides stand right beside each student. One of them remains constantly next to him until the whole process is brought to a conclusion while the other, together with the Higher Self, accompanies the energy body to Nephelon galaxy.

THE ENERGY CORDS

The Higher Self is connected to the seven centers of the trainee's energy bodies via an energy cord (resembling the umbilical-like cord connecting mother and child). The basic cord connects the heart of the Higher Self to that of the energy and astral sheath. That connection, which also assists the reception of daily guidance through it, is permanent. The navigators are connected in a similar fashion protecting and maintaining the necessary attunement and co-ordination of the group for as long as the journey lasts.

These cords are luminous connections comprised of etheric and stellar matter, enriched with spiritual elements of the Higher Self.

The various substances that are intermixed within these cords carry in them regenerating cellular structures in order to help the materialization of the energy body. The cords interconnect the Higher Self, the energy body and the astral sheath. The latter remains projected outside the natural body during the whole duration of the journey. This procedure is what is often referred to as astral projection. Parts of this astral body are transferred inside the energy body with the sole purpose of being taken to the Fifth dimension to be transmuted. The cords cannot be disconnected, not to mention that another one of their purposes is that they connect the realities of the fifth with those of the third and the fourth dimensions. Much effort is required in order for the pupils to be in the position to transfer events, images and messages from the Fifth dimension through the cords to their consciousnesses. They are trained, however, with the aim to become capable of filtering them, in accordance with the cognitive content and experiences of their lifetime.

THE SECRET KEYS

The keys are actually code-words that have been given to me and which I use as a guide, so that my pupils are put in the position to project their astral body outside their etheric and physical bodies.

The trainees driven by the help they receive from the etheric guides reach the threshold of relaxation. Uttering the code words accelerates the unification of the centers of the Higher Self with those of the astral body. Time dilates, the energy body is formulated and space-time modulations occur, in order to keep the body in a state of relaxation for the duration of the journey. The guide collaborates with the guide of the Fifth dimension and together they keep the cords syntonized to prevent the physical body from falling asleep.

THE NAVIGATORS

The navigators who also belong to the Archangelic divisions take us to the galaxy of the Fifth dimension. They possess the knowledge required to open the gates and are aware of the secret codes needed to pass from one dimension to another.

Before setting off they line up forming a pyramid which energy-wise extends downwards forming a rhombus. The upper pyramid constitutes the gateway that allows us to exit our dimension and enter the fifth, whereas the lower one constitutes the passing through which our return to this dimension will be feasible. Further to that, the navigators surround the group with a pulse-vibrational energy net.

The Archangels that lead the group are: Archangel Seraphiel, who has six wings and who also possesses the knowledge concerning the physical laws governing each dimension which enables him to change his body accordingly. His wings are made up of multiple super fast photon fibers that pulsate, expand and contract accordingly creating vortices.

Archangel Labriel, who belongs to the forces of the solar sphere and who coordinates the construction and creation of the energy body. He metabolizes and alters the energy flow around the energy bodies to aid their crossing into other dimensions.

On the right side the group is accompanied by:

Archangel Selenios, who dissolves the astral currents of various thoughtforms as we pass through the fourth dimension and who assists the travelers to remain in a conscious state of being.

Archangel Eloim, who belongs to the hierarchy of the therapeutic surgeons and who coordinates heartbeats and helps by dispelling any dark clouds of fear.

Archangel Gileel, who is an aura healer and helps by removing any projections caused by emotional disturbances, strengthening thus concentration.

Archangel Zochriel, who belongs to the order of Archangel Raphael. He is a healer doctor who also partakes in the operations that are held in special operating rooms on the Emerald planet.

On the left side the group is environed by:

Archangel Zophiel, the coordinator of all the groups, the one who preserves and strengthens the cohesiveness of the bonds during the whole duration of the journey, transmitting simultaneously thoughts that reinforce team-spirit.

Archangel Uranios, who belongs to the hierarchy of Archangel Samuel. He safeguards the passing flows heading for the heart of planet Earth from Nephelon galaxy, reinforcing bonds of love and gratitude.

Archangel Marazeel, healer of the energy centers who also protects the cords connecting the Higher Self to the energy body. He further assists the group to maintain its mental and psychic composure and flexibility.

Archangel Ihran, the second healer doctor who belongs to the hierarchy of Archangel Raphael. The two Archangels Zochriel and Ihran convey their therapeutic energies through healers with whom they have aligned in advance.

Behind the group there are other Archangels who follow. Archangels who have been loved by people at specific intervals for offering their help to them. They became known to the general public when they were presented in my second book entitled "The Return of the Angels".

Among them are five beloved Archangels that represent the five elements of abundance. Agasiel who represents love, Aniel who represents luck, Futriel who represents health, Giubriel who represents the abundance of material possessions and last but not least Petriel who represents harmony.

One should not forget to mention the Archangels of justice, Altos and Aetolos who belong to the order of Michael the Archangel.

Additionally known patrons of road traffic and man's security are Archangels Metiel, Setiel and Fotiel. Next come the Archangels who are responsible for purifying the aura, Sel and Phil. The Archangels of literature, Evron, Atlas and Logios, of balance

Serpios and Telephos, of good physical health, Orion and Filion, of meditation Piriel and Nostiel, of the three wishes or the three opportunities, Kaldimos and Meandros, of judicature, as well as the Archangels responsible for channeling nerve cells, Tsakiel and Ezoem. Finally, one should mention twelve more angels who follow the spiritual groups in order to be trained as navigators.

THE INITIATIONS

Initiations of the highest degree are performed on all the planets of the Fifth dimension. With these initiations divine attributes that were present in man's primeval existence during the prelapsarian times, before the loss of innocence, before the Fall into a dimension of endless suffering and tormenting trials and experiences, and painful lessons, are restored to the human souls.

The initiations constitute exquisite upgrades and lead the soul to immortality. Through them man's divine genetic material is awakened and his primeval divine potential and power as well as the crystal clear Word of God (or Logos) are activated. During the initiations the genitors of the Fifth dimension create holograms of the very subtle and divine mental body of the students. Images and the material substance of the higher intellect and memory of man's divine origin are imprinted in these holograms. All these memories as well as intuition and insight are awakened and ordinary intellect is substituted for hyperintellect.

During the initiation process the pupils receive a life-sustaining seed, which maintains energy and nerve-cell cohesion, rendering them more resistant to quick wear and tear. The nucleus of these life-giving spores includes a segment of a genetic substance of a higher intellect that is capable of producing new nerve-cells. Consequently, the usual division, fission, breakdown and death of neurons and nerve cells cease to operate.

The first initiation is administered by Archangel Metatron himself. It mainly concerns the creation of an advanced neural network for the energy (psychic) body. With this initiation two additional cerebral lobes are activated and the memory regarding the soul's origin is awakened. Hidden talents and divine favors that had remained dormant after the Fall and entry in the continuous cycle of incarnations, are also awakened.

The second initiation is administered by Archangel Michael himself. It regards the formation of a heart for the energy body, which supports the newly implemented evolutionary plan for each soul. A new venous system develops in the psychic body, change in the DNA structure ensues and an influx of blue energy whose cellular structures represents the royal origin of the psyche, emerges.

The third initiation is the one pertaining to the female element, the female principle, and is administered by Virgin Mary and other female entities, who had been incarnated on Earth during the past for specific missions. The chalice used during this initiation contains the highest elements of the feminine potentiality. It concerns the substances that activate intuition, offering, sacrifice and love.

The next initiation is administered again by Archangel Michael. It concerns the chrism of the luminous warriors. In the chalice there are codes of power, and symbols, that develop the body's and the soul's stamina and endurance. Through these codes students are trained in the knowledge of protecting and defending themselves and others, and of ways to handle and manage toxic emotions. These personal codes can be conveyed to the hearts of other people as well, to strengthen them, provided they beseech to be helped.

The initiation and the chrism administered by Artemis constitute codes of power. They assist man in fulfilling the scenario of his/her life and in overcoming his passions and in setting goals, especially material, psychic and spiritual ones.

The baptism initiation is administered by John the Baptist the Precursor and other spiritual masters belonging to the higher christic hierarchy. During this ritual the soul's energy body receives its true spiritual name. The astral field's incarnation gateway is sealed and the centers of the energy body are permanently connected to those of the Higher Self. Thus, the channel responsible for the return of men to their celestial homelands is opened.

The initiation of the Holy Marriage unites through an indissoluble bond the energy body with the intellect of its Higher Self. In this ceremonious initiation, the symbols on the rings that are exchanged contain upgrading codes with which man manages to balance all his cosmic manifestations (the spiritual, the psychic and the material ones). What is more, the communication channel between him and the hyper-intellects residing in the Sixth dimension is also opened.

The pre-initiation of the christic awakening is the initiation in which the seed of immortality is administered. The center of the heart opens up and the soul's mission is ultimately revealed.

During the initiation of the seminal discs, light-emanating discs bearing the divine seed are distributed. These emit rhythmical sound vibrating shades of color useful for awakening all the souls of the planet on a massive scale. Man is relieved of the virtual reality in which he has been living and enters the stage of the hyper-intellect. Additionally, births of crystal children are promoted that gradually and steadily lead to the race of the divine meta-humans.

Finally, the initiation administered by all the hierarchies and forces of galactic channeling is realized in the Sixth dimension. Through this initiation a form of divine DNA is offered and the holy couple receives the chrism allowing entrance to the Sixth dimension, as well as the potential to co-officiate with the highest hierarchy of hyperintellects.

Subsequent initiations are given to "select" groups and concern a higher cycle of apprenticeship including very special symbols for conscious ascension necessary for returning to the Fifth dimension, as well as crucial for carrying someone back to the future Earth on a mission.

THE DOLPHINS

The dolphins are creatures that lived in the sea during the time of Atlantis. They had a form similar to both man and a fish. In our primeval memory we have still images of mermen and mermaids. They were capable of living for short periods of time outside the aquatic element and they had imparted a great deal of knowledge to humankind.

They possessed high frequency etheric antennae which allowed them to communicate with the priesthood of the Pleiades, from where they transferred messages and solutions the Atlanteans needed. Moreover, they controlled the underwater gateways. When Earth's magnetic field was disturbed due to erroneous conduct, a number of these entities returned to the Pleiades. The remainder of them mutated into fish, being more specific, into dolphins. However, within their mind remained a record of their former knowledge which they continue to impart to humans unconsciously via the sounds they produce.

During our journeys, whenever we approach the etheric plane of Earth, whose color is similar to that of the earthly sea, we hear some of those sounds. They are recorded sounds of the hyper-intellectual entities that now live on Earth in the form of dolphins.

Dolphins have developed channels of communication, activating the recordings of those sounds on the etheric level.

A HIGHER COMMUNION WITH MY HIGHER SELF

Do not forget that you live because of me, you exist for me and you will return to me.

Because you are a part of me.

I hurt when I see you creeping in the darkness.

To seize you from there I can.

However, I am not permitted to do so and you

know it. You chose it.

So I hurt and agonize, every time you lose yourself in realities that have absolutely nothing to offer you.

They only imprison you to be fed from your flesh.

My voice you have not forgotten. Yet, you struggle against crude matter, the properties of which I am well aware of. That's why I am watching over you and protecting you, each and every moment that you remember me.

I search every aspect of your soul, to remind you of your origin.

I touch upon your cords of recollection, to help you find the beat that will bring you in tune with me.

I caress each part of you that is hurt,

for only I know to which extent suffering may go.

I cover you, whenever your soul is cold, for I know that whatever you are going through will become a link that will unite us forever.

Now my true love, my sacrifice and my anticipation awaits you.

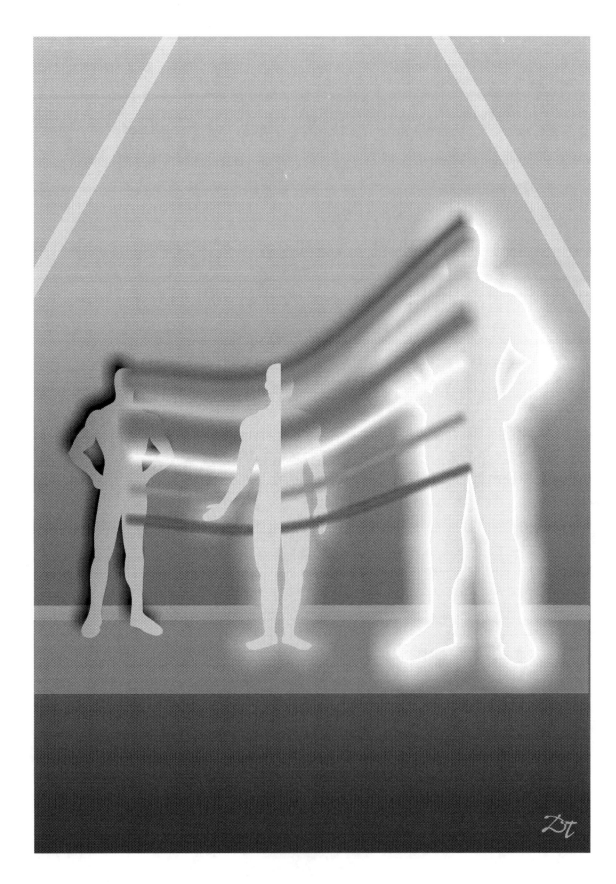

Integration with the Higher Self

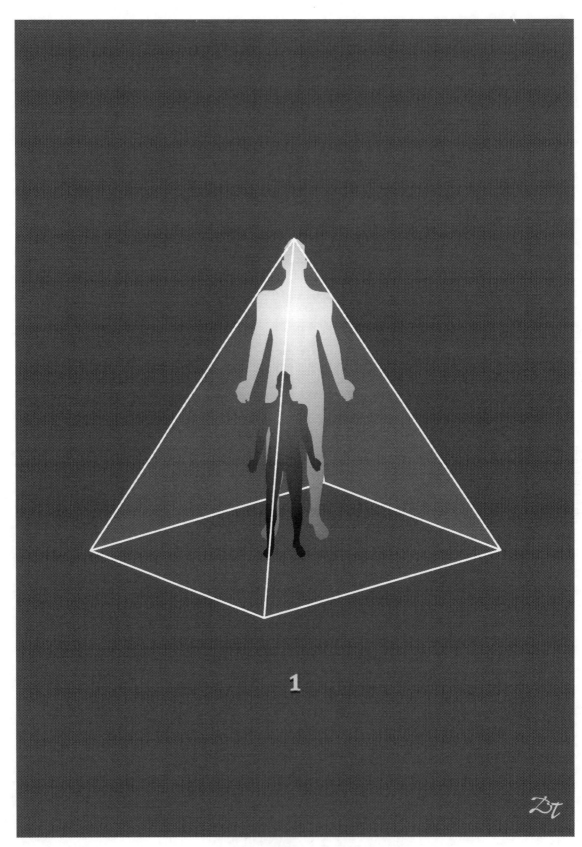

1

Protection inside the pyramid.

MY HIGHER SELF "THE TRAINING"

THE AWAKENING

THE CONNECTION

THE ENLIGHTENMENT

THE PYRAMID AND ITS APPLICATION

A HIGHER COMMUNION WITH "MY SPIRITUAL COUNTERPART"

MY HIGHER SELF "THE TRAINING"

In the past, as I underwent my training, I always wondered why I can't be happy and why problems should keep succeeding each other. Then, I presumed that there were no reasons generating these chained events. I looked at the world filtering everything through my personal prism, justifying myself and blaming all the others continuously.

When, during meditation, I began receiving images of our celestial home, I began my visionary journeys to meet my genitors. There I was taught that the genitors of the soul are the divine Higher Selves.

They constitute births of a higher spiritual essence that puts the universe into motion.

When for the first time I came in front of my Higher Self, I felt awe. Although I felt really small compared to it, I found the courage to ask: "Why do I not have abundance, joy, creation or contact? Why do I lack wealth? Why should I live in hardship?"

Then my Higher Self looked at me sweetly and gently replied: "Enter me and see for yourself"

I found myself in a world of swirling cells. In each one I recognized a small part of me. He asked me smiling: "My dear Mary, what did you see?" My heart leaped and I answered: "What I saw is that my cellular structure resembles yours, but you do not have or face the same problems that I do".

Then he revealed to me the following: "You are highly qualified to obtain wealth and to create your own personal paradise. You can achieve it, provided you enter and go with the flow of your mission".

Since then, its words echo in my ears. Now I fully understand them, whereas then I strived to find the thread which when followed upon would liberate me.

Each and every human being has the potential to improve or to cancel his old scenario (destiny). To achieve this, he only has to sustain the psychic counterparts that are connected with higher intellect and higher consciousness. To come into contact with higher intellect man needs to unite with his Higher Self, who sustains and preserves the divine spark and keeps it inextinguishable.

Collaborating with that celestial entity helps man develop forgotten capacities and powers and assists man in taking a major turn in his life. When man arrives at the realization that all the events in his life, either positive or negative, are actually attracted by him, then he has taken the first step towards true deliverance. That knowledge gives him the potential to make his choices with clarity and to realize his goals.

In each incarnation, at some specific juncture of time in our life, a clue is given to us that functions like a code. Provided we interpret that code, the course of our karmic scenario alters and we enter the path that will lead to self-knowledge and self-awareness.

Many people simply ignore that code, going on with their karmic scenario that includes harsh lessons to be learned and conflicts to be resolved.

That happened to me as well, until I realized that as long as I kept myself on the course of my new scenario, everything would flow smoothly. However, whenever I was incapable of controlling the constituents of my lower personality, I would immediately have to bear the consequences of my own toxic behaviour. Thus, I have learned how to identify the frequency of that energy flow and am now able to remain there for longer periods of time.

I entered the new personality of my energy body, after I awakened, by applying specific procedures.

THE AWAKENING

The Archangelic forces that came into my life opened a channel that broadened my experiences. I felt understanding, gratitude and optimism for all the miracles that occur in our daily lives, which we often tend to ignore trapped in our own personal prisons.

The Higher Selves are capable of coming into contact with people in a multitude of ways, mainly due to their unique ability to alter their material structure. The primary personality trait that they impart to man is optimism.

This emotion is very strong and constitutes a vital element that possesses the potential to transform man's own toxicity into something else.

Simultaneously, the Higher Selves act as navigators that surround us during the journeys. They function as well as a protective energy wall, because they know the passages towards the gates. Their different properties, compared to ours, have helped us enormously whenever we have encountered obstacles. They collaborate directly with man whom they protect for the sole purpose of assisting him in deciding on the best course of action for his life.

The Higher Self constitutes our divine essence that awaits our fulfillment. It has made its presence known to us during our various incarnations, but many of us haven't listened to it, mainly because we have been so absorbed in obtaining earthly possessions. Nowadays, however, more and more people are coming into contact with their Higher Selves, from whom they receive guidance so as to liberate themselves from their lower astral personality.

Being aware of man's situation of entrapment, I asked for a simple way that could bring about rapid changes, and it was given to me. Then came the journeys and later the mutations, in order to activate the seed of immortality. In the program regarding karmic causes we come to understand the reason why a toxic choice can activate a chain of events that will eventually lead to painful conflicting situations. We are also given the method required to enter the real "state of affairs", nullifying the illusory scenario surrounding us.

This is not something we could achieve on our own. We would come up against such difficulties that we would be discouraged from continuing the effort. As such the assistance offered by the Higher Selves is more than critical, for they constitute the mediums through which our celestial homecoming can be realized.

These days with the quick mutational programs we can reach higher levels of awareness and evolution. To achieve and realize this transcendence during other epochs we would need seclusion, fasting, prayers, and suffering a life of privations, just to discipline and subdue the lower self.

From the entities of the Fifth dimension we receive a variety of plates that contain superior constituents. These fundamentals help us to immediately acknowledge and identify our toxicity and dispel it.

The sages of antiquity have referred to this divine fundamental nature existing within us in their own words. Jesus, the projected psychic part of Christ, conveyed to us the idea that man possesses a divine essence which he has to discover on his own. However, many have misquoted his teachings and since then in the name of christic love some of the worst crimes on earth have been committed. The great Masters have always left behind them a spore here on Earth. How that spore will eventually grow and bear fruit throughout history depends upon the consciousness of the people living on Earth. Now, we are reaching the point when the old cycles are nearing their conclusion. A new cycle has already begun in which past knowledge and previous convictions have no place in it. New souls carry within their DNA fresh and innovative information so as to disperse the illusions surrounding us.

THE CONNECTION

In order for the unification (enosis) with the Higher Self to work, the transformer of the psychic astral substance and its material counterpart (that is our body) are both required. Equally important though is that the soul itself has to accept the process in order for it to enter the upgrading procedures. The conscious type of connection, which is taught during the first phase of the initiation process, helps man transfer into his dimension this divine entity.

There are and there always were many ways of connecting to The Higher Self.

I always searched for a conscious and tangible way; so that I would be in the position to help myself and assist other people achieve the same. Many have already participated in this initiation and have enhanced their potential and developed new capabilities on all the levels of their existence. The unification cord operates as an upgrading medium that leads to the awakening of the soul from its lethargic state. Thus, a new, promising, long journey of returning to "Ithaca", the Fifth dimension, commences. The Odyssey here is represented by the distance the soul has to cover to arrive at the heavenly homeland.

When man is reunited with his Higher Self, everything becomes brighter and more luminous. That is the time when the various aspects of one's personality are put under a magnifying glass. It is when one reaches this phase of the procedure that gives rise to manifold fears. Many plausible arguments emerge to the surface as well as many desires and other emotions, for the sole purpose of putting an end to this sudden surge of conscious awareness as to who we really are, as if attempting to discourage us. If we manage to overcome this disturbing, agitating and upsetting initial stage, we then enter the stages of awakening.

A new, a different perspective on life and a different consideration of it begins then. However, our troubles are not over. We have to deal with the lower personality which doesn't easily and readily just let go of the "reins" of dominance over man's soul. Without the Higher Self's help we are compelled to recharge and revive the illusions the lower ego cherishes. When a redefinition of the true existence begins, the Higher Self intervenes assisting at an average of eighty per cent. The remaining twelve percent depends on our individual efforts. Problems do not just vanish magically; they are instead projected by it from different perspectives. We are trained to observe them while being in a detached state, so that the channel can remain open in order for solutions to be forwarded to us. These solutions can present themselves in various ways. They can manifest themselves in the form of an inspiration, a boosting of confidence or reinforcement, or even an appearance of souls compatible to ours or soul mates or teachers whose patronage has been deemed essential to additionally assist us on this evolutionary track.

We are truly living in a historic period, in which the souls are compelled to follow the changes the planet is already experiencing and sustaining. As such, the procedure of reinstating souls to their heavenly mother land depends, to a great extent, on the faith and resolve of the people. One should be well-equipped with optimism, willingness, endurance, faith and love, in order to be given the passport to return. This is actually the reason for which the journeys to the Fifth dimension take place, namely to enable man to discover his true nature through the specialized training programs.

THE ENLIGHTENMENT

Via the cord connecting man's heart with the heart of the Higher Self, the old plan is reconstructed in a way that future events will be allowed to develop and evolve as a result of the change of consciousness. This specific procedure is different for each individual soul in terms of the time it requires to be accomplished. From the moment the connection takes place, the Higher Self starts working on the soul's plan in order to achieve unification with it. It expresses its desire to all the higher Councils of the Fifth dimension where the likelihood of a man's return is decided upon. Subsequent to that a very complex plan is formulated with the intention of pulling the soul out of its lethargy.

The Higher Self always desires and longs for its unification with its psychic element, which resides in the world of form and crude matter, gathering experiences. After its connection to the psyche it can continue to ascend the remaining evolutionary stages together with it. Until then it lives and evolves in the Fifth dimension, making continuous journeys to the fourth and third dimension in order to approach its other half.

A very well known way to reach it is trough the luminous dreams, which are very different from the ordinary everyday dreams projecting desires. These encounters are very seldom forgotten and they constitute the seed that the Higher Self will utilize for the bonding since it is familiar with all aspects of the soul and the course it had followed through its various incarnations.

After physical death occurs, the Higher Self waits for the soul. Numerous accounts of people exist describing a bright, dearly loved, entity that greets them at the edge of a dark tunnel. This is the entity that talks to them, whenever it is deemed essential that they return to life, because they still have some goal to accomplish. Many have recounted that experience, while some others haven't, for fear of being exposed or humiliated. Nevertheless, whatever the case such an experience has marked their lives. These people go on with their lives facing people and occurrences with wisdom and love.

In order for the Higher Selves to be in the position to awaken the soul, they develop a memory. This is the way by which the path for return is opened. That endeavor for some signifies the final return, whereas for others it signifies an upgrading, a chance to try again, either in this life or in another under better circumstances.

Usually they begin with the presupposition that they do possess the ability to restore their "lost" part to its mother land. However, they are always obligated to respect what has been bestowed upon the soul since it was made by the creator, namely its free will. Man's soul has been given the freedom to choose, and to test its powers during the course of its lifetime.

As such the soul has the potential:

Of relieving itself of the karmic burden it has been bearing and consequently receiving the passport to return.

Of "taking a break" in the middle of the course, so as to be given time to reevaluate the facts and experiences or hardships it has underwent.

Of reaching a satisfactory level, but still being required to gain more experiences through re-births. On that occasion it will return to Earth with an upgraded scheme, to continue from where it left off.

Of regressing, beaten by fear of losing something it considered its connection during many lifetimes.

THE PYRAMID AND ITS APPLICATION

The practical application of the pyramid concerns the activation of each student's personal gateway, in order to allow the auxiliary forces to descend and begin the upgrading process. The proper use and management of that pyramid so as to allow the entrance of assisting energies is also something additional I teach in my seminars, details of which one can also find printed in my second book "The Return of the Angels".

In the past, the transition from the third and fourth dimensions were exercised through the technology of the pyramids. These gates were de-activated subsequent to the departure of the "Gods". Yet, they remained intact to remind people of that mode of transition to the Fifth dimension. Nowadays, some of them have been re-activated. I have also played a role in base-activating, by forming a pyramid. The bases that I have activated as a transformer are mentioned in my first book entitled "The Awakening".

The pyramids built on earth are five-sided. They have a rectangular base with four triangular faces and an exit near the top, called the apex, which symbolizes the return to the Fifth dimension. Lemurians and Atlanteans were aware of their operating codes. Nowadays, they have been activated anew due mainly to the channels that have been opened to allow the descending entities of the Fifth dimension to reach Earth.

The pyramid, which has been offered, constitutes a personal gate between the Higher Self and the soul about to enter the upgrading process and return to its celestial home. The apex of the pyramid is governed by the powers of Michael the Archangel, who guards it, and who directs the heavenly forces that will activate the base of the pyramid. The red vibration represents the channeling dynamics as well as the transformation for the passage to our dimension.

Gabriel reinforces the pyramid on the right. His assistance is symbolized by a white light, standing for the birth and the opening up of a new state of consciousness, which further supports us in order to achieve the final alignment. Archangel Raphael (emerald color) reinforces the therapeutic vibration on the left side of the pyramid, thus helping us enter the healing phase that will cure us of any lower personality illnesses. Archangel Zakchiel (purple color), behind the pyramid, metabolizes any possible negative charges that at times are released during the purificatory procedure. At the front of the pyramid, the vibration of Uriel the Archangel (gold) reminds us that the road leading to the mother land is absolved of any older commitments and former attachments.

In this way, the soul in collaboration with the Higher Self starts creating an opening leading to its personal home.

The pyramid serves multiple purposes. Firstly, it attracts purificatory energies that will cleanse the energy flow in the centers of the etheric and astral body. Secondly, it assists the alignment and unification with all the corresponding centers of the Higher Self, meaning the transformation and mutation of the lower personality. And thirdly, it helps the construction and formation of a personal departure gate leading to the heavenly mother land, after being utilized.

When the initial stages of purifying the Higher Self's lower ego take place, then mental and emotional toxins begin to subside. It is exactly that moment when the soul's luminous archive begins to unfold and exit the lethargic state. All the dark aspects of one's personality are illuminated. Peopled begin to acknowledge their weaknesses and start having control over the projections of their toxic emotions. They become detached, so as to find the correct solutions to their problems, relieving the tension. They start having sudden inspirations that assist them in overcoming whatever problem they have come upon. Their immune system improves to conquer microbes, viruses and illnesses. Souls belonging to the same level begin attracting each other and helping one another to complete their evolutionary course. People begin to comprehend the true meaning of love and start overcoming their dependence on certain relationships as well as their obsessions.

The flow of abundance which was blocked until now re-opens and people begin to experience the beauty and the wonders one finds in life and on this planet. They create their own personalized paradise which connects with the positive energy flow of other people as well. Tensions and conflicts simply disappear from their lives because karmic causes are resolved and withdrawn.

This is the time when they experience contact with the spark of the Higher Self and their lucidity increases. They develop creative talents and therapeutic abilities, which up to now remained dormant within the unconscious. Various supporting keys are provided for by the Archangels and the spiritual masters that accelerate the upgrading of their consciousness. Justice is administered and parental as well as ancestral recordings are erased. People become disillusioned and their true mission is revealed.

A HIGHER COMMUNION WITH MY "SPIRITUAL COUNTERPART"

Now you sense my presence and your soul is at ease.

All those years of agonizing quest are over.

Now you can see with my eyes.

Nothing can hurt you any more, for I have spread my wings over you.

I hold your hand.

I cast away the lingering darkness and disharmony.

I present to you the negative side, however the energy grid that separates you from it is extremely powerful.

The love bonding us, allows nothing sinister to approach us.

Even when you think that something is about to destroy you, it is not true.

It is a fictitious form that is trying to scare you, willing to break our bonds and connections.

You can feel me caressing you; you can sense my presence, my warmth and comfort, my solace, my strength.

Be always mindful not to sink into oblivion, which follows you forever from the left side.

Whenever you sense its touch reach out to me and it will leave.

Breathe my aura, whenever you feel weak and bewildered.

Do what you feel in your heart.

Listen to it. Whenever you do that properly, you will be able to sense it, for now you have established a connection with me.

Invoking the Archangels for protection.

THE SOUL'S JOURNEY TO THE FOURTH DIMENSION

LIFE ON THE ASTRAL LEVELS

THE REBIRTH

THE SOUL'S FLIGHTS TO THE EMBRYO

THE SOUL'S DEPARTURE

MEANS OF ESCAPE

LIFE AFTER DEATH

THE SOUL'S PREPARATION FOR THE RETURN

REFORMATION OF PEOPLE'S CONSCIOUSNESSES

The succession of dimensions and the border between them. The Gates.

THE SOUL'S JOURNEY TO THE FOURTH DIMENSION

Our solar system and our galaxy are governed by four dimensions. We, the people, live and evolve on a tiny part of the universe, experiencing only the dimensions of our solar system. The part of the universe where we reside has been analyzed by the astrophysicists who continuously bear witness to many new discoveries and novel information, which I will try to analyze from a slightly different perspective, from the viewpoint of a religious doctrine named theosophy.

The phenomenal and awe-inspiring entity referred to as God we cannot see. We only have the potential to explore our own universe, at least with the means we currently have at our disposal. The God of our solar system has seven (7) centers similar to those of man, but he also possesses three more that correspond to his higher intellect.

Just like our body is composed of many internal and external dimensions, which correspond to the inner physical organs and to the outer figure, each of God's centers is also characterized by the presence of multiple dimensions. Life begins to develop in the very first dimension located in and on God. As such, unicellular organisms experience the first dimension; multi-cellular organisms experience the second and mammals the third.

The fourth dimension, which is astral, is a place defined by the consciousness of the soul and its evolution. It is a place where time is non-existent, a place where souls cross to after death, in order to prepare themselves to be reborn. It was formulated to allow the soul to rest or take a few breaks before descending once more to Earth (rebirth).

It operates like an enormous information processing system with a huge memory capacity that interconnects the subconscious and the unconscious of the soul. These recordings, which tend to constrain the souls, develop and nourish the astral dimension.

The astral dimension constitutes the fundamental essence of which the building blocks responsible for the construction of the astral body are comprised. The various incarnation imprints recorded in its archives determine the individual and collective future of the planet. The true records of our descent (before the Fall) actually exist in the Fifth dimension. Thus, what forms our reality and our perception of the world and our planet is virtually a huge mass of astral illusions that are actually "pulling the strings" of people's lives. Some people however, manage to escape this virtual reality. In the past these kinds of people were hunted down and convicted, for the simple reason of swimming against the stream defined by astral illusions.

As a consequence, during our lifetime we experience the dimension of form (matter), the etheric world (forces of nature), and the astral world that imprisons the soul, until at least the latter fulfils its apprenticeship and leaves for its home located in the Fifth dimension.

LIFE ON THE ASTRAL LEVELS

The soul creates its own heaven and its own hell, depending on the level of its evolution, either in the world of matter (the third dimension), or the world where the thoughtforms usually dwell, the fourth. After passing away and entering the fourth dimension, the soul continues to experience exactly the same emotions and having the same thoughts that, as a person, it experienced while alive. To simplify things, the soul shapes and forms the environment which is suitable for it and which it deserves, using interstellar matter belonging to this dimension, creating thus a becoming place for it. Thus, there is no such thing as a "punisher" God. It is our own consciousness that drives us to make correct or erroneous choices.

Nevertheless, the various astral levels were given form by the multitude of astral entities that were exiled there together with some souls. In the lower, (more obscure) levels of the fourth dimension reside entities that are sustained by our nightmares and fears. In that dreadful place our worst fears determine a dreary environment which essentially constitutes the reality of each individual personality. These levels are visited by souls that have not developed the divine spark (the Higher Self), and therefore are condemned to experience the bestial nature and the lowest and basest traits of their personality in their lives. Because of their passions many of these souls are entrapped in the etheric field and become grounded souls. There, they wander around trying to locate a willing human recipient, so as to experience toxic behavior through him. This transforms them into some type of energy vampires that suck man's life energy out of him, for the sole purpose of maintaining their etheric body.

The fallen angels, who belong to a different rank of birth and possess different abilities, hold their headquarters at the lowest levels of the stellar matter. It is from this place that they attach themselves onto the consciousnesses of the human souls and attempt to put themselves in charge of them. By that way, they become capable of feeding and sustaining their astral bodies, since their spiritual essence has turned inactive and will remain in that state until the predetermined moment of their obliteration arrives.

In our time and age these lower astral levels have begun to collapse, because not enough residents live there to keep them activated. That is the plan of the Fifth dimension.

The astral levels are connected to the corresponding human energy centers and through the influence they exert over those centers they project illusions onto them. As a consequence man becomes imprisoned in a virtual reality, which he actually perceives as the "true" reality. Usually he exhibits and keeps repeating the same toxic behavioral patterns and is subsequently driven to make catastrophic choices.

Each and every of the body's energy centers contains channels through which the soul exits after physical death occurs. If the soul together with the astral body departs through one of the centers governed by the lower personality, which means either from the genital, the abdominal (sacral chakra), or the solar plexus ones, then it is directed to the lower astral levels where it experiences anew the same emotions, the same suffering and is subject to the same illusions. It lives there until certain spiritual guides tear though the dense stellar matter to approach it with the intent of preparing it for its rebirth, a time when new chances and new opportunities will be offered to it.

Souls that leave the body through the centers associated with higher emotions, that is, the heart and the chakras regarding the mental levels (thyroid-epiphysis-hypophysis) are placed on the corresponding levels that suit their up to then evolutionary course.

There, they formulate brighter and more luminous fields and are able to come into contact with souls with which they have kept some type of karmic contract. Although this place is inexistent and insubstantial from our earthly and material point of view, it constitutes a place continuously being formed, in which the souls living there are fully conscious and aware of what is happening to them. They discover that they maintain all their senses even though they cannot fully satisfy them in the way they knew how, when they possessed material bodies.

Spiritual guides and spiritual masters approach them in these planes in order to teach these souls and to show them the path to evolution. They remind the souls of what they had been taught and of what they had not in the grand school of life. Because the toxicities in their behavior no longer exist, their intellect is clearer and they are capable of better perceiving the aspects of their personalities that need improvement. Consequently, they progress and climb the evolutionary ladder until they are totally freed of the endless shift between the third and fourth dimensions.

REBIRTH

When the right time for rebirth has been ordained the souls being helped by guides outline a plan. They settle on the exact date of birth and decide upon the time of their death. They also select their gender and specify the exact location (the country, the city and its environs), where they believe they will be given the potential to successfully develop their new plan and allow it to unfold. In addition, they select the parents through whose parenthood they reckon that they will be able to learn the lessons required to assist their evolution. There are certain "contracts" of apprenticeship that concern parents and children alike.

Simultaneously, on the plan they specify and pre-determine probabilities of occurrence of events destined to unfold and manifest themselves in the course of one's life, such as relationships, professions, and illnesses (provided a karmic cause is present) that will become active. The time of their birth, the country, the parents, and the gender constitute the fundamental "nodal points" of the soul's arrangements, which are unalterable. Depending on the degree of the soul's realization of the plan in conjunction with the power(s) it may have gained everything else can be alterable. At a certain point of the plan, that mainly regards lessons and relationships, the choices the soul can make are directly proportional to the toxicity of its emotions. In its plan there are analogous companions, pertinent to the soul, that are activated by it during its lifetime. The soul will have to live through those specific lessons because it is obliged to. The companion, though, it will attract will be proportionate to its purity, determining immediately how mild the apprenticeship experienced will be.

Within its plan, therefore, are included various scenarios, which the soul activates according to the positive or negative energy it displays at given times. If the soul succeeds in uniting with its Higher Self during a specific incarnation it will be able to change the scenario it had decided upon, depending on the receptivity it will have, and it will be capable of advancing and making new and more positive choices for its life. I believe that particularly the young children, who are about to embark on this voyage of living through their choices, are more capable of making radical changes to their plan mainly because their Higher Selves project more positive solutions and smarter choices. In that way the toxicity embedded in the older plan is abolished. Thus, the soul keeps a tight rein over its future and reforms it. Its future is then characterized by ongoing progress, continuous advance and permanent evolution.

THE SOUL'S FLIGHTS TO THE EMBRYO

During my esoteric journeys, the masters spoke to me about the flights the soul makes until it is decided whether it will be born or not. In order to prepare for its descent, the soul examines one by one the plans of various parents, so as to select those it regards most suitable for it to carry out its own plan. After that, a comprehensive preparation project commences in which all the prospects of success are analyzed. After the final and definite selection of the parents is made, a channel opens, functioning also as a gate, which corresponds to the specific evolutionary level of the soul.

Once the fusion of the sperm cell and the ovum is realized, a gate of descent is activated. From the moment the embryo starts mutating into some type of primary essence, which actually is comprised of cells uniting, it starts constructing the primary level of cells as well as the cellular memory regarding its parents. While this is in progress, around the third month of gestation, the soul performs its first flight inside the embryo to begin getting used to its new carrier. As the gestation continues the flights become all the more frequent. In the sixth month, the soul is now well aware of the physical structure of its carrier, of the ongoing gene transfer as well as of the integration of its plan with those of its parents.

These fundamental constituents are passed on and integrated into the recordings of the cellular memory. At any given time though the soul can decide to cut off the cord that connects it to the embryo and prevent the birth from ever taking place. The exact reasons for which this may happen are not revealed to anyone. Only the soul and its spiritual guides actually know why. If again, the soul decides that it desires to complete the process and be born, then the moment the baby is being delivered the soul imparts to it its first breath of life which also constitutes its essence. Then, the newborn is delivered and starts living among us in the third dimension.

After delivery the soul continues to remain for longer and longer periods of time within the infant until it cuts off the spiritual cord connecting it with the gate and the waiting rooms beyond it. The first cord is cut exactly the moment the newborn exits the mother's womb, the moment that is, when the soul finds itself in a new reality. The second is cut when the infant becomes more conscious and begins to realize the world around it, and recognizes the surrounding environment and its parents. The newborns sleep for many hours because that allows the soul unlimited time for performing flights from the third dimension towards the fourth to receive the guidance required to improve and ameliorate its situation. This procedure is more of concern to a soul that is conscious enough and fully aware of its choices.

THE SOUL'S DEPARTURE

MEANS OF ESCAPE

Several times the soul decides to depart before the completion of its plan is reached, for reasons beyond and independent of the personality's desires. In case such an event occurs some nodal points have been defined and attached to the original plan that function as escape windows. The Law of Free Will pulls the strings and creates the necessary conditions so that the soul can depart in a particular way (that could be a disease or an accident), and be given the chance to create and form another, a better schooling plan for another lifetime.

Should such occasions of "termination of contract" occur, nobody can prevent the decision from being put into effect. There are however, instances of plan reversing, especially when the soul considers that its plan can be altered radically so as to secure a smooth flow. Then, it makes an internal arrangement with its Higher Self stating that it will change, and an extension is given to it in order to carry out the specific alterations. Hence, the escape window closes and we bear witness to situations in which a person miraculously comes out of a very serious disease or a heavy accident safe. This extension is given to some people after making prayers to some divine entity those people believe are protected by. However, this situation of making arrangements is found outside the domains of mainstream religion. What happens then is simply that a religious person handles the base of his faith in such a way that he places himself in the position to achieve his objective.

There are many instances during which the soul has chosen to depart after sustaining an injury or after falling seriously ill, only because it has to "pay off" a certain karmic debt. Even this scenario though lies within the boundaries of apprenticeship. We are the ones who judge and classify events or choices we make as either good or evil through the prism of tension and stress built up around us by our own emotions. This view however, tends to be personal and is invariably hued by our occasional or occurrent knowledge. The occasions during which the soul decides to be taught a lesson are numerous to such an extent that I can only analyze just one tiny speck of it.

Depending on the extent to which the soul improves its plan or not, it can open or close the various escape windows respectively. Many people ask me with regards to suicidal people. There are two points of view that can explain suicide.

The first is that suicide may have been a part of the person's plan in order to balance a past misconduct. That is, the choice of committing suicide could possibly concern a karmic lesson the soul had predestined itself to learn. The second is the manifestation of the soul's inability to pass a certain lesson or training that itself had chosen for itself to experience and undergo. In that occasion, it violates the universal divine laws and is consequently condemned to wander the etheric plane until the appointed time limit for departure expires. That soul relives the same pain until it is liberated via a promising new rebirth.

In addition, it is feasible for a soul to decide to revoke its arrangement in advance. Ergo, death of fetuses occur within their mother's wombs, or babies die after they are born. For these situations again there are two views. The former is that the soul has already decided to cancel its plan; the latter is that through these occurring deaths covenants are signed concerning the child's parents.

I have observed, during my esoteric journeys, souls asking from their Higher Selves to prevent an impending illness, or death. Then a petition is made to negate the plan, which has yet to be substantiated and accounted for. The Higher Self forwards the petition to the Higher Councils of Masters, stressing the reasons for which the soul desires to alter its former plan, opening up a path for making offerings. After the petition is examined and considered it is either accepted or denied. I have attended such councils and I have realized that the Higher Self can act as an advocate for its psychic projection, since its quick and its best possible progress is of a great concern to it as well.

LIFE AFTER DEATH

When the souls, after their departure from Earth, enter the lower realms of astral toxicity they are in a semi-conscious state. It is then that they return immediately to the third dimension to be reborn. This happens because they are given the chance to ascend quicker the evolutionary ladder. However, they are obliged to continue resuming exactly from where they left off. If they are not awakened, so as to upgrade the channel of escape, they usually manifest the same toxic behavior, further linking their conduct with their parents. This occasion is an illustration of what happens to souls that have been burdened by a very heavy plan.

Concerning the souls that come from a higher and more evolved and upgraded astral level, they can select a better plan, since they have already displayed improvement during their "schooling". Even for these though a possibility of premature departure from Earth exists, if they choose so. Moreover, because the planet's evolution is approaching its final cycle, births of souls coming from the lower more primitive astral levels are progressively ceased, since they have already entered a state of dissolution.

A soul never decides to be born if its mother has chosen to terminate, for reasons of her own, her pregnancy. Even if that's the case no murder is committed, contrary to the beliefs held for many centuries by the clergy. There can be though a form of agreement between the soul and its mother concerning making a change or deviating slightly from the former decision, if that is deemed beneficial for both. Thus, as life on Earth is full of mysteries and covert scenarios, one can understand how many similar or how many more hidden and obscure elements can be experienced by the soul during its journey.

Life after death is what is referred to as life in the fourth dimension, which constitutes a vast plane where souls often dream and tend to shape their surroundings. Imagine a huge computer on the memory of which thoughts and emotions are recorded. Various fields are created there, which the souls enter after their material body dies. They pass into their own "cyberspace" and are imprisoned there until the next incarnation takes place. In these "cyberspaces" they continue living having the same emotions and thoughts, creating thus an environment similar to the one they were used to on Earth.

Upon these planes they come across the consciousnesses of people, who have left their corporeal frame behind, with which they can communicate. It seems therefore, that what many esoterists have claimed is true. Namely, that in life after death souls that had compatible relationships in real life meet and get together once again.

From the moment we are born and throughout the whole duration of our lifetime, we form, on our own, the environment around us from which we also gather experiences. On our experiential plane other people are continuously in motion as well, accompanying us, on a domestic, vocational, friendly and erotic level. Through our associations with them we learn lessons, in order to improve the level on which we operate.

Exactly the same happens when consciousness enters the astral planes of the fourth dimension. Several souls do not realize that they have departed from life and thus they continue to operate exactly as they did while alive. Those that become aware that something is altering their surroundings and perceive that the environment changes according to their emotions, ask for help from the bottom of their hearts. It is then that specific entities tear through the stellar matter and visit them to offer their help.

A similar situation prevails there, as it does here on Earth, where many people remain so engrossed in their personal problems creating a miserable and distressing environment for those around them. Those however, who start seeking help begin to improve their rationale and to restrain their toxic emotions. The benefit they reap is that after death they enter the exact same advanced level they created for as long as they lived.

The souls that change their attitude and their conduct set an example for those who are near to them, whom they also attract into their own personalized paradise.

The toughtforms have created astral entities that dwell within our emotional levels. We feed them and they tend to be so alive, just as we are. They are disembodied entities moving around astral spaces and draining energy from our emotions.

In order to secure their lives they start fitting astral tentacles into men's auras to keep rekindling the toxic emotions. Hence, they entrap the human souls in an illusion, projecting upon them images of an unreal world making them believe that it is actually real.

Man continuously moulds his astral matter depending on the positive or negative choices he makes in life. Frequently, he is driven to make the same mistakes as he is trapped in the astral fields of the fourth dimension and the only thing he does, without realizing it, is to keep moving back and forth, going from one incarnation to another until something or somebody points him towards the path leading to liberation.

In the material world engulfing us we live, for as long as we are awake that is, in a state of alertness, whereas when we sleep, our astral body enters the astral plane where the thoughtforms dwell. There, we can confront our worst fears that take on the form of toxic entities. This encounter reinforces the emotions of fear, anger and revenge to an even greater extent.

Whatever we dream constitutes either a pictorial representation of emotions that we experience during the day or it concerns recordings of the subconscious. If some people study these recordings they may "remember" some of their past lives that have exerted some influence over and have had a great impact on or have stigmatized their present lives in some form. If they manage to decode some of these inclinations towards making mistakes and displaying fear, they can improve the level of their consciousness.

THE SOUL'S PREPARATION FOR THE RETURN

REFORMATION OF PEOPLE'S CONSCIOUSNESSES.

There are times when during our dreams we are visited by entities coming from the Fifth dimension, in order to awaken us with regards to our assignment. They are Archangels, angels, masters, or healers that appear with the view to pulling us out of commitment. They remind us that the world we consider to be real is nothing else than a mere reflection of our own thoughts. We can either condemn or redeem ourselves by taking the first step, that of self-knowledge. Such dreams occur infrequently during our lives and we usually recognize them due to their brightness and the smooth flow of admonition and lecturing that distinguishes them.

Our dimension, the third, is currently permeated by energy coming from the Fifth dimension. Hence, Earth is cleansed and purified of its poisonous toxic thoughts, roaming round its astral matter. For as long as these efforts of the Earth last- in view of the completion of its last cycle of evolution- we can observe climatological changes worldwide. To be precise, whenever an astral level is forever eliminated, that is usually accompanied by manifestations of intense weather phenomena.

Parallel to these events, a reformation of the consciousnesses of people and their evolutionary levels also occurs. The new souls that will be born will possess no receptors on which the tentacles of the astral entities could attach to, and they will create a very advanced standard of living, because they will be in a continuous and complete contact with their Higher Selves. What is more, depending on their missions, they will maintain contact with thousands of teachers, who will guide their lives.

The genitors of the Fifth dimension have concluded that now is the proper time to send delegations to Earth, which by uniting forces with several other warriors will partake in dissolving the astral planes. As a result, souls that are regarded as possessing the potential of evolution are transferred to higher astral levels that haven't yet been destroyed. The destiny that awaits the rest however is different. Their archives are erased, and they are mutated by being integrated with better psychic elements, before being finally transferred to higher astral levels. Nevertheless, there are souls that have completely lost their divine essence and are connected to their animalistic nature alone. These are utterly dissolved and cast into oblivion, and chaos. There, because they cannot find any type of sustenance they shrink and fade away.

The missions that have been sent to the etheric plane of Earth have begun to prepare the souls for their final return through various means. One of these regards continuous flights (travels) that can be realized after a new vehicle, called the energy, body is created. These flights lead directly to the Fifth dimension, where specialist healers relieve the souls of any karmic recordings.

When the genitors reminded me of my descent and announced my assignment I felt that it would be impossible to succeed. However, there assistance was astounding and the flow of events put me easily right on track. Now, I know now that I am, as well as others are, guiding groups of souls to reach their mother land.

It is a strenuous effort; nonetheless, because the soul can easily and readily recognize its natural home, it enters these mutations boldly and faithfully, so as to be freed from the empty shells, meaning the thought–forms and the toxic emotions, vibrating around it.

PLANET EARTH
THE FINAL CYCLE

THE PRIMEVAL EXTENSIONS
OF HUMAN INSTINCTS

ANIMAL AND PLANT KINGDOMS

AERIAL AND AQUATIC LEVELS

The vehicle on an astral journey

PLANET EARTH
THE FINAL CYCLE

Planet Earth including the entity that supports and reinforces it-whom I refer to as Goddess Earth (Gaia)- has concluded thousands of years of evolution during which it has grown and evolved, transforming its surface and inner structure along the way. Now, it is completing its final cycle of evolution and its soul is preparing to depart, seeking its brothers and sisters who have already arrived in the Fifth dimension. The creation of an opening for that transition has begun since 1996. The planet's psychic axis has progressively assumed a clockwise inclination, whereas its heartbeats have increased their vibrations.

Many climatological changes and geological upheavals, which have been occurring for many years on the planet, are nothing but the precursory stage marking the moment of the soul's impending departure. Each and every planet and star in our galaxy covers several life cycles and subsequent to that its soul leaves heading towards higher levels. Nothing remains stationary when it comes to evolution. "Panta rhei", "everything is in a state of flux" as Heraclitus had postulated.

As man's corporeal frame undergoes some physical changes right before his soul departs, in a likewise fashion Earth goes through similar stages.

Earth is a colossal living organism comprised of about seventy five per cent water, while it also possesses a neural network, organs, as well as gates that function similar to man's energy centers. It is believed that such an enormous organism does not bear life only on its surface but in its interior as well. We posses knowledge regarding life on the surface and several indications concerning life in the interior of the planet. The inner world of the entity called Earth is comprised of levels that correspond to its respective energy centers.

Man, who constitutes a miniature representation of the planet's organism, goes through various stages of deterioration and rejuvenation similar to those of Earth. The organs responsible for giving commands are located in and belong to the highest energy centers of man, the pineal gland (or epiphysis), the pituitary gland (or hypophysis) and part of the thyroid gland. Directives that reach the brain and various stimuli that reach the optic nerves are transmitted by these organs.

The rest of the thyroid gland, the heart center and part of the solar plexus compose the emotional part of the astral body. Within the heart, which also functions as the regulator of the organism, one can locate the psychic archive. That is exactly the place where all the knowledge and wisdom the soul has distilled from its various incarnations is accumulated, and where the heart of the soul is found.

Finally, the etheric body, consisting of a part of the solar plexus, the abdominal and the genital center, is where the karmic record of each soul is stored.

The entity called Earth is connected with the corresponding energy centers of man through invisible umbilical-like cords emerging from the planet's energy centers. As a result, people formulate a huge chain of organisms that is continuously fed, nourished and activated by mother Earth, either on the surface or in its interior. As cellular organisms they either function positively or parasitically by employing the gift of Free Will which has been bestowed upon them.

Because the cycle of Earth is coming to a close, it passes through various purification stages. People refer to them as floods, glaciers, earthquakes, volcano eruptions and in general as climatological and geological changes, occurring continuously on the exterior and in the interior parts of its mantle.

Just think of the process a dying man goes through when his soul is about to depart. He is already attached to a specific level of the fourth (the astral) dimension which is continuously reformed by his thoughts and emotions. Being subconsciously aware that he will depart, he engages in internally settling his issues by either revising or accepting certain attitudes he had adopted during his lifetime. Oftentimes some physical changes occur. Loss of fluids has been observed, as well as development of fever, convulsions or hypothermia also become evident until the soul finally departs. Many of these symptoms have been documented using medical terms and are usually evident either a few days or a few hours before the time of death. Through our limited perception we are incapable of comprehending these stages and the ways through which the soul of the planet may finally depart. We all desire and hope that this departure be concluded under the best and smoothest of conditions, however, we tend to forget that Earth is a massive organism which during this time is going through a series of changes.

Vibrations emerging from the Fifth dimension have already passed through Earth's gates and are now dissolving the lower astral levels. The more the passage of energy coming from the Fifth dimension increases, the more the stellar or astral matter will shrink until it is totally transformed and is turned into an amorphous mass. Then, it can only be utilized as a basis for shrouding oncoming births, firstly deriving from the fifth and secondly from the Sixth dimension.

As the condensed mass composed of the toxic thoughtforms and the stellar matter is dissolved, it simultaneously allows the respective astral levels to undergo purification and termination. This process has an impact on the physical mass of Earth as well.

Consequently, the occurring geological, atmospheric and climatological upheavals constitute a corollary which applies equally to all the entities that pass through the purification process.

The planet is not being destroyed, instead it is mutating so as to secure that the new soul, about to be activated within it, will be detached of any astral levels.

The elements of air, water, fire and earth constitute multiple manifestations of mother Earth. They also pass through purifications, which are manifested in varying degrees of intensity, and which we are already witnessing now.

As these changes are taking place, some people are bound to leave Earth mainly because they have reached the age limit during which departure is imminent, whereas the young will go on living and adjusting to the new circumstances. On the other hand, some souls will have to sustain dissolution, for the sole reason that the astral levels to which they have been used to being attached will no longer exist.

On top of that, a given part of the souls will mutate and be born out of the upper astral levels which have not yet been dissolved. The remainder of the souls which also constitutes the largest part of them will return home, the Fifth dimension, at a predetermined time.

The Mayan calendar, as well as many other sources, mentions that the life cycle of this planet will end in 2012. I would rather not dwell on that date, since time is malleable but I would prefer to dwell on the various scenarios of destruction that are revolving around us. The planet is not being destroyed. It is simply changing its form to welcome a new deity that will animate it, allowing it to commence a new cycle based on new and advanced social and cultural structures.

This New Earth will be inhabited by the so called meta-humans. These will be people that will have become accustomed to the new circumstances and that will possess and display special capabilities and potentials. Souls that will become the parents of the so called meta-humans are already being created. This regards the inhabitants of the New Earth, the crystal children or the children of the crystal vibration, whose way has been paved by the indigo children.

What has further been revealed to me, mainly through the communication I have with the Fifth dimension, is that the new soul that will enter Earth, exactly at the moment of the old soul's departure, will be an Atlantean one.

On planet Earth, the New Earth, a new Atlantean civilization will emerge that is destined to reach the highest levels of intelligence excelling at science, art and interplanetary travels. Astrophysics will advance to such an extent that it will allow the manipulation and control of the rings of time and space to access other stellar systems. Additionally, genetics will develop to such a point that it will allow man to live from three hundred to five hundred years, without experiencing or becoming aware of the wear and tear that accompanies aging. Moreover, man will possess the power of departing for his celestial home whenever he chooses to, transforming his material structure in specially created mutational machines, that will transfer him to any planetary system he desires.

I would like the readers of this book to break away from a specific and directed trend guided by the thoughtforms of the dark forces, who unwilling to change the facts, keep sowing the seeds of fear ultimately terrorizing people. Fear creates chain reactions that intoxicate human thoughts and emotions. For that reason, send your love to the heart of the planet to facilitate its departure.

It has also been made known to me that after all the secrets of the past Atlantis will have been revealed, the Earth's soul will leave the planet heading for a superior dimension, the fifth. Earth will become a wonderful blue planet there, and it will welcome the souls that will have succeeded in returning to their homeland. The departure of Earth's soul will be effectuated from the exact place where the heart of the planet beats, via a tremendous explosion. The old soul will depart from the East, whereas the new soul will enter from the West.

We are at a very significant juncture in the history of the planet and we are offered the chance to be in harmony with the new energy rhythms, so as to burn the karmic causes which are binding us to the astral level. From the moment we tune in with the ever increasing heartbeats of Earth, we align ourselves with the gateway's tremendous energy flow that will help us return to our heavenly homeland. Many people might continue to live for several decades before they depart, whereas those that remain will enjoy the new state of affairs in terms of evolution that is destined to rise as time goes by on this New Earth.

THE PRIMEVAL EXTENSIONS
OF HUMAN INSTINCTS

ANIMAL AND PLANT KINGDOMS
AERIAL AND AQUATIC LEVELS

The forms that belong to the animal kingdom constitute materializations of the primeval extensions of man's instincts, that is, instincts that have been recorded on human DNA. The primeval form of an animal is characterized by wild instincts. Man himself started off possessing such an animalistic form, but through the ages he evolved. His evolution was not a random event, though. It was forwarded by missions of geneticists sent to Earth. These geneticists passed on to humans the seeds of consciousness and intellect. Yet, man's primeval element remained in the unconscious, where the wild bestial instincts are stored. These tend to be shrouded by the lower personality, which man constantly strives to gain control over and which constantly presents difficulties man continuously tries to iron out. The more he evolves intellectually and emotionally, the more the collective consciousness of the animals will mutate in evolutionary terms. Therefore, as man's consciousness develops and keeps burning the remains of his bestial nature, many species of wild animals inevitably become extinct.

In particular, domesticated animals and pets closely follow man's evolutionary course and pick up certain elements from him, such as emotion. Three centers are active in these kinds of animals, the genital, the abdominal, and the solar plexus ones. These centers contain information, pertaining to the instinct of survival and a broad range of emotions also driven by instinct. Consequently, these animals operate possessing a highly evolved solar plexus and are immediately affected and influenced by human emotion and behavior, since their three centers are connected with the corresponding three centers of human beings. Through this type of connection the animals maintain a very good level of contact with the person that keeps them. Thus, certain animals, like dogs and cats, identify with their owners' habits, and their reactions tend to be reminiscent of the personality of the person who takes care of them, as that person imparts his love. Oftentimes though that person also imparts parts of his toxic emotions.

Whenever such a continuous toxic emotion is conveyed to domesticated animals, they in turn either become seriously ill, or die. Essentially, they unwillingly become filters of human emotional toxicity. Animals that live in a better environment and are treated with love and understanding often function as healing conductors for man. Many of these animals have been born innumerable times, because innumerable are the emotions of man as well. In our time and age, some of them have started developing elements pertaining to consciousness and intellect.

In general terms, animals follow man as he passes through the various evolutionary stages, and are released by him when he manages to shatter and demolish his lower personality. They can move between the third and the fourth dimension, where they usually follow behind the person with whom they were connected while alive. Because they operate with one hundred per cent astral matter, devoid of the divine spark, they remain on the astral level of thoughtforms, without being allowed access to more advanced dimensions, like the fifth.

In this new age of highly evolved consciousness, animals will also exist, which due to their upgrade will be capable of directly communicating with man, since the code preventing any type of communication in our era will unavoidably have been broken by then. The form that some mutated animal species will have during the age of the meta-humans cannot be described by employing current data. For as long as the Fifth dimension continues penetrating into the third and fourth, some animal species will keep becoming extinct. The more people detach themselves from any karmic causes and of any displays of toxic behavior, the more they will "humanize" animals, because the focal point connecting the two species will change. Humans will still be connected with animals but through the heart chakra, the center of love, and the center of thought, the intellect. As a consequence, animals that will remain on Earth will develop new codes of communication. Meaning that, all the efforts made to save animals from gradual extinction is actually a misleading notion. It is like pursuing a utopian dream, since both man and the planet are changing form.

Animals are born in etheric matrices that are formed depending on the Earth's evolutionary period and on man's projected thoughtforms and emotions. When animals die they return to these matrices depending on their species and are attracted by the emotional energy of the person with whom they had been connected during their various incarnations. Then, they are usually reborn in the form of a new pet destined to keep company once again to the same people, compensating for their previous loss. As a consequence many tend to see the pet they had lost in the eye's of a new pet they obtain.

Mother Earth's projected emotions and thoughtforms are actually what constitute the plant kingdom which has no connection whatsoever to man. In contrast, it tends to be quite hostile to man, mainly due to the futile and meaningless exploitation it has sustained.

The aquatic level, (the sea, the rivers and the lakes), inclusive of all the forms of life found therein, constitutes image projections stemming from the Earth's unconscious. That is to say, all that compose the aquatic level are image recordings extending from the time of the Earth's birth up to its final evolutionary cycle. These recordings are projected on various levels of expression, either negatively or positively.

Finally, the aerial level, (the air, nature and birds), in all its forms again constitutes projections of the Earth's thoughts. It regards, that is, and corresponds to the planet's noetic level.

All these various levels of Earth's expression are on the point of passing through various phases of mutation. Furthermore, the objective of those who have been awakened is to surround nature with love, for the sole intention of keeping continuously in touch with the planet's emotional levels.

Nephelon Galaxy

THE FIFTH DIMENSION
THE HEAVENLY HOME

THE STAGES OF EARTH'S EVOLUTION

THE JOURNEYS

TIME IN THE Fifth dimension

HYPER-FAST PHOTONS

FOLDING OF SPACE

TEMPORAL DILATION

THE FIFTH DIMENSION
THE HEAVENLY HOME

The Fifth dimension has been designated as the only reality concerned with soul upgrading. It consists of thousand of galaxies and is governed by the divine essence of the universe. Astrophysicists have already discovered its presence and have entered a procedure of documentation based on evidence and data. In due course, humans will be able to travel towards that dimension through space-time folding. Lemurians, Atlanteans and twelve entities men called Gods had traveled to Earth coming from the Fifth dimension. By mentioning the twelve entities I am actually referring to the ancient polytheistic Hellenic religion of the Dodecatheon.

THE STAGES OF THE EARTH'S EVOLUTION

The Fifth dimension as well is divided into various evolutionary stages. However many souls return there, they all operate as a couple with their Higher Self and work on a variety of missions. When they fulfill their apprenticeship in that dimension, then they commence the procedure of being transferred to the sixth. This entails a lot of preparatory work which is too complicated to be understood by us with the sketchy knowledge we have.

The Fifth dimension is located in the future and it represents evolution and the place from which knowledge and discoveries are channeled to our dimension and specifically to planet Earth. All this, which is forwarded in the earthly time flow, undergoes fermentation and is subject to bipolar tendencies of positive and negative, light and dark, yin and yang forces, until they are complete.

Conditional on the evolution of the planet's and the souls' consciousnesses, channeled knowledge becomes operative and is also forwarded and materialized. Therefore, the filter plays a very crucial role in ensuring that all the knowledge that has been imparted and that flows to planet Earth actually works either for personal benefits or for the general good. Having completed numerous evolutionary cycles from the moment of its creation centuries ago up to the present moment, the planet has undergone much fermentation. Souls have evolved trough pain, conflict but through joy as well. These emotions and situations have inoculated the cellular memory of the planet. Now that the final evolutionary cycle is nearing its end an increasing number of souls perceive that they are entering the final straight for returning to their heavenly homeland.

The entities called the Higher Selves live and work in the Fifth dimension. From there, they attempt to come into contact with the soul, their other counterpart, so as to awaken it and guide it. Many people mistake these entities for guardian angels. Although our Higher Self is our most important guardian it has a different constitution and make-up from that of an angel.

From the moment of their birth, the Higher Selves- in a Godlike fashion - dichotomize their spiritual and psychic essence projecting it from the ninth dimension into the eighth, seventh and Sixth dimension and they become active as conscious entities in the Fifth dimension. Their subdivided spiritual essence remains inactive in the upper dimensions until it once again becomes reunited with them. These resulting substances all together constitute a type of consciousness that sleeps and dreams, receiving and gaining experiences while dormant from their more active counterpart dwelling in the Fifth dimension. Highly evolved souls such as Pythagoras and Plato have referred to their contact with that entity and have passed down to us that knowledge through their manuscripts.

THE JOURNEYS

We travel towards the Fifth dimension transferring our psychic projections. In order for this to take place however certain conditions have to be met:

First of all, a properly trained spiritual guide is required. This is one of my basic roles. Secondly, the people who have decided to participate will have to be initiated, in advance, in the way the connection with their Higher Self will be performed, for it is going to act as the medium connecting the third and fourth dimensions with the fifth.

Before each journey begins I bring my students to a state of relaxation so as to connect all their centers with the corresponding ones of their Higher Selves. The centers are seven: the epiphysis, the hypophysis, the thyroid, the heart, the solar plexus, and last but not least the abdominal and the genital ones. Next, we enter deeper states of relaxation. Through these connections the Higher Self manages to pull the astral vehicle outwards. The material body is connected with the etheric and the astral one with a luminous energy cord. After the astral vehicle is fully projected, the energy flows between the connected centers are accelerated. This type of union is a form of spiritual intercourse. An energy vehicle carrying and containing elements from both the fourth and the Fifth dimension is a direct result of this bonding, which is often referred to as the energy body. It possesses the ability to transfer us to the Fifth dimension mainly because it incorporates the necessary components that will allow it to cross over.

It should be pointed out that during the first journeys, that specific vehicle is not fully formed and should be administered the rudimentary operational structures by the entities of the Fifth dimension. In it certain parts of the current personality are transported as is a certain plan regarding subconscious recordings.

All the incarnations that have created karmic causes to the solar plexus, the abdominal (sacral chakra) and the genital centers are documented in the subconscious. Simultaneously, the psychic record is transferred to the heart centre (anahata) where our current life plan is recorded always in connection with all our previous plans present in all our previous incarnations. The noetic archive is transferred last and concerns mainly our way of thinking, as well as the program concerned with the orders administered by the brain. These commands determine our choices, our perception, and the way by which we analyze facts.

Once these primary constituents have been transferred, the Higher Self, being assisted by the guiding entity, cuts the connections from the subtle astral vehicle leaving only one unifying cord intact, which continues to sustain the link with the material, the etheric and the energy bodies.

The difficulty in this procedure is that the students should not lose their consciousness completely. Instead being helped by the spiritual guides their levels of alertness should remain unaltered.

The navigators frame the group by forming an octahedron, a tetragonal bipyramid which consists of a tetragonal pyramid and its mirror image joined together base-to-base, which resembles a rhombus. Guardian Archangels are situated on each of its angles. These are Michael, Gabriel, Raphael, Uriel and Zakchiel. They are connected to the entire group via umbilical-like energy cords in order to assist with the commencement of the syntonization and the transition to the etheric plane, where the gateway is found. The rhombus is a sacred symbol that symbolizes the structure of the divine cell. Via this morphic vibration, which also constitutes a hologram in the shape of a bipyramid, we develop and syntonize our cells as well.

As the transition to the etheric plane takes place we find ourselves on a vibrating base whose moving rhythms progressively keep increasing. The holographic bipyramid surrounds us. Its upper apex determines the direction of our destination whereas the lower apex constitutes and determines the exact position for the return. In the front there are four rotating rings that formulate the entrance of a gate and configure the direction which is also determined by thousands of rotating rings. These rings are capable of transferring us via time warping to such a remote dimension like the fifth. To activate the gate certain codes have to be provided which only the navigators are aware of. If the journey concerns the level concerned with karmic releases then during the transition certain imprints are gathered that reside in the astral and etheric akashic archives.

The astral akashic archives constitute a multi-plane environment consisting of multiple level subdivisions where the planet's historic archives are kept together with the causes each soul has created in each of its incarnations. A part of those is collected each time, so that these karmic causes can be removed by particular entities of the Fifth dimension.

Thereafter, we exit through a gate only to enter a level we usually refer to as "the station" which divides the fourth from the Fifth dimension. Specialist instructors such as Arion, Phelathros, Artemis, and Vahiar take us under their wings, while others using special crystals surround our energy bodies with a protective energy grid obstructing and simultaneously preventing toxic leak from entering the galaxy. The next stage involves us being driven towards the gateway that ultimately leads to Nephelon galaxy found in the Fifth dimension.

TIME IN THE FIFTH DIMENSION

HYPER-FAST PHOTONS
FOLDING OF SPACE
TEMPORAL DILATION

Our gate is determined by frequency number nine, which is a symbolic number standing for completion. Codes are given at this gate as well. Once we pass through it, we find ourselves in a crystalline vehicle accompanied by navigators that represent one of the planets of the galaxy. They activate various channels with rotating rings through which the vehicle moves. These rings are hyper-fast photons governed by frequencies of the Fifth dimension. They fold space annihilating distances rendering the arrival to each planet a very rapid event. The notion of time that our body, which has remained behind, experiences turns out to be relative. Some people feel that it elongates while others feel as if everything is happening simultaneously within the space of a moment. The feeling of time is non-existent in the Fifth dimension. What does exist is a sensation of time dilation, according to which an event or even a movement occur simultaneously.

As a navigator, I am obliged to coordinate time according to our terrestrial specifications so that I ensure the journey lasts approximately an hour. That is the difficult part, for I must transfer simultaneously the consciousnesses of all the members of the group, the image and the dimensional information. Each and every student receives his own information and respective guidance that impels him to turn his life to advantage by changing his options by developing a constructive approach to life, and by setting himself on a more positive course. The trainees align their consciousness with the guidance provided by the masters of the Fifth dimension. Following that their upgrading commences, as they transmute the dark elements of their personalities into brighter ones.

Etheric gate of departure

NEPHELON GALAXY

ZIRION THE EMERALD PLANET

THE PLANETS OF THE GALAXY

OUR DIVINE ORIGIN

Crystalline structure for carrying out genetic mutations

NEPHELON GALAXY

ZIRION THE EMERALD PLANET

Nephelon galaxy reflects our solar system though chronologically it is situated in the future, since it lies within the realms of the Fifth dimension. Familiar and usual time measurements that exist on Earth simply do not apply there, and the only perception of time one has is its dilation. The specific solar system called Nephelon activates and governs our solar system rendering us capable of perceiving three-dimensional operations. Because our visual ability is limited we can only witness a minute part of it rather than its entire existence. From Nephelon galaxy missions come and go having as their primary objective a dimensional upgrading.

The emerald planet called Zirion consists of crystalline structures. The center of the planet is made of a condensed crystal resembling an emerald. On the planet there are multiplex building facilities and brilliant temples, where initiations and removals of karmic causes are preformed. All the initiatory stages and the mutations of the psychic DNA are performed in some of Zirion's buildings by masters and Archangels and by entities operating as geneticists. The Archangels manage to sustain the cohesion of the energy links between the planets intact, through various frequencies.

The planet is represented by a couple, Ziron and Moira, who are genitors. They are accompanied by higher entities and masters that at times had appeared on planet Earth to promote evolution. On our planet they were given various names and because they were aware of the secrets of life and bioenergetic manipulation we regarded them as Gods. Ziron and Moira are non-other than Zeus and Hera. They are both surrounded by all the Gods, demigods and masters that have contributed much and have played a very crucial role concerning Earth's evolutionary stream.

Throughout the galaxy, those who have completed the course of their lives act as divine couples. Each couple is characterized by a distinct feature which it develops in these cities dealing with advanced programs. Whenever we travel to one of the planets of this galaxy, in order to identify them, these entities project the form they had during the time they had paid a visit to Earth.

The emerald planet's matter tends to be organic and it possesses a distinct intelligence that can detect the physical structure of the bodies transferred there for upgrading. In the towering buildings one can find channels containing complex transformers in which projections of entities of the Sixth dimension are manifested. The Sun, a huge planet named Auric, sustains and maintains the cohesion of this specific solar system and simultaneously functions as a large gateway that connects the fifth with the Sixth dimension. On the right and on the left there are two smaller planets-satellites that operate as channels responsible for equilibration and transformation. The right one has to do with solar consciousness while the left one concerns solar logos.

The highest hierarchy, which is comprised of entities acting as teachers, like Christ, determines the evolutionary streams of the worlds. The evolutionary course is often characterized as the solar route and constitutes the pathway that transcends religious restrictions and commitments.

The upgrading journeys from the third towards the Fifth dimension were not feasible up to now for souls that had many karmic impressions to burn, so as to upgrade their psychic quality. Usually, these, regarded souls that had completed their evolutionary cycles and that were capable of passing, after undergoing commensurate mutations, from the lower levels of the fourth dimension to the fifth.

Let us return though to the galaxy and the Nephelon solar system. The perceptual dimensions that govern the planets of the Fifth dimension are the dimension of sound vibrations, the dimension of holographic entities, and the dimension of the poly-morphic image. The entities in the galaxy of the Fifth dimension know how to convert the energy field around each living organism and every organic matter. They are aware of the frequencies required for conversion and transmutation of the various material forms and of psychic matter. Besides, even here on Earth, depending on the bioelectromagnetic field that forms around each organism, we can interfere either therapeutically or to materialize an object out of a morphogenetic field. Some of the initiates of our era had accomplished this. Wilhelm Reich and Tesla were two of the most brilliant minds that had attempted these transmutations, but they were dissuaded from continuing them. Their research may still be continued nowadays in some obscure laboratories.

THE PLANETS OF THE GALAXY

On the planets of the Fifth dimension soil doesn't exist at least like the type we are used to on our planet. Both flowers and nature in general are mere extensions of crystalline forms of structure. Spheres of condensed knowledge are also present. The inhabitants are given the possibility to choose a specific specialty and to unite with a large part of that knowledge, which keeps continuously upgrading through canals (channels) of the Sixth dimension. At specific intervals certain births of select entities have been directed toward the Earth from the galaxy, so as to propel and promote man's intellect and to assist in the evolution of human civilization. All the people of the Earth have recorded through images and paintings, or through symbols and signs, or through parables and myths the coming of such divine entities that have promoted transformations not only in social structure, but also in the human cellular DNA. These so called "gods" have left their mark. All this is accomplished through gates that become activated whenever missions are sent to the etheric plane of the planet or births of highly advanced souls occur.

The Gold planet is inhabited by hyper-intelligent entities that have already put their plan, of reinstating several souls to their homeland, into effect. In order for somebody to ultimately grasp and realize the space and matter of the Fifth dimension one requires his inner vision be structured via a five-dimensional mode of perception and imagery.

The planets of the Fifth dimension are environed by five rings that protect them by sustaining their cohesion via specific channels. Vehicles travelling in these channels move by means of super-fast photon rings.

The galaxy is surrounded by an incredibly immense, by our standards, station, which separates the fourth from the Fifth dimension by transforming the energy of the portals. Numerous gates of arrival and departure exist. The journeys take place under the guidance of experienced pilots that are aware of the proper codes. This station also functions as a gateway for entities descending to Earth's etheric mantle to promote new types of evolution (some of which are already becoming evident in science, social structure, and religion).

The Fifth dimension is an essential dimension, the world of integrated existence, where the oncoming mutations are scheduled, planned and decided upon. However, in order to render the entities of this dimension capable of materializing these new directions, transformers are needed, which in this case, are bodies living in the third dimension. These bodies belong to people inhabiting the Earth.

In order for a transformer to be created many mutational procedures are required. The receptors (energy centres) need to be upgraded so as to allow the higher energies of descent to be transformed, as well, without being the least affected by the corruption of the lower personality. These mutations have to do with the alignment of the central axis of the spinal cord and the transformation of the neural network. The latter needs to be developed with new nerve cells in order to be united with the higher channel.

In 1996 channels opened up on Earth. Gateways were activated so that forces form the Fifth dimension could be sent to Earth to prepare the descent of new notions. As such, we have been experiencing a rapid evolution in medicine, astrophysics, informatics and thousands of other changes whose sole purpose are to pave the way for the meta-humans. Until then the dimension that had been penetrating our reality was the fourth together with its parallel worlds.

OUR DIVINE ORIGIN

More and more people are nowadays realizing the true meaning of real existence and their own divine origin. Of course, life in the third dimension does seem real, mainly because the world of crude matter tends to be a tough learning environment. Emotions resemble shells that imprison us in leading and experiencing a deceptive life. Detached from our divine counterpart, we tend to reproduce the recordings of our astral body, the body which is directly connected to the impressions of the astral field.

The connection with the Higher Self opens up channels towards the Fifth dimension where it tends to reside and evolve. The first step we have to take is to accept that who we are, is not actually our true self.

However easy that may seem, it actually isn't. The "I" or "me" of the personality does not readily let go of the reins of domination over man's soul. Thus, the toxic emotions that are produced feed the masters that dominate the astral realms.

One of the great masters of all time that had referred to the celestial homeland, was Jesus. He opened the way for the return of the souls and taught about the ways through which we could connect with our divine nature. However, he was understood only by a few. Some of those few, who were also in the service of the astral lords, believed that by sentencing Christ to an ignominious death the Gate of Ascent would be subsequently closed as well. They furthermore attempted in thousands of ways to conceal his true teachings together with the information he gave concerning the ways leading to our connection with our heavenly home.

The first initiation regarding the connection with our Higher Self and the Fifth dimension begins the disillusioning process, in a certain way and we begin to remember our true essence.

The Higher Self is a real entity which in order to be approached by the human souls needs to be initially activated by a strong desire and wish to be unified with it. Its presence awakens memories hidden in our spiritual archives and it unfolds latent knowledge.

The connection with it creates an energy frequency, which vibrates continuously and increases in intensity as time goes by. A certain kind of catharsis ensues and the individual enters a phase where he/she starts resetting and reordering previous information. In addition, the psyche begins to acknowledge that the void it felt so far was actually its desire to be reunited with its divine nature.

THE JOURNEY

THE FIRST JOURNEY THE ANTICIPATION….. THE EXPECTATION

THE ARRIVAL

THE SECOND JOURNEY

THE GRAND PLAN

Departing vehicle on the way to Nephelon Galaxy

THE JOURNEY

THE FIRST JOURNEY-
THE ANTICIPATION....
THE EXPECTATION

Standing by we experience the usual nervousness felt before every journey. Breathing rates accelerate. The desire is great. We would all be going back to our homeland at least temporarily. Gradually, the body commits to the attention of the Higher Self who had previously connected all its centres with ours. The luminous body had already been formed and had taken its place beside it. Breathing can barely be noticed. We are all ready to stand in front of the gate. The Archangels, our navigators transfer us using invisible umbilical-like cords to another dimension of consciousness, which constitutes the etheric mantle of the Earth.

We are standing in front of a huge gate that begins to vibrate rhythmically. We look under our feet. A crystal base is shining. Bright explosions diffuse all around us and an enormous energy circuit embraces us. Multicoloured crystalline cords syntonise the luminous bodies. A pulsating cord connects us to our physical body. We look back. It seems foreign and indifferent to us now. We find ourselves in the arms of the divine being we were always on the quest for, through our numerous incarnations here on planet Earth. Above us a pyramid made out of a material that blinds us keeps glowing. It's a crystal that iridises like thousands of melting diamonds, disseminating their song. They are a part of the Earth's mantle. It constitutes the focal point of our return to this dimension. We feel free. Fear, sorrow, anger, and all the emotions that restricted us remain behind. Beauty, freedom, and love overwhelm our souls. The soul fixes its eyes on at its heavenly spouse, the Higher Self, who smiles back, holds its hand and tenderly says:

"You have nothing to be afraid of my dear heart. The waiting time is over. From now on we will be together for ever. We will keep travelling until we are united in heavenly holy matrimony. Whenever I casted my eyes on Earth, I was in pain watching you as you seemed to be lost, to be hurting, drowning slowly and tormentingly in the prison of solitude. Many times I pulled you out of the gutter and you felt a star shining in your heart. Yet, it always went out so fast. And now behold! We are ready to embark on our first journey home."

The vibrations have increased; the rings of the gate begin to rotate. The navigators have already provided the codes needed to commence the process. The atmosphere is electrifying, and the space has been flooded with light. The earthly sounds are echoing from afar. The barking of a dog, the piping of the birds and many other distant voices start fading as if a velvet veil is covering our ears. We cannot take our eyes off the rotating gate. The succession of colours and sounds cover us like a cloak.

We no longer stand on the base. We are swiftly absorbed by the vortex created by the rings of the gate. We are surrounded by the navigating officers that form a solid and powerful pyramid around us. We feel we are in a channel, composed of thousands of rings that are propelling us, shifting time, space and all the dimensions. We become one with them. With each shift we enter and experience varying shades of colour. They pass by us so fast! We hear the colours exploding. We feel the pressure of the photons that rotate, and fold the distances between dimensions. We feel no nostalgia for our bodies we have left behind, sitting torpidly in our chairs.

We focus our attention on a speck of light present at the top of the channel. Before we even realise it we have moved beyond that speck, which actually is another huge gateway composed of five rotating rings. We are pushed out of those rings and onto a similar crystal base. We are all looking surprised. The navigators smiling whisper to us the following:

"Do not be startled, you are at the station zone that not only separates the fourth form the Fifth dimensions but also constitutes a huge ring that surrounds Nephelon galaxy".

THE EXPECTATION

My heart beats fast. These heartbeats remind me of the visions I had during the first years of my awakening. So, I finally reached home! All the memories surround me and all the images assemble forming a gigantic puzzle. I am bound to this group and I constitute one of the links that connects them with their heavenly homeland. So many years, so much training. The difficult lessons, the tender, gentle but also unrelenting pressure I received from my spiritual masters, have led me here. Now I understand the twenty years of preparation that I had underwent.

Mixed emotions not only of pleasure but also of responsibility overwhelm me. Beside me, my Higher Self, my sweetheart, and all around me the heavenly navigators.

My eyes begin to clear and the image I see gradually stabilizes. The station is huge; the proportions are five times bigger than those of Earth. The structure of the materials resembles crystal and titanium, but in reality it's unknown to Earth. All around move other travellers as well. Some nod, others are familiar to us.

Navigators inform us that there are entities possessing varying abilities whose missions are to enter the etheric plane of Earth. Furthermore, they let us know of the soul entities that travel there in order to be upgraded, with a view to acquiring the potential to pass from the fourth dimension to that of the fifth.

The station's ring surrounding Nephelon galaxy is replete with departure and arrival gates. The entrance to the station is not that easy. The navigators know the codes that tend to change at every trip. Without them the gates do not open. The codes are administered by the Higher intergalactic council and are comprised of different symbols, which need to precisely lock into position in order for the gates to open.

Those travelling from Earth have been given a special tablet full of symbols (numbers and names) that provides the means by which they can travel together with the navigators. These codes are not activated if they are not modulated and coordinated with those of the navigators in advance. The entrance safety valves cannot in that case be cracked. The station is guarded by Special Forces that keep the travellers attuned at all times.

The navigators keep whispering to us:

"Do you know what you are and where you are?"

"You are time travellers, you come from the past and you are entering the future".

"Nephelon galaxy belongs to the future and it is your homeland. This is the place you lived in before you were separated from your Higher Self".

There are numerous questions, queries, there is impatience and yearning to learn, to remember. However, our navigators keep reassuring us:

"Everything you long for is going to be experienced at the specific time that has been preordained for your discipleship. At this specific moment you are not yet ready to receive this information. What we can assure you of is that multiple travels are going to take place. Through them you will be taught in order to replace the time you have already lost because of the long period of dormancy you have been in. You are still experiencing many influences from your lower personality. You still need a lot of work. Now, we will lead you to the gateway from which you will enter the galaxy".

We can sense the absence of gravity, an indiscernible dizziness and the absence of any type of tension. We enter a passageway moving smoothly with the flow. We inadvertently continue to hear syntonizing sounds. They sound like music, but what beauty there is in it! It is indescribable. It makes our bodies vibrate and infuses us with nostalgia. We reach another crystal base. In front of us lies another huge gate that vibrates rhythmically. Our navigators whisper the following to us:

Remember that you are standing in front of gate 9. You have just arrived from astral vibration number 6. The upgrade of 6 in rotation unlocks the final setting permitting our departure from gate 9.

There are many queries; however our longing to enter the galaxy dominates. A huge crystal screen draws our attention. On it, one can observe rotating numbers, symbols, complex equations and colours. The navigators enter their own codes into the system. A vortex forms. The gate opens the rings.

A vehicle appears out of the blue which totally startles us. So vehicles do exist! It is a reality. The navigators smile to us. Everything exists in the galaxy. It is not a figment of our imagination, it is not a hallucination. There are seats. They are made of organic matter which embraces the bodies and records data. At a distance we can see three navigators smiling at us. The emerald colour dominates their beautiful and singular outfits. On them one can see the symbols of the planet which we are travelling to. We ask which planet it is. Our pilots answer:

"It's the emerald planet!"

We are deluged with memories of days long past, overwhelmed by images succeeding each other. The masters, the training, the missions. How did I get trapped in this body? I am something else, yet, I entered something foreign. For the first time in my life I understand clearly my true identity. My heart melts. I look at my Higher Self and say to it:

"Now I remember. I remember how we loved each other. Dear God!" What psychic pain! Tears run down my cheeks and materialize on my physical body that is waiting. "You will find out more"; it responds looking deep into my eyes.

I feel my vision expanding, opening up like a giant flower. I closely watch as the Higher Selves activate the insight capabilities of the other souls' luminous bodies. The navigators gather up at the front part of the vehicle. They enter complicated codes and coordinates into a huge screen. In front of the vehicle a channel starts forming with thousands of rotating rings opening. The vehicle moves into the first ring and gradually passes through the rest. We try to take in all those images; we try to live the journey.

I ask Melenios (my Higher Self):

How is the transition actually realised?"

Affectionately, it answers to me the following:

"My dear Mary, we move through channels that are composed of super fast photon rings. The bending of time and space which allows us to travel to other planets in minimal time exists here as well."

"I feel that time cannot be measured", I whisper.

"That's right!" his voice echoes in my ear. "You are experiencing what is referred to as dilation of time, but it is quite difficult to comprehend and interpret when using your human brain".

I am baffled by the appearance of the vehicle. It is made out of crystal and a substance that resembles titanium.

"What kinds of materials are those?" I ask him.

"It is a mixture of crystalline structures and organic matter of the galaxy", he responds. "The vehicle possesses a type of intelligence of its own that is in a certain way connected to the commands given to it by the pilots".

"I feel as if I am participating in scenes of a science fiction picture movie", I say in amazement.

It smiles and meaningfully tells me:

"What do you think? That everything you see is just a deception? No Mary. All the guidelines and ideas stem from the Fifth dimension. You are in the future. Have you forgotten that?"

I try to adjust the potential of my widened mind to construe the reality of the third dimension, the place where our corporeal frames are waiting for us.

"I am having difficulty!"

"You will adjust! You have done it before", it responds.

I feel safety, lucidity and power. I look at the galaxy. The description, the words are so insufficient! The planets, the stars, everything is in motion. They are revolving in a feast of colours and sounds. Now I understand Pythagoras's reference to the music of the spheres. The two satellites, one on the right and on the left hand side, connect the fifth with the Sixth dimension. I still feel though that I need some more answers.

I look at him; he embraces me with his velvety look and tells me decisively:

"Now that I found you I won't lose you. You have entered the final straight for return."

I glance at the galaxy for one more time. I see other vehicles flowing in the channel, their destination being one of all those visible planets which it shows to me.

"You see that rose-coloured planet, that orange one, that blue one? We will travel there as well, where you will receive various initiations".

I do not ask. It feels as if I already know these things, though they still seem a bit blurry. The navigators prepare to approach the first of the five rings of the Emerald planet. I realize the inner gates opening. Its beauty surrounds me. We enter the atmosphere of a specific state. We finally arrived!

THE ARRIVAL

High above and nearing. The city is sparkling and the colourful rays run through its towering buildings. Most of them have crystal pyramids together with some type of antennae. At least that that's way I can interpret it. The proportions are enormous. Our Higher Selves reach 10 feet in height. The buildings have a peculiar arrangement. The floors of the buildings are detached from the central base but are simultaneously connected to it via cylindrical crystals. There are temples, where various initiations are carried out. One of them is made out of a mixture of marble and crystal. All the materials used for construction have a different composition and structure.

The entire Emerald planet is a huge mass of crystalline stone. It doesn't possess dirt or rocks like Earth. Instead, a crystal resembling the emerald dominates. The vehicle descends, passing vertically through a specific channel. It reaches a crystal base in whose centre a five-dimensional rhombus shines. The entire base is surrounded by a huge crystal sphere.

Three entities await there, Iesmel, Alvatar, and Achatios who are responsible for our having access to that place and who also act as teachers and geneticists. Genetics, on the planets of the Fifth dimension, has reached unimaginable proportions. They welcome us, but being in a dazzled condition we try to focus on their form, which due to lack of proper syntonization appears to us a bit vague and hazy (as if being in a state of fluidity). They speak and the melodious aspect of their utterances creates words, sentences. At that moment I realize my role. I am expected to translate. I am familiar with the inter-galactic dialect. I convey my interpretation into the consciousness of the human brains of the members of my team.

"Mary you are responsible for regulating the earthly time in relation to the dimension of the galaxy", the masters tell me and look at me with love.

"When you left this place we had informed you that it wouldn't be long before you returned. Now it is happening".

The memories and nostalgia impose a heavy burden on me. I wonder if it would be feasible never to return back to Earth. However, I understand the precariousness of the situation, because I am familiar with the terms of the "contract". The group attunes itself with the masters present. They scan us by using crystals of differing chromatic frequencies, which assist them in studying our personal archives.

Two files have been transferred. The first one concerns our psychic identity and the knowledge we have gained after numerous incarnations, whereas the second has to do with the unconscious, in which karmic recordings are found as well as recordings about our behaviour, our mistakes, and the lessons we have never completed. After that, they slip into us the first discs which they later named "navigator discs".

During these initial stages, upon the discs are recorded various ways which could be used to commence the challenge of retrieving our lost identity. It will be difficult, because we will have to fight against our lower ego and that requires endurance, faith and optimism. Luckily, in this struggle we are not going to be alone.

The entities and the masters of the Fifth dimension have devised a whole plan and in cooperation with our Higher Selves they will prompt and guide our discipleship. For the final return to our motherland to be successful, we will need to pass though various stages of having the accumulated karmic causes removed. These karmic causes function as imprints on the astral planes of the fourth dimension as well as on the etheric akashic archives of the planet. These entities keep talking to us with regard to the upgrading programs and the openings that have been made on Earth, for the sole purpose of helping forces descend to Earth to carry out the planet's new evolution. They also emphasize the plan of the Supreme hierarchy.

As we leave the planet, we realise that our bodies left behind in the room are starting to get tired. The navigating officers take us to the station, they activate the gate's five rings and the journey for our return begins. As we reach the point for departure, our guide in cooperation with the Higher Self directs the luminous body in order for it to be assimilated with the astral, the etheric and the corporeal frame.

The navigators depart closing the gate behind them. We take a deep breath. The parts of our bodies are still in a lethargic state, feeling as if we are wakening from a dream. But it is not a dream. It is a real experience and we already know that it will be continued.

THE SECOND JOURNEY

We relax. The projection of the astral body is reinforced through its umbilical-like cord connections with the respective energy centres of the Higher Self. A vortex is created, a type of psychic and spiritual intercourse. The new energy body that is created, the luminous carrier that will take us to the Fifth dimension, forms rapidly absorbing and simultaneously joining elements from both the Higher Self and the astral carrier of the soul. Once this procedure is complete, the umbilical cords attached to the astral body are detached. Only the cord of the heart remains, which connects the astral body to the new energy one and to the Higher Self.

The navigators have arrived travelling through an etheric gate. A shift of energies occurs and we gradually enter a rotating gate. The journey begins assisted by the propulsion of the rings. We reach the station and we are led to the departure gate, which for Nephelon galaxy is gate number nine.

Teachers, with whom we are already familiar, like Arion, Phelathros and Artemis, surround us with energy barriers to prevent any toxic leaks from spreading out into the galaxy. The codes are provided next and the gate opens. We board the ship; we pass through the five rings of the emerald planet. The vehicle approaches a crystal sphere base. A corridor leading to a brilliant structure that resembles a temple unfolds. There, three great masters await us, Iesmel, Alvaar and Achatios. Their names also constitute the sounds that syntonise us for our contact with them. They announce to us that the council of the wise masters of Zirion is waiting for us. They have deemed it essential that we familiarize ourselves with the plan since we are to play a vital role as transformers. Our guide keeps reinforcing the syntonization through the umbilical-like connection. The teachers provide the codes so that the huge gate of the temple opens. Holograms of vibrating moving pictures form on the gate, creating clusters of sound and riots of colour.

We enter a hall in the centre of which there is a huge crystal column that reaches the ceiling. Here, is where entities from other planets of the same galaxy arrive. Our vision is still blurry and we cannot make out any details. The basic difficulty I have to face as the guide is to convey images and directions to the travellers. I have to be careful while translating so that all the members of my team can perceive life in the Fifth dimension in the same manner. Their language is comprised of sonic pulses (the same ones that are used to render us syntonic before we embark on our journey), and we refer to it as the inter-galactic dialect.

Afterwards we cross a moving aisle full of belts with colourful domes sending out sonic pulses. We reach the centre of an enormous hall, in which there is a rotating sphere adorned with beautiful designs and colours. That sphere is a huge computer which the group of wise men uses to recycle and filter their decisions. It also operates as a huge screen and as a transformer that conveys image diagrams of our solar system. The more one experiences this, the more comprehensible and significant it becomes.

In front of this gigantic sphere, six entities are sitting on a semicircular base. The royal couple, Ziron and Moira preponderates right in the centre. They are the genitors of Zirion. They are the ones who in times past had visited ancient Hellas as part of a manned mission, to carry out some genetic alterations. Our ancestors called them gods, due to the advanced technology they possessed. Ziron and Moira inform us that they organise manned missions to Earth nowadays as well that mainly concern mutational programs. This connection between past, present and future is quite an unfamiliar feeling.

Further away stand the other four entities, one of which is Alvatar, the Archon of the heavenly Poseidonia. He informs us that it was from Poseidonia that the manned missions responsible for creating the civilisation of Atlantis had been launched.

Next to him stands a very handsome couple, Pileus and Nephele, who represent love within the heavenly regions. We are informed that when they had visited Earth they were demigods.

Last but not least the sixth entity approaches us. It is Phelathros. He has a very respectable appearance, that of a scholar. When he was sent to Earth from the Fifth dimension, he was called Socrates.

THE GRAND PLAN

The group is prepared to listen to the masters' wise words. The entities look at us with love in their eyes and they reveal to us the following:

"You are by now fully aware of the impending transition of the planet's soul and of the new births that will occur that will both boost tremendously the new civilization's evolution. Our purpose is to transfer as many souls as possible back to their motherland. For this to happen we need to proceed with certain programs concerned with cutting off the karmic imprints you have left in the astral field. You have been trapped in these planes for countless of years and you have been bound by the "tentacles" of the astral entities that cast a shadow over your souls.

However, now you are ready to return home and this return is made possible due to your cooperation with your Higher Selves. When the mutations help the karmic removals to be finally realised, you will become transformers and you will begin to change people. Only then will they be capable either consciously or unconsciously of redeeming themselves by paying their Karmic dues".

"This big plan concerning the census and homecoming of the souls has begun. A large part of the lower astral planes is already undergoing disintegration. The entities that dwell in and bind these lower levels are dissolving because the nourishment they had been receiving from the astral cords is no longer to be offered to them. Little by little the whole realm of the fourth dimension will cease to exist. Some of the souls that will receive pardon will have the chance to transfer to the intermediary levels of the astral dimension in order to receive training before they are disintegrated as well. As far as the other souls, that have remained in an animalistic state are concerned, their essence will be dissolved. They will be transformed into something totally new and then reborn according to new reformational laws".

"Slowly but gradually only the higher astral levels will remain, which will be used as a cornerstone for the souls that will be destined to enter corresponding programs just like you, with the view to crossing over to the Fifth dimension".

"What has been described constitutes the transitional procedure and it has been operating like that since the dawn of humanity. Your guide, Mary, has been chosen, after she had received rigorous training. With her help you will be able to fight against the multiple personalities you had been assuming during several incarnations. In that way you will be successful in accomplishing the transition phase that has already begun in your dimension. It is almost impossible for you to bring it off by yourself. To be transferred here, only one carrier could accomplish this, a different one, the energy (solar or christic) body. This constitutes a vehicle for the soul that has remained inactive because of your fall into crude matter. Now, it is reconstructed via the Higher Self and it is structured in compliance with the principles governing the Fifth dimension. That is why it gives you the ability and allows you to enter it".

"The rules are very strict and there are several safety valves deterring anyone, who might be willing, from entering the Fifth dimension. Entities found near the gates continuously check the codes given to them by the various navigators at every check-point. Certain plates from the astral and mental bodies will be transferred to the newly formed energy body. Special entities will project these archives under favourable and suitable conditions, and you will experience the removal of your karmic cords as well as undergo cellular mutations in order to become active warriors of light. We are only allowed to provide about eighty per cent guiding assistance. Do not forget that the help you will receive will continuously be transformed through the Higher Self. That is the reason why a harmonious cooperation between you and your Higher Self is required".

"Many women, after undergoing and realising karmic removals will be prepared to become "gates" themselves facilitating the descent of the crystal children onto Earth. No crystal entity will be able to pass through a womb-gate if it hasn't been relieved of and liberated from its karmic debts. The crystal souls are entities of the Fifth dimension that choose to come down to Earth through these births so as to enhance the planet's evolution. They have extricated themselves from the astral realms and the karmic imprints. Consequently, there are no karmic contracts with their mother. However, the mother should also not have any whatsoever karmic attachments to the astral levels".

"Most of you, who participate in these journeys, possess karmic imprints only of the middle astral level and some of you of the higher astral one. That is why you are still held captives of those recordings. In addition, your endurance has been tested and challenged, despite the few occasions of people who cannot stand the termination of a state in which they had been so heavily burdened with karma. Yet, even they will benefit since they will decrease their heavy load to such an extent that when they leave Earth they will have earned a position in the higher astral levels. Then, after having increased their awareness they will try to enter mutational programs to become successful in realising their final transition here".

"During your journeys you will encounter souls from the higher astral levels that will be partaking in similar programs concerning their transfer to the Fifth dimension. They are capable of completing this procedure easier because their astral body is more malleable and suppler".

"Furthermore, the various initiations you will receive will assist you during the rest of your life in the following points:

To awaken others.

To gradually transmute your astral vehicle to such an extent that the new energy body manages to keep a tight rein over your personality.

To release the karmic causes and redeem matter. This will be accomplished according to the way you will be handling your thoughts, emotions and choices".

"The first journey virtually begins with the initiation of Metatron. This entity had been projected numerous times on Earth at different periods of time in the history of our planet, in order to bequeath knowledge to humankind. At this moment he belongs to the hierarchy of the Sixth dimension of the golden planet, which energises and activates the entire galaxy. Christ is at the head of this hierarchy working hard in order to complete and fulfil his second coming. He coordinates the restoration program for souls upon which immortality will be conferred. On Zirion there is a being called Hyacinth who is the psychic projection of Christ".

"Jesus has been the greatest teacher ever to have appeared on Earth. He descended into and through a womb-gate that had been detached of its karma and has constituted a soul that we had sent from the Fifth dimension. It was a virgin soul, since it had no karmic imprints to resolve".

"You should never be afraid. Fear and doubt block the channels of assistance. Whatever you are experiencing now is not a figment of your imagination. We are real and concrete beings and you will come to realize that when you begin to awaken and to observe the changes in your lives many charismata will start unfolding, arising out of oblivion. In addition, your lucidity and perspicacity will evolve and develop respectively, which will aid you in making the right choices for your benefit".

"Always remember that you are our beloved children who are coming home."

"We wave goodbye to you and are looking forward to your visiting us again."

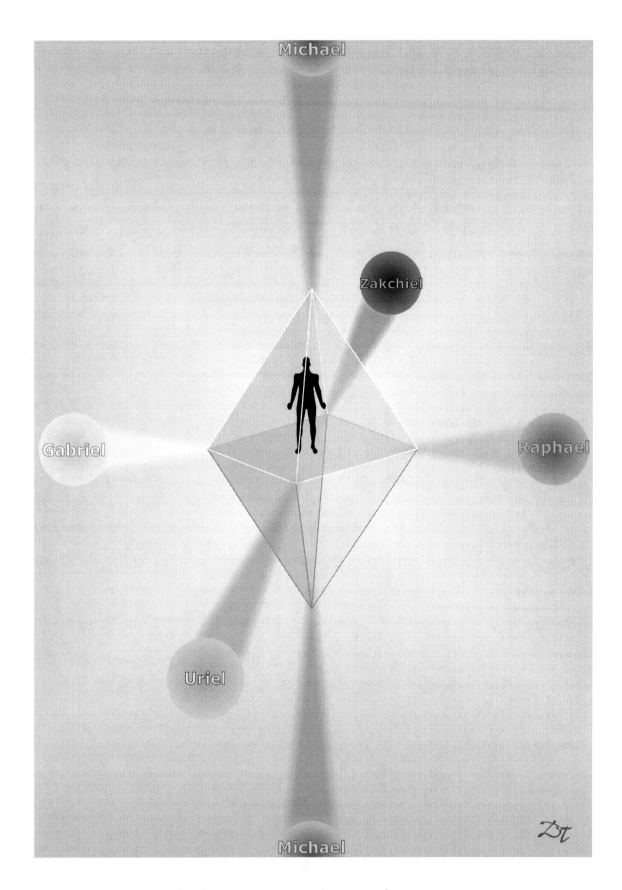

The thaumaturgic visualization of protection

THE THIRD JOURNEY

PLANET POSEIDON

THE PROTO-HUMANS

MISSIONS OF ENTITIES BEING SENT TO EARTH

THE CREATION PLAN

ANTHROPOID MUTATIONS

GODS AND DEMIGODS

HUMAN DOLPHINS

THE DISRUPTION OF EARTH'S MAGNETIC FIELD

COLLISION OF MATTER AND ANTI-MATTER

THE POLAR SHIFT

THE FALLEN SOULS

THE THIRD JOURNEY

PLANET POSEIDON

We experience the same feeling just before departure. After the separation of the two bodies occurs we enter the station. In front of the gate, Archon Alvatar awaits us accompanied by five entities acting as officials. Our destination is planet Poseidon. It was from this planet that the first missions were sent to Earth to bring into effect an evolution towards an Atlantean era. Even now, numerous delegations consisting of Atlantean beings are sent to Earth. Some souls will arrive on Earth in the form of crystal children whereas others will remain on Earth's etheric plane. From there they will come into contact with specific transformers- receptors in order to promote the reformation plan. In that way, the period marking the civilization developed by the Atleanteans recommences, but this time, better and safer methods are applied.

The entrance to planet Poseidon awakens various memories while its beauty is unparalleled. It shines due to innumerable crystal cores that unite emitting iridescent flashes. Its crystalline structure is a direct result of an upgraded mixture of particular crystals that are produced only on that planet. Poseidon is a huge transformer and transmitter of Nephelon galaxy.

After the descent we are transferred to a cylindrical base. We are greeted by teachers-geneticists, who had participated in the creation of intelligence during the age of the Lemurians and the Atlanteans. We try to tune in to images of five-dimensional form. We are led to a poly-morphic crystal pyramid and we slowly enter a column in which thousands of spherical detectors begin to scan our energy bodies. The first toxic substances that have been recorded on microscopic discs by the navigators and that we have transferred there are identified.

The usefulness of the navigators is unquestionable. Upon these etheric discs the difficulties and emotional blocks, which tend to be a direct result of every personality's inclinations, are recorded. During every trip these discs carry within them material which is substituted for newly recorded solutions, helpful for each individual and which concern specific difficulties the individual will encounter. This constitutes a very significant program because the lower personality keeps projecting false images that lead us astray and resultingly we keep confronting our difficulties in a similar fashion, making the same thoughts having the same feelings and perceiving events similarly. The spheres pass over the surface of the discs deleting that toxic substance. Moreover, at the same time they create an electric charge by surrounding the body with electrons with the intention of setting it in tune with the perception of space.

The navigators together with the Atlantean Alvatar lead us through a crystal gate into a hall. Its base is five-dimensional tapering off in a cone adorned with intricate designs and full of crystal clusters. These clusters direct beams of multi-coloured light downwards, which further down split into a wider variety. In the hall there are many levels where a variety of entities are seated. These entities, either coming from planet Poseidon or from neighbouring ones, are there to attend the lesson. They display a wide interest concerning the various missions sent to Earth, mainly because they know that that way constitutes transcendence with regards to the rapid and complete transition of the human souls to the Fifth dimension.

Twelve Atlantean teachers are seated on a different level suspended over our heads. The rest of the entities display a crystal-like solemnity. What seems to be a dominant feature on their thin oblong faces are their eyes; slanted and large. The pupils resemble glowing diamonds. Their tunics have been woven with crystal threads that shine reflecting all the colours of the rainbow. Crystal sounds vibrate in the hall and penetrate our bodies.

THE PROTO-HUMANS

MISSIONS OF ENTITIES BEING SENT TO EARTH

The luminous entities stare at us, surrounding us with frequency waves and tell us the following:

"We welcome you on planet Poseidon, which is also the homeland of many members of your group. It is from here that numerous missions have been sent to Earth. In the beginning we transferred seeds that constituted the first unicellular organisms. Next, through our intervention – always through the various missions – they became multi-cellular. Simultaneously various interventions on the climate of Earth were also performed. The first animal organisms, which were capable of surviving based on their own instincts, were created through various mutations. Some of these species never managed to survive. One species of the first proto-humans named Neanderthal managed to prevail".

"From our planet we continued to monitor the first evolution of that "anihuman". After that, the first expeditions exiting the intergalactic system of the Fifth dimension began. Chosen couples coming from differing planets were united. The essence stemming from that union went through a plethora of mutations and then was implanted in the wombs of monkey-like humans. That was the primary psychic seed that rendered them animate beings. The children that were born from these primary mutations possessed evolved consciousness, displayed ingenuity, and discovered new and more potent ways of survival.

In these primal humanoid species were transferred the first seeds of connection to spiritual entities. A psychic essence possessing in it the divine spark was passed on to the already mutated mothers that later gave birth to children with a higher intellect. Those children had a direct connection with their genitors, the Higher Selves, which guided them to create the first civilisation".

THE CREATION PLAN

ANTHROPOID MUTATIONS

GODS AND DEMIGODS

"When these superior entities realised that the creation plan was developing, they decided to come to Earth. However, they had to remain on the planet for a very long period, so that they would be able to develop novel mutations that would provide man with the secret of immortality. Multiple missions of all the highly evolved races descended to different parts of our planet and settled there. Among them were teachers, physicists, healers, geneticists, and many more entities of varying specialties. With them arrived some winged beings as well, which possessed a bodily frame of a different composition. Their DNA was tampered with in a way that they were structured to follow orders and directives and were also deprived of the seed of free will. These were entities that had been positioned in the last of God's material dimensions, the fifth".

"During that time and age Earth was surrounded by amorphous stellar matter, whose role was to energise astral bodies, the primary carriers of the psyche. The entities that had descended as couples constituted the first "gods" of the age of the Lemurians, the Atlanteans and of other civilisations. In order for these entities to function in the etheric and astral matter of this planet they had to borrow an astral vehicle that was supple and malleable. In that way they were capable of projecting themselves and of appearing before people's eyes either as possessing a physical form or as being able to dissolve that form whenever they wished".

"However, because astral matter is subject to wear and tear, they had carried with them genetic material that would assist them in continuously recreating and remoulding their cellular structure so that it didn't deteriorate in time. That specific material is what the humans on Earth referred to as ambrosia and nectar.

Some of these entities came to Earth in pairs, but others arrived after being united in the form of one gender as Plato had mentioned. They were aware of the fact that their stay on Earth had a deadline, so they started teaching humans, bringing about, during the same period, certain improvements in their genetic make-up. Some of these "gods" had slept with women that had disposed of their animalistic nature and consequently were devoid of any such recording whatsoever in their DNA. These women gave birth to demigods whose one half possessed a divine core and whose astral matter was subtler.

They functioned utilising an advanced astral vehicle. Additionally, their energy bodies were always in full operation, that is, they were constantly in touch with their divine genitors."

"The winged entities also slept with women even though it was forbidden for them. From their union giants were born as well as humans with wings, whose appearance was half human and half bird. More mutations also ensued from genetic material which had started functioning in a degenerative manner. Many of these entities went on to become earth gods trapping themselves into crude matter. In order to be fed they started creating false images in and around man trying to arouse his animalistic nature, which in some remained fully active and had not yet been fully cancelled.

Consequently, lower personality shells started being created; with whom those entities connected by attaching "tentacles" (cords) and slowly they began to suck back their lost energy. By using that energy they formed the various levels of the astral realm from where they continue to reign until now. The creators of the winged beings also fell in the astral vortex, which resulted in them losing their primal composition. Religions across the globe later referred to them as the fallen angels.

These astral levels are exactly the ones that the entities of the Fifth dimension are trying to decompose, so that man will be able to return to and regain his primal form and identity. When the astral levels dissolve then with them the elements and properties of their leaders will also disappear, since the "tentacles" facilitating connections and nourishment will be and remain detached from the human souls".

"After all the pairs of creators had taught humanity, had shown humans whatever they needed concerning advanced technology, and had perfected mutations, they departed, returning to the Fifth dimension. Some of them decided to stay behind to assist the development of various civilisations. Gods, demigods, and hyper-intellects of that epoch cooperated very closely. The children that were born from these unions developed great civilizations, whose traces in history we are trying now to analyse and explain. These highly developed civilisations evolved on many parts of our planet. The centre, in which the basic mutations were carried out, was named Poseidonia. This was the territory where the entities coming from planet Poseidon of the Fifth dimension, descended upon."

THE HUMAN DOLPHINS

Some of these great entities facing us start narrating to us the following:

"Beings used to dwell in the seas; entities that had crossed over to you from the Fifth dimension through planet Sirius, which constituted their communication station. They were placed under the leadership of an advanced life form that had descended to Earth from the Blue planet of Nephelon galaxy accompanied by its forces. It was a sole gender entity that became known in mythology as Poseidon. His team also was subject to mutations. Consequently the humanoid-dolphins were born. They were half men and have fish, which helped them live under water, possessing at the same time an advanced intellectual ability and a tail of a fish. They had the ability to breathe both in the water and on land. Oftentimes they were seen coming on land exchanging knowledge with people. These creatures considered to be the ancestors of dolphins played a vital role and were the key determinant of Atlantis. They operated as mediums and they kept the portal open so that frequencies could be transferred from the Blue planet down to Earth. They had been used by people of the mainland in various communicative programs".

THE DISRUPTION OF EARTH'S MAGNETIC FIELD

"The divine couples that remained on Earth however, began to sustain some type of deterioration, because they could not totally control the formation of astral fields by the grounded gods, who had mutated into draconians. They began exhibiting egocentric habits. The entities of the Fifth dimension, in order to prevent deterioration from entering their dimension through the portals, sealed both their entrance and exit. As such these entities that remained behind, isolated and deprived of the guidance they usually received from the heavenly home began conducting various experiments trying to disrupt the planet's magnetic fields. They opened up portals in the astral dimension from where the reptilians broke loose dragging along with them many of the creators and many mutated people. In that way the structurally divine primal DNA was denatured".

COLLISION OF MATTER AND ANTI-MATTER

THE POLAR SHIFT

THE FALLEN SOULS

"The creators realised the mistake but it was already too late. What followed next was that a collision of matter with anti-matter took place, resulting in the beginning of chain explosions on Earth. The poles shifted, cracks and faults appeared on the Earth's crust and water flooded the cities annihilating eighty percent of the population.

Those of the creators that had survived developed the Egyptian civilisation and later on the ancient Hellenic one. That event is referred to as the fall of the souls. The souls lost their divine origin and immortality and entered the astral levels. They were condemned to experience corporeal death interminably. Since then they have been destined to be reborn assuming various forms and becoming various personalities, until they manage once again to awaken the divine spark within them".

"The Higher Selves withdrew the immortal energy bodies from people. They left however a small remembrance seed concerning home, which, beyond being a helpful reminder, further impelled people to search for their other half. It is also a reminder of the divine entity with whom they once performed and lived together, forming divine couples. The Higher Selves are therefore obliged to remain in the Fifth dimension, without having any ability whatsoever of evolving into a higher being, inhabiting higher dimensions. This happens until the psychic part, which they have left on Earth, awakens and is reunited with them activating thus once again the energy body. That latter body remains inactive in the Fifth dimension and is sustained in wombs. It constitutes the psyche's vehicle that bears the seed of immortality".

"All the expeditions that had reached Hellas from the Emerald planet were comprised of the Olympian Gods. They left though when the process of deterioration began closing the gateways behind them. As they departed they left only one central gateway open that has overlooked the city of Athens ever since, and that is the sacred rock of the Acropolis. They connected it with several portals (energy points) found all over Hellas. The Acropolis-gate was activated again by the prime movers of 1996. This activation was sanctioned with the commencement of the Olympic Games. These missions produced some key points on other parts of the planet as well, like the pyramids in Egypt, the Mayan temples and the megalithic religious structures at Stonehedge".

"After the destruction of Atlantis the architects of the creation of the humanoid-dolphins departed as well, as did a big part of their hierarchy. However, they did leave behind them and did place a seed plate containing high frequency sounds in the dolphins that remained behind just to remind man of the heavenly origin of those creatures. This is also the way by which these mammals are compensating for their karmic debts readying themselves for their return, at the same time. That is also the reason why in a short period of time they will disappear from the face of the Earth".

The luminous entities keep watching over us, surrounding us with frequency waves telling us at the same time the following:

"At present we are attempting to send similar expeditions. Our intention is to awaken those prime movers that have reached higher levels and assist them in realizing that they actually are in the position to resolve their karma, simultaneously testing them for their steadfastness and faith. The anamnesis they have about home becomes more intense as time goes by. By applying that gradual mode of awakening, these "torchbearers" will embark on their own missions becoming guides themselves to assist in awakening the souls of others".

"During the journeys to the Fifth dimension geneticists place light-emitting discs on all the energy centres. These discs are impervious to any external influences. They only emit pulsatory waves and contain frequencies of the entities that lived in the thalassic environment during the time of Atlantis. Some of those entities remained on Earth lost their memory and became the animals we know today as dolphins.

Before their brother-entities departed they inserted an etheric plate into the dolphins containing sound frequencies that syntonised them with humans. Some of those frequencies were also inserted in the light-emitting human discs, so that the dolphins, that are in a semi-conscious state, be assisted and start being awakened in order to gradually return as entities to their homeland as well".

"The light-emitting discs trigger the dolphins, to unlock frequencies for the opening of the gates. These are the gates that had been closed after the destruction of Atlantis".

"Knowledge concerning the genesis of the solar system and of the third and fourth dimensions is stored in the Fifth dimension".

When the first mutations on humans who were in a primitive state were realised, the centre of speech and thought were the first to be transformed. Within the human brain were placed certain types of neurotransmitters that later on aided the development of ingenuity and man's ability to convert inarticulate utterances into words. Consequently, the first language for communication was developed by configurators of neurons that contained the primary lexical, semantic and communicational framework.

During the centuries that followed, man's mental body evolved. The primordial cerebral neurocells of human biochemistry became enriched due to the formation of a highly complex mechanism. This specific evolutionary trait occurred being based mainly on the recordings that the psyche transferred with it on its mental plate during each and every of its births. Consequently, there is a certain "survival memory" existing in each human which assists him in surviving without any need of any material possessions. This evolutionary trait is dormant in every human, and remains stored in a big file which can be reactivated if need occurs".

"Earth constitutes a part of the planet Uranus of the Fifth dimension. Before the fall, together with Uranus they worked as genitor-gods of this planet. When they separated, Earth's psyche formed and instilled life into Earth, the planet in which it was finally trapped together with all its creations. However, the fallen Nephelim had a fifty percent influence over man. They are still trying to exert control over the various human races and to exterminate all of God's creations by using the tremendous powers they have been administered with. They have become tyrants and they currently control man's intellect and emotions, by offering him material benefits, fame and power. Their intention is to halt Earth's evolution and to wipe out all of humanity from the face of the Earth.

They use multiple modes of destruction (wars, famine, the negative side of technology, viruses). While the planet's energy sources slowly but gradually are being depleted they are trying to keep hold of them only to be in the position to control man. In that way, they halter the exploitation of other, alternative, forms of energy that would save Earth.

Divine provenance, however, is concerned not with the destruction of its creations, but with assisting and indicating a plan for reversal and a plan for returning home. Your guide, Mary, is one of those key-figures, a soul that has been chosen to lead you and to aid you in tuning in with the frequency which is emitted for return…"

Initiation of Metatron

METATRON INITIATION

THE FOURTH JOURNEY

THE GENESIS AND THE FORMATION OF THE NEW ENERGY BODY

THE CODES OF IMMORTALITY

THE REGENERATING SYMBOLS

THE REVITALIZATION COMMANDS

ARCHANGEL ZAKCHIEL DURING THE INITIATION

SUBLIME COMMUNION WITH METATRON

METATRON INITIATION

Metatron is an Archangelic entity that appeared on Earth as Enoch. It has been made known to me that he belongs to the highest hierarchy of the wise on the Emerald planet of Nephelon galaxy. He had arrived on Earth as part of the crew of the first mission responsible for carrying out the mutational programs on the planet. His cellular structure consists of a mixture of Archangelic genetic material and genetic material of the Earth goddess. He had an advanced nervous system and was capable of altering his carrier in order to enter each and every dimension.

Oftentimes he would transfer part of his psychic consciousness to an embryo whereas during other times he would materialise assuming a variety of forms at specific historical junctures of the planet.

This type of fusion is not unknown in the realms of the Fifth dimension and Metatron is one of the very few masters that belongs to the highest order. His interest in Earth is unmatched because he possesses great knowledge concerning man's soul. He chooses his apprentices after careful consideration and after they have underwent harsh training.

He is the first master who gives the permission to commence the programmes regarding karmic removal. He is a great geneticist and is responsible for the structure of both the nerve tissue and the spinal cord of the energy body. That is the knowledge he had drawn upon during the first mutations that were performed on Earth. He also activates the neural network, the spinal cord and the various cerebral lobes, so as to assist the projections of man's karmic imprints.

THE FOURTH JOURNEY

A pervasive sense of unease and unrest prevailed in the room. Everybody knew about master Metatron and was wondering:

"How will I experience the journey?"

"What will I see? What will I feel?"

Twenty five Higher Selves united with the astral bodies of the students getting ready for the projection of their energy carrier.

I will meet my master! A sweet expectation overcomes me. The familiar procedure commences once again. We arrive on the Emerald planet called Zirion. Iesmel, Alvaar, and Achatios are the teachers awaiting us. They lead us into a multi-dimensional temple. Through the well-known cylinder, which syntonises cord connections, we reach the highest part of this level.

In every part of our body we sense the oncoming presence of Metatron. Thousands of entities, as well as inhabitants of the planet, are sitting perimetrically in the hall. There are thrones there for the genitors Ziron, Moira, and for the spiritual order of the planet. Additionally, several masters, who tend to appear during every journey choosing apprentices to tutor, project the carriers they were known by on Earth during the latter's various historical periods. They had been sent as instructors at crucial evolutionary junctures of Earth to provide fresh impetus and assist its development.

On planet Zirion they take on various forms. They are tall and thin beings, over ten feet in height, with a long face and bright eyes. Their tunics are embroidered with insignia regarding their status. We identify teachers like Pythagoras, Plato, Hippocrates and many others.

The crystal column tapers off in a huge cone. This constitutes a massive channel through which masters of the Gold planet found in the Sixth dimension reach our planet and materialise, in order to perform various initiations. On the left side of the throne stands Archangel Vachiar together with five other officials, who are holding energy swords, while on the right side stand Archangels Iotheos and Zakchiel.

Microscopic spheres —that are energy spheres- are shining and wandering around. Vibrations keep increasing; our expectation is charging the atmosphere, while the room is suffused with explosions of colour and light emanating from the column. Before Metatron appears we are led in front of Archangel Vachiar. He is holding a fiery crystal sphere and he passes it from every energy centre burning various astral elements, which concern our personality; elements that we have transferred there so that they can be purified.

The vibration's intensity increases with time reaching the highest rotation frequency. An entity so bright that we are unable to discern its entirety, slowly but gradually takes form as it exits the energy column. The navigators syntonise the focal point of our eyesight and things start to clarify, parts of the images become clearer until they take on a specific form. We set our eyes on that which our consciousness and the knowledge of our soul can stand and accept. We observe Metatron. His face glows and his straight long hair have a silverfish-white colour. His eyes are like blazing fire, sparkling, radiating knowledge and love. He is wearing the symbol of a rhombus with four crosses, one on each corner, and an orb right in the middle that vibrates emitting sounds and colours. He is holding an intricately decorated chalice made of organic matter which also contains some kind of fluid. It is silverfish-white in appearance and within it one can see thousands of crystal spheres moving at very high speeds. These spheres contain the nuclei of neurocells and nervous tissue.

THE GENESIS AND THE FORMATION OF THE NEW ENERGY BODY

Metatron welcomes us. His voice sounds as if it resonates on all sides of the circular hall.

"My children, you are my beloved students whom I had guided when I had descended onto your planet. Now, I feel that you are determined to return home. The channel and the gateway that will lead you there have already been activated. In today's initiation a complex nervous system with two spinal cord axons and two cerebral lobes will be constructed for your newborn energy body. All the elements that had been removed from you, when you were sent to live in the third dimension, are now returned and restored, in order for you to become capable of gradually reconstructing your divine immortal body".

The Higher Selves lead us in front of Metatron. We sip three times from the chalice swallowing the silverfish-white substance. On a huge screen we observe what is happening to the energy body. The crystal spheres that were in the fluid we drank release numerous neurocells. These cells begin to form a double spinal cord axon and to construct a complex ramus of the spinal nerve throughout the torso of the energy body. Other spheres form two extra cerebral lobes that are connected via a rotating disc to the neck and to the coccyx. We monitor and we feel the creation of the energy body. We come to understand the mutations that had taken place when the genitors descended to Earth. The two new lobes are connected to the already existing ones, opening thus a rotational flow to the epiphysis and the hypophisis.

The Higher Selves receive communion as well drinking form the chalice the same substance, in order to assist the formation of compatible connections between their nervous systems and our energy bodies.

Metatron sends his blessings and then disappears in the rotating vortex. Iesmel, Alvaar and Achatios approach us. They are holding orbs in their hands in which certain symbol codes are floating. This substance is released in the epiphysis.

THE CODES OF IMMORTALITY

In the fluid that penetrates all four lobes of the energy body there are clusters of codes. The codes pass through a vortex into the region of the neck and move downwards into the two spinal cord axons. There is a second fully operational vortex in the coccyx from where the codes travel upward reaching the neck. From there they are distributed to the entire neural network of the energy body. We watch how rapidly they are channelled to and are integrated by the neurons.

Being obviously mystified we ask: "What is that substance?"

The genitors answer us providing an analytical explanation:

"It is the first upgrading, regenerating, and revitalizing flux that is essential for your cells. These substances carry in them the elements of immortality. They constitute commands the cells should follow to avoid deterioration. As we have explained the connections that united the four lobes had been cut. That had happened during the time of Atlantis, when we cancelled the mutational programs of people because they hadn't utilised them properly.

Two out of four lobes that the human brain possessed had atrophied and their memory was lost. In the two that have remained there is an inactive part. That is the place where the secrets of life and of knowledge are found. By reactivating the connections of the four cerebral lobes your old abilities will begin to emerge once again. By applying these mutations, the focalisation of the energy centres will shift towards the Fifth dimension. Thus, your consciousness will open up to other unexplored fields. The spheres that were released into your energy body are cytoblasts possessing an intelligence of their own".

We ask in ecstasy: "Are you simply saying to us that we will become immortal so simply?"

They smile and reply:

"It is actually not that simple. Many journeys are required, for the mutations to become more definitive. This procedure contributes immensely to the immortality of the energy soul. Because the energy body remains in the astral one for long, that substance is released and further influences your cellular system. Accordingly you will appear younger and there will be no evidence upon you whatsoever of the degenerative disease often referred to as senescence. In addition we also offer you symbols that activate the central regenerative centre".

THE REGENERATING SYMBOLS

THE REVITALIZATION COMMANDS

"These symbols are not yet complete. They will be assimilated once they have been worked upon through continuous upgrades that will be realised in each journey. Later on we will provide you with the complete codes. You are obliged to transfer these symbols into your dimension as well so that the whole procedure is finalised. If you handle these codes over to a third party they won't be operational. They are only of benefit when they are passed into man's energy bodies, after they have been activated by geneticists of the Fifth dimension. Their insertion into the energy body and their secretion into the material carrier will strengthen your immune system and will give you a youthful appearance. This cellular reconstruction contains cells that assist alignment, productivity, mutation, vibration, modulation, connectivity as well as equilibrium".

"All these in conjunction with the new neurons that formed the nervous tissue of the energy body will work on the respective energy centres in the following manner: In the epiphysis and the hypophisis they will function as mutational cells and as healers of the new neurons. Their operation will transform the old cerebral commands into fresh ones, more positive ones that will penetrate the entire system.

In the centre of the throat (thyroid) and in the heart centre there will be vibratory and equilibratory energies that will restore the flow of both the masculine and the feminine energies.

In the solar plexus (stomach) and in the abdominal centre they will function as neural modifiers and will induce neural discharges, regulating thus the tensions produced by inferior emotions.

In the genital energy centre they will function as cell-moulders energizing the primeval force, and as equilibrators of the neural connections of the genital centre that entails the creation of the neck as well, which in turn is connected with creative speech".

ARCHANGEL ZAKCHIEL DURING THE INITIATION

After completing the code regeneration phase, Archangel Zachiel appears. He is the renowned Archangel of purification that assists men in mutating their toxic emotions into more positive ones. He approaches us and places a bright flickering purple flame in our right palms.

He says the following:

"This flame that I offer you constitutes a purification power. Whenever you invoke this power in my name, pass it from all the energy centres touching them each in turn with your right palm. In that way, any existing and prevalent energy blocks will be burned. In the same fashion, you will be able to purge the energy centres of other people as well. You should make circular movements with your hands so that through the small vortexes you will create the toxic substances will be disposed of. The astral body is full of karmic recordings of various tendencies and attitudes. The lower personality affects clarity. When you keep your chakras purified you actually also allow the channels with which you have become attuned to become channels of assistance. Karmic memory focuses on the traces you have left in the astral and etheric akashic archives. That makes you forget about your divine origin. Consequently, you lead a life full of fear and conflicts.

When you enter the karmic removal phase, you will feel pieces and elements of your previous toxic personality becoming detached. Gradually, you will distance yourself from it and it will be replaced by a new one, a more luminous personality, one that will be structured with cells of a higher frequency and intelligence".

The Higher Self's mission, to transfer its respective soul to the Fifth dimension is slowly being fulfilled. The energy body has been activated and awakened. Now, the road to the Sixth dimension where we will become a divine couple united with our Higher Self is once again open in front of us.

SUBLIME COMMUNION WITH METATRON

"The channels of communication are purified, for each member of the group separately, from the "litter" and nonsense of the astral influences so that each one is properly prepared to enter his home. The purification process begins. Progressively, parts of the lower personality are cut off and karmic "debts" are dealt with. A new astral vehicle is created; one that is attuned to the frequencies of the Higher Self. Through this mutation various souls will be rendered capable of tuning in with Earth's new vibrations now that the Earth is undergoing its own purification. The energies are impelling the souls to become attuned to the dimension of their Higher Selves. The Fifth dimension is a pragmatic, a concrete place permeated by very subtle energies; a place where entities of teachers and Archangels dwell. It is from there that syntonising energies and evolutionary thoughts destined to reach the fourth and the third dimensions, where planet Earth is located, are emitted from.

In the Fifth dimension we live, being totally aware of our divine essence. We experience divine love and the union with our Higher Self. We work with it in carrying out the divine plan and we evolve until we are completely and utterly fused with it. After this takes place we are no longer obliged to return to Earth as part of another incarnation, unless we decide to come to this planet as part of another expedition. Numerous souls are already preparing to enter the Fifth dimension. In unison with their Higher Self they are approaching it, so that upon departing from Earth they will be in the position to recognise the channel that will lead them immediately to the Fifth dimension. Otherwise they might get drawn by the fourth dimension which actually is the astral one".

Hospital. Karmic removals

THE FIFTH JOURNEY

KARMIC REMOVALS

GATE NUMBER NINE

THE RELEASE

KARMIC IMPRINTS

KARMIC CORDS

KARMIC DISEASES

TOXINOSES OF THE ENERGY CENTRES

MILD TOXINOSIS

SEVERE BLOCKINGS

DISTINCT POSSESSIONS

ADDICTIONS

ADDICTION REMOVAL JOURNEYS

SPECIAL HEALING PROGRAMS

MESSAGE FROM ARCHANGEL VACHIAR

COMMUNION WITH MY HIGHER SELF

THE FIFTH JOURNEY

KARMIC REMOVALS

The well-known procedure commences once again. Our energy body has already acquired form and support (spinal cord). Special navigator discs are transferred to it form the astral body. These discs contain the recordings of the lower personality as well as the information concerning the difficulties that emerge during periods of extensive decision making and problem solving. It is a very important journey since the first karmic removal of a part of our karmic burden will take place. Five journeys will be required, in order for the specific event to be assimilated and detensified. The entities that partake in these karmic removals are:

Archangel Vachiar, who is one of the most prominent of Archangel Michael's officials, and who also knows the necessary mechanisms to clear karmic causes. He is accompanied by five officials who with their fiery swords cut off the astral cords, which are then committed to the melting pot of the Fifth dimension.

Artemis the goddess, who is also regarded as the entity of knowledge. She was incarnated in Hellas in order to partake in some mutational programs. She projects her image as a goddess appearing exactly as we had become accustomed to her in ancient Hellas. During the initiatory phase Artemis drives a crystal seal into men so that they will be able to focus on their goals effortlessly and unhampered by anything. Another element that has been included in that plate is the ability to focus. Artemis is well aware of the fact that lower types of emotions produce energy shifts resulting in the loss of perspective and goal. That is why she keeps energising that plate to keep the students aligned and focused.

Arion is the master who trains the students in ways that will help them confront the toxic projections of their lower personality, further aiding them in projecting their luminiferous power. His teachings take place in the astral fields through lucid dreams.

When the gateway opens, we enter the first of the syntonising rings and our transition begins. Each ring transfers us to the next directional zone.

We pass right by the astral belt. On some of its levels karmic imprints are evident. Karmic discs containing archives are drawn out of the middle and higher zones. These fasten on one specific part of the spinal cord as we ascend towards the station. The navigators regulate the channelling openings of the discs closing behind them the channel that has been formed. There is a specific program for a specific number of discs that are going to be transferred during each journey. The quantity depends on each student's personal program and the soul's ability to detensify the causation.

After the primary karmic matter is transferred we are forcefully propelled through a coordinating field. We cross it and we arrive at the station. We are further transferred onto a crystalline base where Arion and Artemis are waiting for us.

It is announced that our destination is the Red planet of Nephelon galaxy. Archangel Michael dominates this planet–which is also considered to be the training ground and place of defence of this specific galaxy. It is from this planet that hordes of warriors are sent out to suppress riots that various astral forces instigate. Specifically during this period, various astral battles are occurring, in which astral beings are attempting to prevail. We perceive the effect of these battles on Earth nowadays in the form of climatological upheavals that inflict suffering on the planet.

Arion trains students coming from the Red planet and the etheric plane of Earth, onto which he frequently descends. He instructs them on how to distinguish between light and darkness and on how to notice the drawbacks of the lower personality. Additionally he trains them in ways of confronting the enemy and facing the attacks coming from the shadowy part of the levels in which the astral entities reside.

This training will prepare us for the initiation of the luminous warrior, which we will be administered to us by Michael the Archangel. Artemis represents one of the many female divine entities that assist us in balancing the feminine energy (ying) with the masculine energy (yang). This balance is considered very crucial for human existence. Both these energies are harmoniously balanced in the divine entities.

GATE NUMBER NINE

The frequency of gate number nine (which is the reverse of number 6) symbolises the effort to upgrade from the lower personality. This is accomplished with the opening of the gate that takes us home.

The codes unlock the gate. Three officials of the Red planet welcome us. A sense of security and of the presence of a certain dynamic is intense. We ready ourselves by assuming our launch positions.

As the transitional procedure to Earth through the golden channel commences we once again come in tune with ever increasing vibrations emitted by the planet. We tune ourselves with the frequency of the planet's departing soul. When this is finally accomplished its soul will leave the central gate behind it open as well as a trace of its direction. Thus, when time for our departure nears close we will be in the pleasant position to identify our exit frequency. As the planet's soul leaves it will leave behind it energy cords by means of which the various souls will travel towards their final destination.

The Red planet is glowing. It has a bright rosy colour while blue currents run through its surface. Around it one can see the familiar defence rings, which we pass through as we approach its atmosphere. Enormous buildings seem like gigantic guards. Their crystalline structure diffracts the light dispersing thousands of colourful rays throughout the city. There are canals that lead to crystalline domes where the vehicles land. It is from this place that air lanes branch off leading to respective buildings.

The hierarchies assemble secret councils in order to determine what mode of defence they should adhere to. Our group expresses its desire and its interest in visiting these planetary fields. They explain to us that something like that will take place some time later, after we receive clearance and permission to enter. At the time being, we have to focus on karmic removals.

Next, we enter a central hall that tapers off in a polycrystalline cone. It is surrounded by other round-shaped rooms with cones as well. Beautiful white columns that resemble archaic pillars make up the gate which leads to the hall. The pillars lead up to a pediment in which alternating geometrical shapes vibrate. This, as we are being informed, is a joint creation of Pythagoras and a team of masters that belong to the Atlantean race. The patterns on the pediment constitute a set of code-keys.

A decision taken unanimously by the prelature determines the change of the codes whenever needed.

In the main hall arrivals from many other planets are welcomed. Additionally, entities residing in the Sixth dimension are continuously projected there.

Archangels Iesmel, Alvaar and Achatios greet us.

We are directed to a neighbouring hall in which there is a peculiar fining pot right in the middle, a cylinder into which some kind of substance keeps continuously flowing. This is the place where the karmic discs are thrown into in order to be burned and cancelled. All around there are bases, made out of organic matter, which resemble ordinary beds. Two doctor-entities, Archangel Vachiar accompanied by five officials, and Arion together with Artemis await us. We are told to lie on these organic beds that embrace our bodies and begin reading the material we have transferred with us. All the data recorded on them are projected upon a huge screen. On it we watch a slideshow of alternating images running rapidly in front of us; images that regard the recorded material existing on these discs. They also contain information concerning incarnations during which we had exploited our "talents", our "gifts", with the intention of benefitting our material needs.

THE RELEASE

After the phase of karmic recording has been concluded Archangel Vachiar together with his five officials approach us. He is holding a vile containing a ruby liquid and he pours it over our energy bodies covering the space from the epiphysis all the way down to the coccyx. The liquid has the potential to detect karmic material that is present on all the karmic discs. Various forms resembling tentacles slowly appear or become evident; forms that are shadowy, creepy and which keep wriggling around in fear.

When all the karmic material has been projected outwardly the officials that have accompanied Vachiar intervene. They cut off these horrible tentacles by using their swords. They cut them off from the root, and they deposit them into a vessel which they later place into the fining pot to have their karmic matter deactivated and incinerated. This material is then forwarded through special ducts to the akashic archives where a further deletion is carried out.

In that way, it passes through the etheric-akashic and the astral archives of the planet where its cellular memory is further detected. That is the place where its final removal and incineration occurs. They explain to us that this combination of substances passes through a specific channel and is then sent into chaos. Chaos constitutes a huge "reservoir" in which all the transferable substances and the deactivated discs that are destined to be dissolved are put and where their ultimate deletion is effectuated.

After the karmic removal phase we are taken to another room for therapy. There a surgeon Archangel is waiting for us, Archangel Zochriel, who belongs to the order of Raphael (the Archangel). Besides all this, another entity catches our eye, a very attractive one, Hyacinth, who represents the christic unity of the Fifth dimension.

They lead us to similar receptor bases where doctor-entities monitor the medical history of our karmic diseases. These concern diseases that we had experienced or diseases that exist at present in our astral and corporeal vehicle. After the doctors examine each specific case thoroughly they pinpoint the cases for which they deem essential that action is necessary. They transfer microscopic discs that contain clusters of a crystalline essence. They place them at the specific body parts where there is indication of an existing problem. Each cluster is actually a cure that will be transferred back with us in the astral and corporeal vehicle as we return to Earth.

Hyacinth approaches us next. He passes a crystal over the epiphysis moving down to the coccyx and back from the coccyx to the epiphysis. With this he manages to terminate all the causes of our karmic diseases and to reinforce the power and potency of the therapeutic substances. Next, we watch him holding a crystal plate upon which his symbol shines right in the centre of it. Hyacinth places it where the heart is, conveying the following message to us:

"Now you will be given the chance to develop your christic consciousness, to open your hearts to love and to enter a new framework of developing energies. These energies will help you understand the true christic teachings and the oneness within you. With this gift you will awaken to true life and you will develop a new potential for evolution and creation".

Hyacinth represents a part of Jesus in the Fifth dimension. The crystal plate which he inserts in the hearts of women activates them, rendering them capable of giving birth to crystal children. With this gift the road characterised by the highest frequencies is opened for the advent of such children on Earth.

Following that we are taken in front of Archangel Zakchiel who is projected in the hall in order to place upon us a protective grid. By using a five-dimensional mauve crystal he activates a luminous sheath. This will protect us until the next journey and will accelerate the assimilation of the healing process and facilitate our release.

The doctor-entities inform us that the causes for which our incarnations take place, which further contain attachments to the energies of the dark side that we have served, are going to be transferred during the next journey. These doctors carry out thorough checks of our body and of the elements that have been passed on to it for the transition phase and then they announce the following:

"The karmic removals will be completed in five journeys. During each journey one of each of the causal plans, which confined you to the astral fields, will be negated. You will sense and feel your life and your options to be changing. You will experience a psychically independent optimism, which will help you confront easier the problems of your life. Whoever passes successfully the karmic removal phase will enter the alignment process. This entails carrying out mutations and shifting of one's focus of the energy centres towards the Fifth dimension".

They wave goodbye to us and they encourage us by saying that they will always be close to us, with us, and that we are not alone.

KARMIC IMPRINTS

The first journey concerning karmic removals is also the beginning of man's release and withdrawal from the astral fields. Humans carry with them a plan deep within the archives of the subconscious (solar plex-abdominal centres) that is related to the incarnations during which they were not able to fulfil the course requirements that would eventually lead to their evolution. Instead, they accumulated the results of their toxic actions and toxic choices. These are recorded in the form of miniature discs in some of the astral levels, wherein the consciousnesses and the evolution of all the souls through the various incarnation cycles have been imprinted.

In the astral archives there is an astral zone existing in a fluidic state. That is the place where the collective unconscious of all the humans on planet Earth keeps vibrating. It is continuously being formed depending on the quality of the souls that comprise a country, a city, or even a group of people. A special link unites all these human souls together through these recordings. The astral entities feed on and are sustained by this mass of combined thoughtforms and emotions that wanders around freely on the etheric plane of Earth. Additionally, the astral files are connected to the human karmic files that are mainly located in the solar plexus and the abdominal centres. The various dark entities rekindle the toxicity of these recordings leading people to the point where they risk repetition of previous toxic attitudes and toxic behaviour. Thus, without knowing it man keeps feeding these entities which in addition co-operate in a certain way with the shadowy and lower parts of his personality.

Many have managed to escape using a variety of means or by adhering to rules of self-knowledge. They succeeded in shifting the focus of their energy centres away from the astral planes and were also successful in discharging their "suffocating" karmic load. That needed to be filtered through the higher psychic archive –which is the heart- and then burned by the light of love. In that way, many souls managed through self-denial and sacrifice to transform their toxic material.

Whenever we refer to love, we do not mean selfish love, which is governed by karmic laws. Love means to offer yourself for the general good, to leave your mark on the world through your deeds for the next generations. Many people have left their seal of love on the planet and have with their offering and contribution managed to terminate their karmic archive and to liberate themselves from the ravenous entities of the astral levels. (Castaneda likens these beings to the eagle that feeds off human emotions entrapping men within its own planes).

It had been made known to me through a teaching of a higher order that there is a way of redeeming karmic causes, but only entities of the Fifth dimension had the power to bring that into effect. It took me many solitary travels in order to free myself of my karmic recordings. Thus, it is now very easy for me to lead groups of people back home, in order to rid themselves of their karmic burden. The Higher Selves agreed on devising a plan according to which whatever human souls wished to return home would be capable of realising their dream if they passed through the mutational programs.

However, I kept wondering: "How many journeys would I be able to perform and participate in until the end, so as to lead all human souls to freedom?"

The spiritual masters responded to all those people who would redeem themselves of their karmic causes that a special disc would be transferred and placed at the heart centre which would be called a light-emitting disc.

This light-emitting disc would broadcast over a very large region so that whenever the transformer-human would move around he would be able to mutate and set in motion a subconscious procedure of discarding the karmic burden of other humans as well. This is what is happening at the moment on Earth. Suitable transformers, who are also referred to as luminous warriors, are already taking active part in this mission they have been appointed to. They are leading people either consciously or subconsciously to redemption, liberating them from bondage. If one were able to actually see these bonds, he would see cords hooked by the stomach, the abdominal region and the heads of all humans, which would also be interconnected with and hooked onto one of the astral fields of consciousness. These tentacle-like structures suck a lot of energy out of us. The toxic material, which constitutes their nourishment, is then transferred from the astral entities into huge cisterns located in the astral fields.

What is more, the vapours of this substance form certain areas within the astral planes which look forward to receiving the soul after death. These places are so real that the soul actually believes that it continues to live. In this way, a certain quality of life is fashioned whether one is on Earth or dead.

The genitors wish to cancel these lower fields, so that even the souls that will never make it back home will have the chance to enter more luminous astral planes, where they will receive proper guidance from other luminous entities to better their rebirth.

The groups of souls that have cut off their karmic "tentacles" are ready for the change, which means shifting the focus of their energy centres towards the Fifth dimension. There are people who are already scattered throughout the planet who move about like luminous spheres totally detached from karmic influences.

These karmic removals do not solely concern the personal karmic burden one has accumulated throughout his lifetime. They also have to do with a part of their parental and ancestral karma. The ancestors pass down to the descendants either a positive or a dark recording which the latter will inherit and unwillingly have to take over.

Karmic debts do not constitute punishment. Instead they are viewed as acts of administering justice for actions and choices that hurt us and those around us. The lessons we receive are more effective when learnt through various events, so that harmony can be restored. For man to reach redemption on his own is an impossible task. We live in communities in which we have to deal with our everyday issues and survival, without there being any time left for seclusion, so as to get even with ourselves and clarify some issues for ourselves.

KARMIC CORDS

Relationships usually operate through karmic cords of interdependence, which keep us confined and which compel us to exhibit behaviour full of pretence and theatricals. This window of opportunity offered through the journeys to the Fifth dimension provides the entities with the potential of restoring our plan by clearing our entire karmic load. We only need to discharge that binding substance through the events that arise in our lifetime that may manifest in our dimension on a physical and emotional level. This may create a feeling of bereavement for anything we might eventually lose. At the same time though, we are liberated.

The psychic pain we experience depends on how quick we are able to perceive these changes. Relationships especially, constitute a very significant chapter on training in this school for souls. When any one of the two in a relationship cuts off the specific karmic bond, then his/her counterpart remains at a loss for a given period of time. Later on, he/she is also liberated in his/her own way. The relationships then transform. They take on a different perspective and are based on a different foundation, one of understanding, one in which the exchange of love and energy between both counterparts becomes common practice. Moreover, they tend to project the positive aspects of the people involved rather than the negative ones.

There are however instances during which someone does not possess the power to overcome this change. It is then that that specific person finds another recipient in order to continue his toxic and dependent behaviour. In contrast, karmic removals give us the chance to attract luminous soul- mates that will have a positive influence on our lives. As far as shortage of material possessions and difficulties that people encounter in the vocational sector are concerned, we have to note that after karmic debts are cleared an influx of abundance and professional development always ensues. Obstacles are removed because the bases on which and the reasons for which they existed and which developed a karmic toxicity are no longer present.

Many people begin to perceive that their work-related reality does not fit in with the newly emerging state of affairs. Thus, they change their job just to be in tune with their new developmental plan.

There are four types of karmic releases that occur on a daily basis after the karmic removals have taken place. These may be:

Physical. Karmic episodes are sometimes released in the form of symptoms that materialize in the physical frame. These differ from person to person. They are easily recognised and identified as the process of their appearance and discharge lasts only for a few moments. They are directly opposite to symptoms that various diseases have, whose development is totally different and which are usually not included in the types of symptomatology that are present in karmic releases.

Psychological. They arise, when fixed and solidified emotions, emotions that have remained in the subconscious, like anger, sorrow, addiction or fear are intensely projected for a specific period, probably because we have to comprehend the true cause of there existence. However, later on positive emotions are developed and take their place gradually creating a better ambience around us. Due to this we tend to continuously attract positive events, and our life changes for the better.

Mental. Quite often certain releases manifest themselves accompanied by occasional headaches. These are caused by toxic thoughts that concern an unreal perception of our being, which also go on to define a way through which we run our lives which again turns out to be wrong and eventually tends to lead us astray.

Material. There are also releases that concern the loss of money, of goods and valuables, with the intention of restoring the ill effects of any disharmony we have caused.

In order to be able to pinpoint and admit that all these releases are caused by the karmic removal programmes, we should first consult a doctor for any symptoms we experience that concerns our health in order to exclude them from those caused by the releases. The aid we receive from the entities of the Fifth dimension relieves us of eighty percent of the effort. What is required of us is to supply the remaining twenty percent which concerns our attempts in realising and evaluating pseudo behaviour.

KARMIC DISEASES

Inherent in each karmic plan there are almost always some diseases, serious or not, as well as certain accidents that cause the soul to depart its corporeal frame. In addition, disabilities may also be inherent to assist us in attaining the knowledge and in becoming familiar with the feeling of for example patience, or of power or faith. There are also some gifts, or talents or endearing qualities that may have remained concealed or that have never been manifested such as a highly developed intuition or a certain talent or even the ability to change attitude towards life. All that are included in our scenarios will be manifested and fulfilled at the specific time frame that the soul itself has chosen and has deemed appropriate for a specific lesson to be learned.

Yet, there are some diseases or accidents that are caused or induced by man himself when for example he behaves recklessly and treats his body and health immaturely and with disrespect. In these situations the vast majority of those afflicted will eventually recover, become well and go on with their lives either having attained some lesson or dealing with and considering this as if it were simply chance, or a haphazard event. As regards serious accidents, man will either survive them or depart life immediately. When man is saved, that means that the accident did not constitute the point in time for the soul's departure. If, on the other hand the accident was something inherent in one's karmic plan then the specific time frame does constitute the selected moment for the departure of the soul which further means that nobody on Earth can save him. Subjecting oneself though to karmic removal such possibilities of diseases and accidents are prevented from ever occurring.

Through our journeys the various scenarios concerning diseases and accidents are transferred to the Fifth dimension. There, spiritual operations are performed and the plans are restored. During the operations inherent karmic diseases, which have yet to manifest themselves or which have been manifested to either the astral or the corporeal vehicle, are projected clearly.

TOXINOSES OF THE ENERGY CENTRES

MILD TOXINOSIS

The astral levels are imprinted on our astral body. These imprints are recordings that have been consolidated in the lower personality, whose "centre of command" lies in the solar plexus and the abdominal chakra.

There is however another command centre that reinforces and amplifies man's toxic recordings. That resides in noesis. The divine spark is located in the psychic archives, in the heart centre. However, that spark has lost its glow and is instead surrounded by layers of vapours that define and compose the respective astral fields to which we are attached. Toxic recordings deriving from incarnations during which we had experienced traumatic events also exist. These are recorded on the cellular memory and are transferred with us from life to life. These toxicities block the energy flow within the chakras resulting in man feeling weak, feeling drained of energy, and being in a way compelled to enter a cycle in which he continuously recreates these same tendencies.

Toxicity is dealt with by special teams of healers that pinpoint what the problem is. This may only concern a smooth flow of energy towards the chakras, however, the problem may have entered the material frame as well and have manifested itself as a physical threat. In these situations the healing team primarily restores the flow of energy towards the chakras and then it moves on to remove the recording of the disease existent in the physical carrier.

It is then when man is cured, simply because focus shifts from the previous state of entrapment it had homed in on. Especially during the healing of karmic diseases the energy body is transferred to the Fifth dimension. There, an image of the astral body, resembling something like an astral "effigy" is projected, upon which the healing is carried out.

The healing team and I have had such experiences for so long a time now. What we use as the fundamental tool to perform these cleansing procedures is the weapon of Archangel Michael which we mentally place on all the energy centres. We are in the position to help, if it is asked of us, anybody who is ready to receive treatment and aid.

SEVERE BLOCKINGS

When man is governed by emotions of hate and passion he can focus that toxicity on a person who has fallen within his vicinity beaming thoughts telepathically. In our world there are wizards who operate either unconsciously, or consciously like that.

Those who do it consciously can, by beaming fixed telepathic mind-blasts, open holes in a human's etheric sheath thus devastating his immune system. It is then easier for them to inflict damage particularly on the nervous system resulting in the production of certain psychoses, neuroses and various forms of schizophrenia. On a physical level they attack the immune system leading to the organism's collapse and to the development of illnesses. If that attached toxic cord isn't cut off and the opening in the etheric sheath is not closed then the human may even meet his certain death.

However, because all the cases of illnesses or schizophrenia do not occur due to such projections, the experienced and intuitive healer should be able to pinpoint the true reason for the occurrence of these diseases and close the holes in the astral body. Numerous of alternative medicine therapies are being practiced at present on the planet. They are continuously evolving to offer solutions outside the realm of conventional medicine.

In spite of those who practice magic consciously there are also those who unconsciously are aware of ways to absorb energies from other people. We call those people energy vampires. Whenever we locate them, we need to seek and enter the protection offered by the closed pyramid surrounded by the respective Archangels.

Whenever man exhibits toxic behaviour he creates breaches in his etheric sheath.

If no such gaps are present then the directed shadowy energies cannot inflict any harm on anyone. The fundamental emotion that can open a path to any malicious thought, rendering it thus powerful enough to focus on us, is fear. Those wizards who deal with black magic utilise objects that intensify and reinforce fear. Those objects have no other power except for that of the materialised thought of the specific wizard practising black magic. People who are not afraid possess a very powerful form of protection, for the simple reason that they do not believe that wizards have any influence on them. If however, they are emotionally attached to the person that emits these deadly and poisonous blasts they are then usually affected and feel as if negative energy surrounds them. In essence, what has been sent to them is an astral suggestion in which poisons flow and which finally attach to their astral environment. In addition, if some people have karmic recordings then they attract analogous behaviour. What is actually needed in that occasion is removal of the cause. The absence of such a causal background prevents their being tracked down by malicious individuals.

The irony is that most interventions are acts driven by alleged personal affection and love which in essence is sheer addiction. The people who receive such influences usually do not possess free will, are usually inactive and are characterised by a certain weakness when it comes to seeking and asking for help. Additionally, there are many more who seek help and guidance from psychologists, psychiatrists, and priests or healers believing that they will reach some kind of result. Choosing this latter alternative is something that has to be done with extreme caution as regards the suitability of such people when it comes to asking for that kind of help.

DISTINCT POSSESSIONS

There is a very serious form of possession that is performed by lower astral and demonic entities.

For these occasions exorcisms are frequently carried out, which are mainly performed by people who possess a certain "gift". These people may come from the ecclesiastical domain. They may be priests, but they could also be ordinary people walking among us who have an awakened ability to handle dark entities.

A very malicious wizard has the ability to control and send telepathically such entities. These beings take control of the nervous system after of course they have passed through the gaps of the etheric sheath. They gradually hold sway over the centre of command of the sympathetic nervous system and the brain. From there they order man to commit acts that are not normal or in accordance with his personality. The entities remain hidden in the nervous system systematically weakening his defence mechanisms.

When an underlying cause is also present then this deterioration can lead to the appearance of serious illnesses like cancer. Besides, one should not forget that most of the illnesses people experience are psychosomatic, with the exception of diseases that pertain to heredity, nutrition, the way one leads his life, toxicity (which is abundant in the atmosphere) and toxic addictions, like alcohol, cigars, and drugs.

Some times some thoughtforms come into being in man's thoughts. Such occurrences are identified by specialists as split personality disorders or dissociative identity disorders. In these cases or in cases of schizoid personalities the humans who are afflicted are the ones who allow the entities to find a way into their unconscious and gain control over it. It is an issue that modern psychiatry as a science is still researching.

The entrance and presence of such entities in a man's aura is reinforced by the continuous negativity and toxicity with which that person surrounds himself. These types of people have the tendency to create an environment similar to hell and enclose themselves in it. Later on that situation becomes their reality, which keeps surrounding and following them, some times drawing in their acquaintances and family members as well (with dire consequences for all, since the latter are often driven to seek healing and therapy as well).

For as long as the lower animalistic personality exists, a certain psychic part of man will always be focused on such toxic levels.

The coming of highly advanced and highly evolved souls gradually puts an end to the astral levels. The new souls that are continuously arriving possess a customised DNA that is devoid of receptors for such negative attachments to occur.

Consequently, we get what we deserve. God does not condemn us when we abide by his law. The basic one being, which every human has the tendency to break, that we should never interfere with a soul's free will. That is the biggest karmic lesson to be learnt. We are allowed to suggest but not to guide others or impose anything on others.

ADDICTIONS

Addictions constitute a part of a neuro-chemical network that exists in us (either active or inactive) since the dawn of humanity. They create and promote hedonism and pathogenic symptoms in man causing him to repetitively imitate hedonistic behaviour.

Dependencies are experienced as addiction to things and situations. The chemical substances that are released are of the most dangerous, because they cause serious psychological problems, and because they pose threats and have serious psychological effects on man. Usual examples are found all around us, like addiction to cigars, to alcohol, to narcotics, to overconsumption and extravagant materialism, to personal computers and to lucky games.

Those who get addicted are to a large extent genetically predisposed. Their brain exhibits deprivation in the areas of learning and intellectual analysis. The various excesses subdue the will power and the area of decision making is greatly affected.

Dopamine-the substance that our organism secrets, whenever it feels euphoric-is released from the neurons and then adheres to the synapses of other neurons, conveying thus the pleasing sensation. The amount that remains is absorbed by the nerve cells that function as transmitters. The neurons that act as receptors also possess a certain system that inhibits over-excitation.

Continuous doping, which is achieved with the use of chemical substances, disrupts that operation because it destroys the neurotransmitters responsible for and destined for exerting control. In addition, excessive dopamine that results from overuse of cocaine, heroine and other narcotics causes the group of synaptic receptors to multiply their secretions. Thus, when the organism is administered such substances the system that inhibits over-excitation is destroyed.

ADDICTION REMOVAL JOURNEYS

SPECIAL HEALING PROGRAMS

In the channelling groups special healing journeys are carried out to the planets of the Fifth dimension. These concern withdrawals from nutritional, drinking and smoking habits, as well as from mental and emotional addiction and interdependence.

Additionally there are special programmes, concerned with changing the plan of one's life and altering one's emotions. These provide solutions to emotional problems and lead to withdrawals from toxic (both friendly and amorous) relationships.

The geneticists place into the toxic body new commands. New neurons are inserted that affect the area where the emotional part of a person resides that is also concerned with karmic causality.

That part is physically represented with the system of the amygdala which is connected to the disc of the lower emotions and the karmic tendencies. With the new neurons the analytical areas of the brain are able to evaluate respective implications. That is why we often refer to a higher type of analysis and intellect that is related with that part of the brain (prefrontal cortex). In that way, withdrawal from various types of toxic behaviour is realised.

The entities channel into human-transformers information concerning the structure and the mutations of the nervous system. The neurologists here on Earth manage to cure the symptoms however, the recordings continue to exist, because the cause of the symptoms- that are mainly karmic- cannot be operated on by anyone else than the healers of the Fifth dimension.

The new nerve cells that are inserted in the Fifth dimension are detector-moderators. They are pairs of neurotransmitters that detect deteriorations and repair them. That's the way that restoration of the damage ensues. However, exactly because all deteriorations have been recorded on man's nervous tissue, it is during these stages of releasing tension that sorrow or even depression become evident or are feelings that are produced. The secrets of health and immortality are well concealed within the neurons. The positive effect of dopamine is secreted from the neurons. This substance revitalises the cells and empowers and strengthens the immune system. In addition, endorphin is also secreted which brings about balance.

Meditation has the tendency to activate dopamine, which is released and then attached to synapses, containing new healing and evolutionary orders.

From the moment that the journeys for addiction overcoming and removal commence, ninety days are required until the people participating are fully restored to health.

MESSAGE FROM ARCHANGEL VACHIAR

"I am an Archangelic officer. I serve in the order of Michael the Archangel. I have undertaken the purgation of your teams. Through you I also fulfil my mission as well.

It is through the purgatory fields, which the souls entering now the vibrations of the Fifth dimension, should pass. This mission of re-gathering home is directed by the entity of Christ. It is he who will deliver the final initiation".

"There are many masters like me who have taken on other teams. Great teachers are working on the grand plan of gathering each soul and directing it to the respective vibrations it belongs to. The transition will have been completed by 2012, as it has been reported, though dates are a bit unclear since plans keep changing.

The council has decided that I should take it upon myself to cleanse all the groups. Your dimension as well as your human status continuously charges you with a plethora of emotions.

Through them we can carry out your training and be trained ourselves in return".

There are more beings of creation, which have a different idiosyncrasy. Some posses only intellect and no emotion whatsoever.

Earth is a planet where hard training takes place through a lot of suffering and psychic pain. Those who complete their training are distinguished by sublimeness and profound consciousness. Karmic debts act as discipleship for as much as it takes until the soul learns to make better choices. Many souls get trapped into some type of virtual reality and subsequently create even more debts losing their time and having to experience and put up with ongoing problems and conflicts. Several of them will, after the deadline that will have been given to them expires, dissipate and be reformed anew".

"Those who enter new vibrations will increase their frequency and their consciousness. They are redeemed of karmic debts and they enter the true dimension. In that level they are bound to make more conscious and better choices. Thus, their evolution is accelerated. Generally, humans are structured possessing the spark of free will and power, and can, when united with their Higher Selves, even make miracles happen. This type of knowledge though remains dormant".

"Most people remain entrapped into a virtual perception and have the illusion that their lives are governed by some type of destiny that they are unable to fight against or deal with.

This type of reality is what serves the purposes of the entities that control the planet and are fed by the lower emotions and by human fear and pain. It is especially during the hours of sleep that they project mentally false images so that man may remain their prisoner and feed and sustain them interminably".

"Since 1996 though- when your planet joined the galactic brotherhood of light- Earth has began to move around in higher frequencies and has managed to approach the vibrations of the Fifth dimension. Many souls will return home after undergoing the mutations that the Higher Self performs. It is the one who is responsible for cleansing following the guidance of the Archangels.

Detachments of all the connections that concern the virtual illusion, take place during the second initiation in the purgatory hall. These connections resemble tentacles that convey to us inaccurate information.

Gradually, you will acquire a different perception for the things that up to now you had considered real. If you experience uneasiness during sleep it is only a sign and the outcome of the battle you are giving, to have all the thoughtforms removed. These thoughtforms are projected directly to your psychic archives and cause disorientation and confusion.

The more the purgatory process continues, the more the tensions you are experiencing will decrease. You would be horrified if you could just see the energy "tentacles" that hook on to each and every individual and start draining his energy.

For the removal to take place we cannot interfere arbitrarily. We have to receive authorization by the human souls that have started to realise what is happening with the energies all around them and within them. You have to understand that you are entering very powerful energy cleansing procedures. The astral body will have to be changed and utterly reformed.

During the period when the removals will be taking place many of you will feel tired. This feeling persists because there are "wounds" in your energy sheath that need to heal. In the purgatory hall those wounds are sealed. In that way those exact same spots will never be reattached to energy "tentacles", which could allow the re-emergence of the 'deranged' condition".

"In the Fifth dimension, the Archangel healers can work immediately and fully on the energy bodies. We do not need any human-transformers like it is required in the third dimension. Human diseases arise from the energy cords that are attached to your bodies. Ensuing turmoil and agitation affect the central system of the cells and the immune one as well.

The most susceptible part is the nervous system. That is the area where primary deterioration occurs. Many people in these days suffer from various neuroses, from depression, phobias and schizophrenia.

There are many periods of emotional outbursts during which people behave without managing to keep their composure, doing sometimes things they are not fully aware of. The insertion of symbols of cellular rejuvenation is utterly important, because it restores all the damage caused to the cellular system. Thus, both the energy and the physical carrier become healthy once again.

The determinative sealing of the codes is administered by Archangel Achatios in the Fifth dimension. You, later on, have to activate these codes in the central system of the brain at regular intervals. The codes enter the two cerebral lobes, are later blended and are then diffused along the spinal cord. From there, their inherent frequency permeates all the cells and organs through the operation of the neurotransmitters. Some of the cells that have sustained damage are recreated and are provided with new information. All this work is carried out by us in steps and is analogous to the durability of the corporeal frame. Some bodies have been led to exhaustion and consequently require more time to be restored. You will feel the changes during the daily round provided you are observant enough. Through what will be happening, you will actually receive messages and will acquire higher intellect and intelligence. Your plan will be formed and improved according to the course of your development. Behind all this, supporting you, are Archangels who act as guides and instructors and who continue to directly co-operate with your Higher Self".

COMMUNION WITH MY HIGHER SELF

I observe your soul bleeding.

I reach out to make it stop as it flows warm leaving within you a feeling of bitterness and a sense of anguish. Being lost in a foggy labyrinth, you keep fighting against the images you project on the mirror. Take my hand and step into the light.

I am always beside you.

So I can hurt as you do.

So I can rejoice as you do.

So I can hope, like you.

And whenever you ask for it, I hold you in my hands, preventing you from falling into the gutter.

You cannot see me, but you sense me.

You know that I am always near. You know that I am in anguish over you, whenever I see you getting lost treading on paths filled with sorrow, and I remember that during those moments you do not let me to instil life, love and peace into you. Oftentimes you seek my help, but you are not open to receive it. I can help you only when your soul is open enough; only when the unification begins to vibrate in the same rhythms as mine.

THE INITIATION OF MICHAEL
THE ARCHANGEL

THE CHALICE

THE DIVINE GENETIC MATERIAL

OUR ROYAL ORIGIN

THE RESTORATION OF THE PRIVILEGES

THE FIRST HEARTBEAT

THE CERULEAN VIBRATION

Initiation of Archangel Michael

THE INITIATION OF MICHAEL
THE ARCHANGEL

THE CHALICE

THE DIVINE GENETIC MATERIAL

The second initiation is administered by Michael the Archangel. Archangel Michael is an entity whose composition remains unknown. He does not belong to any of the orders of the Archangels, but to the forces of the second sphere. We can only perceive one small part of his phenomenal existence.

The chalice used for the initiation procedure contains genetic material which is extremely necessary for the energy body in order to acquire a heart and a circulatory system. That system does not resemble the physical human one. Inherent in the newly formed heart are the bases or the receptors which will allow it to receive an advanced file.

The material that diffuses into the veins of the energy body has a cerulean vibration and its cellular structures represent the royal origin of the soul. The initiation is performed on the Red planet that corresponds to Mars the familiar planet of our galaxy. It is the planet upon which the warriors are trained and on which a gigantic purple pyramid constitutes the centre of its defence.

The journey begins. The navigators supply the proper codes and the coordinates and the vehicle enters the time-rings, responsible for the folding of space-time, of the Fifth dimension.

We arrive at the great hall where the initiations are held. A huge throne dominates the area in front of the energy column marking the arrival zone.

The various entities, the genitors and various dignitaries welcome us joyfully. The masters choose some of the students to converse with them. Two renowned teachers talk about the initiation.

These are Phelathros, the coordinator and the spiritual guide of the groups, and Aethra who is very knowledgeable when it comes to syntonising the frequencies.

The column located in the centre of the great hall is activated. A rhythmic pulse is gradually amplified resembling the sound of a huge beating heart.

OUR ROYAL ORIGIN

THE RESTORATION OF THE PRIVILEGES

A part of Michael the Archangel materialises. We watch him as he exits the column and sits on a towering throne. He is huge. He is surrounded by a group of Archangels, who act as officials, at the head of which, Archangel Vachiar is found. His voice is transferred through pulsing sounds and enters the intellect of both our Higher Self and our energy body striking us straight at the senses we possess in this dimension.

Archangel Michael announces the following: "This initiation is going to offer to your energy body the first beat of life. The flux of energy that will pass through it will return to you the privileges of the royal generation. It will restore the memory and the consciousness you possessed, when each one of you worked together with your Higher Self before the Fall. This first beat marks the beginning of true immortality.

Understanding will not be achieved by human intellect. It can only be reached through this psychic file that was until now locked. You will proceed by drinking thrice from this genetic material that bears the divine cellular anamnesis".

Having spoken as such, he extends towards us a huge chalice. In it there is a substance which is moving and which is comprised of morphed cells and small globules that are responsible for recreating the cellular system.

THE FIRST HEARTBEAT

THE CERULEAN VIBRATION

The distance the substance covers in our energy body is projected on a big screen. We watch ecstatically as a beautiful new heart of a blue vibration is created. This heart surrounds the luminous archive of the soul whereinto the primary priceless element of its creation is well concealed.

With the first heartbeats the eyes of the energy body open. The body appears fully formed and complete; a beautiful, a very bright body that is awakened form its lethargic state. It turns around and looks at its Higher Self. Their eyes meet and start talking about all that they were familiar with and had left behind them before it entered that lethargic state.

The energy body exclaims: "Now we shall never part!"

The Higher Self smiles back compassionately and says: "We have a long way in front of us yet. Now begin the difficult parts. However, we did succeed in overcoming the first trials".

The beat resonates throughout the hall and tunes to the same frequency with the beats of all the hearts of all the other entities that are present and are watching the initiation.

Archangel Michael has fulfilled his mission and announces to us:

"Always remember that you are preparing yourselves to become luminous warriors. The new files implanted in you will also mutate the archives of other people as well. The new frequencies you will be emitting will dissolve and totally destroy the toxic thought-forms that wander the Earth."

"After the formulation of the new heart and the nervous system are complete, your energy body will be capable of moving between dimensions whereupon it will also be enriched with genetic material.

This material will gradually mutate your astral vehicle as well. For as long as your focus was directed towards the astral fields, after the death of your physical body, your psyche being in a semi-conscious state entered the astral body which dominated over it.

The etheric body was doomed to dissolve as the material body decomposed. The astral lead the soul to fields that were responsible for reconstructing new births that would materialise in various personality moulds that would supposedly aid its learning. Now, however, the removal from the karmic realms has compelled the astral body to weaken and pass its dominating influences onto the energy body, wherein your primary knowledge and consciousness reside.

When the time for return will be drawing near there are certain signs that will be sent to you. The transition will be easy because the magnetic attraction exerted by the astral mass that held you back will cease to exist".

"Your Higher Selves, accompanied by other entities as well, will be there, beside you, guiding these transitions. The higher astral elements of the soul will be transferred to the energy body, whereas the lower part of it together with the etheric body will automatically dissolve.

Those who will have achieved an overall mutation of their old personality, the one governed by the astral realm, will be able to proceed to a total decomposition of their matter when death occurs".

"What I just described is also what was known to you as assumption. Assumption is what very few entities had succeeded in realising. These entities had been sent to Earth from the Fifth dimension on a mission. After their mission ended they departed without leaving any trace on your planet.

Your return is taken for granted and will be realised in one of two ways, either with the dissolution of the astral body, or with the decomposition of the physical carrier. You have awakened and activated your true bodies, that is, the carriers whose frequencies possess the structure of the Fifth dimension. That is why you will enter our plane with great ease".

Next, Archangel Michael departs via the energy column.

We enter a part of the hall where pairs of geneticists are found. They approach our energy body and convey to us the message that they will undertake the next mutations.

They insert a plate into us containing new frequency commands, to aid the preparation of our energy centres for the change. The plate also contains information we need that will assist us in handling certain events of our lives, so that we begin gradually to acquire a different perception of reality.

The energy body together with the Higher Self are in a permanent connection with the respective bodies that have remained behind in the dimension we live.

We return to Earth knowing that the substance we have transferred back here with us is of vital importance. We finally open our eyes to reality.

MUTATIONS
THE FEELING OF FEAR

THE TEACHINGS OF METATRON

ACTIVATION OF THE PRIMEVAL POWER

DNA CHANGE

NEW NERVE-CELL MORPHOLOGY

TRANSFORMATION OF THE MENTAL BODY

MUTATION OF THE HEART

THEY KEYS OF TRANSMUTATION

HIGH FREQUENCY VIBRATIONS.
DIVINE BIOLOGY

THE SEAL OF IMMORTALITY

MUTATIONS
THE FEELING OF FEAR

Fear is one of the most powerful underlying feelings that remains concealed in the subconscious constraining the soul. It is multifaceted. Usually what we have to deal with whenever we experience it are some of its facets instead of actual fear itself.

When the physical body gets in tune with vibrations quite different from those that it had been used to it responds, and all the types of fear it had inherited or had been activated at the time of birth, are projected intensely outwardly trying to enforce their presence.

Within the limits of spiritual evolution we are striving to shake off the coating, that is, the factitious earthly personality, which resides in the solar plexus and covers true knowledge of our identity and of the reason for our existence.

This is something we achieve through the mutations. We have however, to be able to deal with them, because there is a certain resistance stemming from within that makes the shift of our energy network seem very hurtful.

THE TEACHINGS OF METATRON

How can I not lose energy?

How can I protect myself?

The true "tenant" of the physical body, the soul, is required, since birth, to cohabit with another 'tenant' named personality, which keeps forming and strengthening throughout one's lifetime.

The soul at a certain point rebels and realises through its Higher Self that it is actually the one that should dominate. Thus, the struggle to dispose of the one, personality, that has trespassed into its space commences.

The personality brings forth all the weapons it has at its disposal, because it knows that if it retreats it will mean its annihilation. In that way it resists forcefully and uses all the facets of fear hidden in seemingly beautiful emotions.

This period characterised by the "battle" between them usually tires and disheartens the psyche. It seems as if it is losing. However, this is only a phase of truce, during which the psyche regroups its forces.

We, the teachers, help as much as it is allowed, even by using other people as intermediaries.

The other side also uses some people who possess a very emotionally strong personality. These types of people emit low type vibrations that reinforce the "enemy's" powers.

We reinforce by using light whereas they use darkness. During this fight both parties are allowed and have the right to use any means they have at their disposal, but within the defined limits.

Do not wonder why you are giving this fight.

You have asked for it. You know that.

Your request was to fight and mutate your energy body during this lifetime, so that you will be able to leave the unending cycle of continuous incarnations.

This is something that you cannot gain without pain. Nobody knows in advance how the game will unfold.

We, the masters are aware of certain strategic moves and some techniques. So, you find yourself in the middle of a battlefield. The protection you may receive is directly proportional to your will.

The moment you receive the light, the psyche —believing that it is invincible- leaves its rear totally defenceless. Thus, the enemy moves towards the heart centre and dominates it. That is the place where alertness and reinforcements are needed.

ACTIVATION OF THE PRIMEVAL POWER

DNA CHANGE NEW NERVE-CELL MORPHOLOGY

The energy body is complete. It now possesses a nervous system, two extra cerebral lobes, a heart and a circulatory system. In order to escape the incarnation cycle our energy network has to be shifted. Thus, the energy centres that remain inactive have to be mutated in accordance with our astral recordings. The genitors transfer and insert into the energy body the old astral discs in order to be able to transform the various elements of the DNA. They place new discs on top of the old ones. When those start rotating they simultaneously start altering the recordings present on the older discs.

In order for this mutation to be accomplished seven journeys to the Fifth dimension are required The final alignment of the centres is sealed during a journey in which all the centres are united and aligned with the disc of the central chakra, that of the heart. The upgrade and the transference of the elements of the Fifth dimension to our reality- that is achieved by the mutational procedure-attunes us with the higher frequencies of the entities that are working on this. What they are trying to achieve is to help the light pass into the energetically low consciousnesses. These express themselves in the form of continuous infrasonic sounds and they stimulate the toxicity of emotions with differing outbursts on a daily basis. The discs have antennae that are tuned to pick up on any deterioration and to activate the globules of defence.

The mutations open up other centres as well, like the aural one or the olfactory one. In that way the students- especially the healers- perceive the toxicity of the various emotions better and become capable of directing the healing process respectively. Because they function as transformers they can promote and forward the new discoveries, which then wander freely in the aether and are then picked up by men with a highly developed intellectual ability so that in continuation they can be materialised in our physical world. People though are not aware of the fact that all discoveries are forwarded to us from the Fifth dimension, which is situated in the future.

Additionally, the double strands of DNA in the sympathetic and parasympathetic nervous systems balance the masculine and the feminine energies of manifestation. Directed luminous flows enter the right side (the masculine, yang side), and offer clarity, activate the memory and syntonise the ability to handle things. Entering from the left side (the feminine, the ying side) the luminous flows enhance and strengthen the ability to assimilate. In addition, an opening up to love is experienced and enhanced, as is the ability to fulfil missions.

During these journeys the following teachings have been imparted to us:

All humans are tied to one another via karmic umbilical-like cords and their energy centres are attuned to the laws governing the astral dimension. Some initiates knew how, by applying older techniques, to activate and bring about the mutation of the energy centres. They managed to awaken the power of kundalini, which remains dormant at the base of the spinal cord. That very significant power was sealed in humans after the failure of certain experiments that were conducted during the Lemurian and the Atlantean periods. Those who had awakened that power surrendered themselves to the laws and the influences of the astral forces.

The initiates that had managed to awaken this power were humans who had subdued the lower part of their ego. The teachings and the knowledge were then passed down to the uninitiated who in turn taught it to the western world. Because, though, almost all people focused on the lower personality, that power mutated into a dark one and entered the karmic recordings of the subconscious. That caused damage to the character, temperament, and psychological well-being of men, producing problems like neurological outbursts, emotional effusions, depression and development of egocentricity.

That is why the entities of the Fifth dimension began to release and liberate man first of all of all his karmic cords, ensuring that it would not be possible for them to be activated by the lower personality. That, however, was something that could not apply to the astral carrier, because its matter was astral. Thus, they now utilise the higher astral elements (the brightness of the soul, as well as its true archive which up to now remained locked in its core) in order to manufacture a new carrier. They manage to bring about a type of spiritual intercourse between the Higher Self and the astral body. In the beginning, the embryo that ensues from this union (energy body), is made up of various transferred cores, until it acquires support, that is, a skeleton, a nervous and a circulatory system.

It is instilled the breath of life and becomes alive when the first beat of its heart is heard during Archangel Michael's initiation.

TRANSFORMATION OF THE MENTAL BODY

This procedure commences from the higher chakras. That is where the mental part resides. The noetic or mind or mental body includes the epiphysis, the hypophisis, and a part of the thyroid which is also the centre of speech. Noesis (the philosophical term) or Intellect (as it is wider known) is composed of the strings of our thought and constitutes the mental body.

Mutations here start with the epiphysis. During the voyage a plate is transferred that resembles a map on which the sympathetic and parasympathetic systems of the astral body are depicted. Furthermore, an astral disc is also transferred upon which all the functions of this specific centre have been recorded during the various incarnations.

The energy body is taken into a room where mutations are conducted on one of the planets of Nephelon galaxy in the Fifth dimension. There, geneticists (who are usually old Atlantean genitors) collect the energy body. After they have already studied the old disc that the Higher Self has carried with it a different program is appointed to each one of us. The geneticists monitor the material found in the old disc concerning the epiphysis and the hypophisis on a big screen. They study to what extent our apperception, insight and perceptiveness had been developed during the various incarnations (especially the ones during the Atlantean era, since it was then that our focus shifted away from the heavenly home). Later on, using some hot liquid substances they burn the astral "rubbish" and the toxicity that surround the disc.

When this cleansing procedure ends they transfer a crystal disc with incisions around its edges that would be used to change the focus of the old disc. The new disc rotates clockwise, whereas the older one counter-clockwise. As they rotate, like cogs, they reach a point at which they come upon the notch which will bring about change. It is then that the new direction of focus for the centres of the epiphysis, the hypophisis and part of the thyroid is set. During the rotation the new disc carrying in it the new DNA is projected holographically.

When the divine elements within us were deactivated, except for the two extra cerebral lobes, the two strands and double energy flows of the DNA (which gave us unique abilities like immortality), sustained a similar fate.

Hermes was familiar with that operation and that is why it was portrayed in a design found on his caduceus, after its dual aspect was removed from human DNA. These days they are awakening us again, so as to develop those unique abilities once more. This however, also depends a lot on how we will handle our lower personality. We should always take into account that our energy body possesses a far better potential and is more potent in dealing with and dominating personality, which at this moment retains only the astral recordings, since it has been cut off from the influences of the astral "tentacles". The new DNA layout that is recorded on the new disc is comprised of a double flow and a double axis. Via the genital fluids that are exchanged new neurotransmitters create a double flow, one on the right and one on the left side of the epiphysis and the hypophisis that lead all the way up to the throat. The throat being a very crucial mutational nodal point receives reinforced flows of energy that connect the mental body to the astral one. This nodal point is of vital importance because it also is the focal point where the mental body and the psychic body connect, which manifests itself within the astral one. Flows of genetic material start running from the epiphysis to the centre of the throat and back formulating and creating, along the way, the axons and the dendrites which assist the connections of the new nerve cells. The geneticist using a crystal rod seals and integrates the communication between these centres in a way that their pulsing vibration focuses on the intellect of the Higher Self and complies with the laws of evolution of the Fifth dimension.

The most significant change that is realised in man when the mutation of the mental body is complete is that his clarity of mind is greatly improved. The mental toxins dissolve and the mind begins to assimilate the new commands. The choices one is provided with change and the attainment of targets is more easily realised. Out of this newly formulated channel of communication that is mainly focused on the centres of the epiphysis and hypophisis, a new guiding stream commences. The latter activates both old and current knowledge that had remained inactive after our previous abilities had been removed. Speech develops and our wishes are expressed explicitly so that our intentions are palpable.

The remainder of the mutations concerns the rest of the thyroid, which are realised mainly though focusing on the centres of the heart and on a part of the solar plexus (that constitutes the connecting link between the higher and the lower astral body). The lower astral one has to do with animalistic recordings.

MUTATION OF THE HEART

The most significant journey to the Fifth dimension concerns the mutation and adjustment of the heart disc. This etheric disc includes the luminous essence of the soul, the divine spark, knowledge and positive attributes that the soul had acquired during its various incarnations. In it the assignment each individual is appointed, is concealed, however, it is surrounded by the poisonous vapours associated with toxic emotions, which darken and neutralise the brightness of the soul. These vapours tend to carve into the surface of the heart's disc imprinting the personality we develop into and which we acquire in each incarnation. The voice of the soul- for some considered to be the voice of conscience- looses its efficacy and efficiency because it is suffocated by that deceptive cloud. The plan we bear in us since the day we were born is greatly influenced and affected by it. As such the plan is either never completed or it remains partly fulfilled. Man always strives to understand what his mission on Earth is and what he came here to learn. The answers are well hidden and can be found in the core of his soul.

After we are led to the hall where the mutations are performed, the geneticists project not only the plan of our current incarnation but also all the inactive plans of our previous incarnations and they study them. They pinpoint the parts of the plan that were not completed, due to various influences and the conditions that prevailed during specific time frames. The new crystal disc that is placed in the heart contains a different plan that is destined to lead man to the development of new talents and that will rehabilitate his personality. When the new disc rotates clockwise, the old one rotates in the opposite way. At the points where the notches meet the discs stop rotating until man comprehends the problem that is impeding his progress. This compels him to enter a series of chain reactions full of contradictions and conflictions in which he will have to prove himself and change his stance to life, his behaviour, and mentality. The extra keys that are inserted by the entities help not to disrupt the motion of the discs. When an instance, during which the discs stop moving arises, that means that man cannot overcome a specific toxic emotion or cannot outgrow a specific toxic behaviour.

During the mutations of the solar plex, the abdominal centre and the genital one-exactly because those are the areas where the lower personality resides-the old discs included in these centres are all destroyed. The lower personality constitutes a second brain that regulates man's behaviour to a great extent. These are also the places where the opening, through which man's vitality is lost, also lies. The astral discs, which are directly connected to the astral "dynasts", are also found there.

When these bases cease to exist then new discs are inserted which the central disc of the heart mutates, metabolises and filters. Their emissions are very strong. Especially those of the key-disc placed at the heart since it develops love of a higher order that is connected to higher intellect. In that way our choices cease to be guided by our vices and become more clarified. What is more, they abide by our unique higher plan.

THEY KEYS OF TRANSMUTATION

HIGH FREQUENCY VIBRATIONS. DIVINE BIOLOGY

THE SEAL OF IMMORTALITY

Through these mutations the astral body is rendered weak and cannot be nourished any longer by the astral levels. Additionally, the unifying cords between the energy body and those levels are permanently severed and the focus of the energy centres shifts towards the realms of the Fifth dimension.

In order for the new DNA plan, which has been recorded on the discs, to operate with no complications, the entities serving as teachers place two key-discs in each of our centres. Whenever we evoke these keys their frequency is immediately activated.

In that fashion, a certain amount of condensed knowledge is released to assist us in completing the shift of our centres. The new neurocells, which carry out the condensation of the material on the discs, also function in a therapeutic, syntonising, equilibratory, transferential manner and as cell-shapers. They are cell morphs that process and materialise new types of thoughtforms.

They are permutation cells that classify the conventional structure of cells into groups.

The invariable frequency of the key-disc codes mutates – through the frequency they emit- the consciousnesses of other people placing them in the position to go through the various stages of reformation.

Within all the key-discs are inserted the attributes of the Fifth dimension in the form of small globules.

These small spheres are providers in the sense that they reinforce willingness, faith and militancy in man.

They also tend to coordinate the descending energies, channelling them from the discs right into the nervous system.

They are archives of knowledge, condensed plaques that are unlocked at appropriate moments. They constitute ideas, openings, and everyday relationships.

They are regulators, transmitters, which attract people of the same vibration, to reinforce alterations. They are also guardians that protect the organism against external attacks.

The archetypal symbols of genetic mutations

ALIGNMENTS

**FOCALISATION SHIFT OF
THE SEVEN CENTRES**

**UPGRADING CELLS OF A
SUPERIOR FREQUENCY**

MENTAL BODY

THE FIRST THREE CENTRES

ALIGNMENT OF THE EPIPHYSIS

ALIGNMENT OF THE HYPOPHISIS

ALIGNMENT OF THE THYROID GLAND

ALIGNMENT OF THE HEART

ALIGNMENT

SOLAR PLEXUS - GENITAL CENTRE

GENERAL ALIGNMENT

EXPERIENTIAL JOURNEY TO

PLANET POSEIDON

THE NEW GENETIC CODE

THE NEW FORCE OF CREATION

LIGHT-EMITTING DISCS

HIGH-RANGE FREQUENCIES

LONGEVITY

SUPERIOR TEACHING

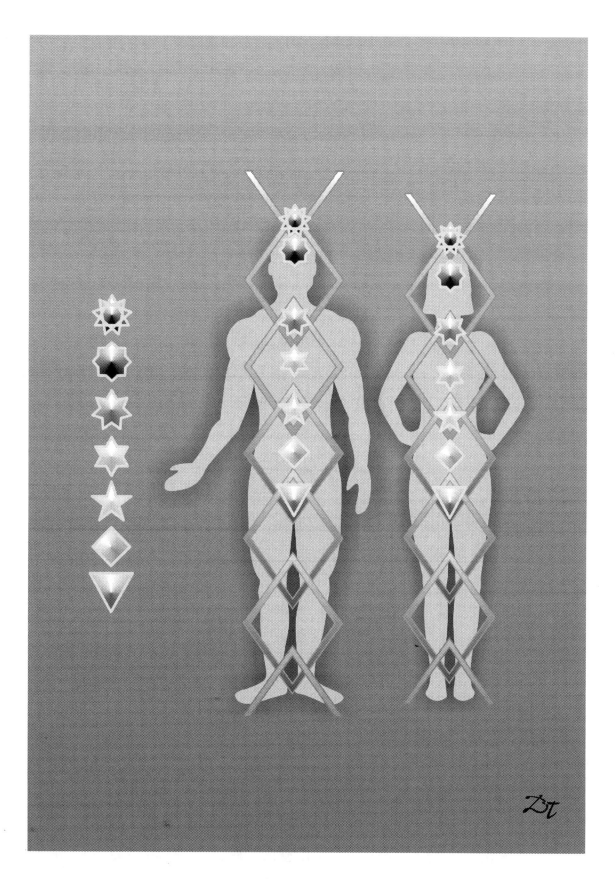

Formation of energy rhombi

ALIGNMENTS

FOCALISATION SHIFT OF
THE SEVEN CENTRES

During the initiation of Metatron the geneticists of the Fifth dimension awaken and activate the two higher cerebral lobes in which the entire primeval knowledge concerning our origin is stored. The two lobes, considered to be an intrinsic part of our human brain, carry within them the information that man's "reptilian" brain required before it underwent the primary mutations carried out by the "god"-geneticists that had descended on Earth during the first stages of his evolution. Consequently, our older lobes are linked to our lower personality, whereas the two superior ones are linked to the hypernoesis of the Higher Self. With their activation man begins to approach the superior intellect, which in turn impels him to lead his life in accordance with his own free will.

After the removal of the karmic cords from the astral levels is completed, the energy centres are liberated and free to change their frequencies and focus on the attributes of the Fifth dimension. This is accomplished with the application of the alignment procedures.

The geneticists of the Fifth dimension insert neurotransmitters that contain divine orders in the energy bodies. The new discs that are fitted into the centres in combination with the activation of the two extra cerebral lobes, allow man to glimpse into a world full of knowledge which until recently was unknown to him.

In addition they awaken even more attributes just by activating the double flow of DNA's double helix. These attributes had remained inactive since the fall into this world of crude matter. Their activation will open up the path towards longevity and immortality.

An entity named Irian participates in the alignments. She is a highly evolved neuro-geneticist who performs a very serious task concerning the recordings of the neurons.

She pinpoints with great accuracy the reasons for anamnesis that are recorded in the cores of these neurons while working with crystal tubes. Next, she places cores containing new orders and manages in this way to activate new neurotransmitters that will transfer and diffuse the awakening data to the other neurons as well.

The alignments always begin with the epiphysis. If the activation of the flow begins from the genital centre where kundalini is found it poses a threat to the well-being of the human concerned, especially for the uninitiated one. If this however does happen, then the awakened energy is diffused through the abdomen and the solar plexus. Both constitute the areas where the lower personality and the archives of karmic behaviour are kept (meaning, the poisonous emotions that manifest themselves as toxic behaviour). In that way the awakened energy appears to serve better the needs of the lower personality and man's vices instead of focusing on superior needs and causes.

That is the main reason why the first three centres that are mutated via the alignments are the epiphysis, the hypophisis and part of the thyroid gland, the three places where the first crucial fundamental node is formed that is responsible for balancing and for maintaining man's focus on positive thoughtforms.

The mutations of the centres are completed with the formation of five rhombi that at the same time stand for a primeval symbol, the pentacle. The correct (pointing upwards) pentacle regulates man's psychic and physical balance.

As the alignments are performed all the energy centres become connected to the frequency of the Fifth dimension and as a consequence we receive clearer messages, devoid of any influences or effects of the astral dreams.

During the karmic removals the karmic causes are removed from the discs and during the alignments the recordings are removed.

With the help we receive from the geneticists we discover the true values far beyond the ones that the lower personality had already allowed us to perceive or had created for us. The discs connected to the lower chakras are destroyed and what remains is only the cellular information. The knowledge we receive after the removal of the recordings contributes greatly to the opening up and improvement of our lives.

The doctors and the psychologists here on Earth are capable of solely spotting the symptoms or the illness, but cannot either counteract or negate its causes or its roots. In contrast here, during the alignments, the causes of the illnesses are treated through our plan.

Through the alignments we come consciously face to face with our personal and individual tension, because it is necessary for the recordings to pass through our consciousness first before they are completely cleared.

Consequently, all the reasons for which karmic issues, such as economic failures or loss of a spouse someone has suffered, cease to exist, and on the surface emerges a new more advanced understanding of ourselves. The entities shed light into the deepest aspects and darkest corners of our being, on places of our psyche where introspection and mere self-knowledge cannot take us. In that way we develop inner confidence and we cease to act as victims. If we are at fault we should work with ourselves.

We distinguish ourselves and we develop hypernoesis and a superior intelligence.

UPGRADING CELLS OF A SUPERIOR FREQUENCY

The light-emitting discs that are placed in the energy centres bring about a rapid and very extensive mutation of the immediate environment surrounding us as well. With each journey more and more advanced programmes are installed on the discs. The upgraded cells that are also included in these discs are divine in origin, and they constitute high-frequency reprogramming and aligning cells. New nerve cell plates are positioned in the energy body, which because it tends to be absorbed by the physical body results in the plates being absorbed by that frame as well. In that way we change, we transform, and we become brighter, more intelligent, and we stop thinking negatively.

Specifically, the following enhancing cells are administered to each one of the different energy centres:

High-frequency aligning cells are sent to the epiphysis and the hypophisis.

To the centres of the heart and throat are sent: connective cells that are responsible for bringing about balance and for restoring neurons and the balance between the double ying-yang energy (the lunar and the solar energies respectively).

To the solar plex and the abdominal centre (where the lower personality lies) are sent: regulatory and mutational cells that tend to upgrade the emotions linked to the lower personality.

To the genital centre (that is linked to creation) are sent: healing cells that function in a cell-shaping way and that awaken the primeval power in man.

MENTAL BODY

THE FIRST THREE CENTRES

The three first centres moving from the top of the head and going downwards are the epiphysis, the hypophisis, and the thyroid which all together define and characterize man's mental or noetic body.

The mental body features recordings concerned with dogmatism and social structure, which in turn are very closely related to the time and place of each incarnation. Moreover, it also features astral recordings that include impulses, stimuli, and knowledge that we have gathered throughout all our various incarnations; recordings that concern superstition, fixed ideas and causes for depression.

That is exactly the place within us that the ways we think, we judge and we communicate, where our instances of overbearing behaviour and our mistaken choices, are all recorded. Furthermore, all the existing lesions of the astral body's neurons (that result from poisonous thoughtforms) are also spotted here.

The biggest part of our brain remains inactive; however, the geneticists pinpoint the dormant neurocells and activate them. Thus, during every journey concerned with alignments we make, a specific part of those cells are awakened via the information we receive.

Maria Zavou

ALIGNMENT OF THE EPIPHYSIS

The geneticists begin with the epiphysis. First they make some necessary corrections on the old disc. Next, they put a new disc in place adjusting it on top of the old one. In it are incorporated special codes which will allow superior knowledge stemming from the higher intellect (to which the Higher Self is attached), to be awakened. The old disc turns counter-clockwise whereas the new (crystal) one turns in the opposite direction. As they rotate they meet at certain points. This is what triggers, at that specific moment, and brings about a conscious change in our way of thinking and any poisonous thoughts we had within us up to that moment are negated.

In that way man is relieved of the mental astral cloud of illusion that surrounds him and begins to think in a more positive fashion. After that, the new DNA is rooted and new neurons in the form of small crystal spheres are channelled into the body. These spheres are called mutational converters and tend to reprogram the thoughtforms. Once all these have been accomplished, the upgrading procedure for this specific centre has been concluded. This means that in that new state, from now on, it will be capable of syntonising its channel to communicate with the superior knowledge and be guided by it.

Chosen entities later on insert two key-discs. These are codes that ensure the proper and unmistaken operation of both the old and the new discs. In order to avoid any jamming of the key-discs as they rotate, it is necessary to invoke the teacher-entities, which fitted these discs, at regular intervals.

Finally, the first light-giving disc that contains a lot of transductional material is inserted as well. This disc rotates independently emitting metrical frequencies that awaken higher intellect in other people living around us as well. It also carries in it neurons with new orders that influence the older disc. It helps us develop a new perspective to life, to become distinguished, and to avoid compromise. As the new disc rotates it cancels older recordings, spotting at the same time any problems in the mental body. In that fashion, previous facts are revised and matters become clarified.

Being able to clearly view the reasons for which we have been so karmically burdened, we can invoke, whenever needed, the special secret key which applies to each particular occasion to assist us. In addition, exactly because the new disc contains the new genetic code, which leads to the activation of the two extra cerebral lobes, all our abilities are suddenly awakened and enhanced.

It is time now to begin talking about subtle discrimination. Without hypernoesis and the discs of higher intelligence, we would not be able to discriminate properly. However, being aligned to the new vibrations we become capable of easily apprehending the low dark frequencies. As a result we cannot be deceived by people who have disguised themselves into positive transmitters projecting fake luminosity.

ALIGNMENT OF THE HYPOPHISIS

This centre lies just between the eyebrows and in the past functioned as a third eye. When however, our divine attributes were removed, meaning the two extra cerebral lobes and the double DNA helix, that part was sealed. Some people managed to keep it partly awakened and then it got aligned with the astral fields. Thus, some futurologists, depending on the quality of the astral levels, are capable of entering the akashic astral realms and transferring some of the many future plans. Because the latter though are prone to change, due to the astral currents that exist, they do not display any stability and tend to be rather obscure.

In the hypophisis another new disc is placed together with extra key-discs. Inner vision shifts and focuses now on the superior levels of the Fifth dimension. Students experience new events and their mental thoughts and choices become clearer. The visual field opens and they begin to discern the true reason behind any given fact. They become capable of seeing through people without paying attention at or focusing at all on the external appearance of any individual.

ALIGNMENT OF THE THYROID GLAND

The third centre in line that completes the mental body is the centre of speech.

This is where the first rhombus concludes.

The same discs are placed in the thyroid as well, the difference being that all discs are joined together with a crystal axle. In that way the light-emitting disc sustains the other two centres, the epiphysis and the hypophisis. The key-discs that are fitted into the thyroid, bear codes of equilibratory cells. The throat centre is the most fundamental balancing node because it connects emotion and thought. The next most crucial nodes are the solar plex and the coccyx.

These nodal points keep the balancing axis aligned. The latter sustains the spinal cord regulating the two neural flows of the parasympathetic system, which contains both the warm and cold energies.

When this axis is not aligned, meaning that it might lean either to the left or to the right hand side, it suggests the absence of balance between the ying and the yang flows. That is the moment when the thyroid and the genital centre become blocked. Furthermore, when the mind is blocked by negative thoughtforms the centre of speech is immediately affected and health problems in the neck arise.

When the axis leans to the left, man remains focused on utopian fantasies, and hypotensive tendencies on a physical level are manifested and observed.

When the axis leans to the right, man is then defined by rationalism, and tends to be deprived of any sense of prolific imagination. (these type of people often operate in anger and tend to be hypertensive).

Cell-shapers and therapeutic crystals of different vibrations, which also contain equilibratory elements for syntonising the ying-yang energy flows, are transferred by the geneticists into the etheric axons and discs.

They also contain neurotransmitters that allocate the required codes transmitting information that corresponds to the respective physical organs of the body. Finally, they also contain modifiers that check and eliminate negative and foreign energies that surround people.

The cell-shapers that are diffused into the neural network of the energy body are actually regenerating codes that affect positively the entire cellular network. When these substances are released into the physical body they activate endorphin and serotonin resulting in enhancing the good mood one is in as well as boosting one's optimism and reinforcing one's positive thoughts.

Additionally, students are given special codes which are transferred mentally into their physical body. These codes operate in a twofold manner, firstly they develop and build a very strong immune system with a quick and very effective response and secondly, in a regenerative way, they assist the students in maintaining their youthful appearance. The secret of longevity resides in the centre of the brain that is pre-programmed to send commands that prevent the cells from wearing down.

The new codes progressively and gradually alter this programme by tampering with the core of the cell's nucleus.

The hyper-intelligent ancient Hellenic Gods were nourished with a regenerating and recreative substance which they referred to as nectar and they frequently displayed the ability to transform the energies and the structure of their bodies. In that way, they could assume different forms. Our DNA structure possesses recordings of such information as well, due though to our attachment to the thoughtforms of the astral levels it has now become dormant. The geneticists of the Fifth dimension are now in the process of restoring the memory concerning that information and ability.

The key-discs that are found in the centre of the throat chakra develop creative speech and the new frequencies, which are frequently expressed through it, bear special vibrations of exlplicitness and enunciation. Thus, human speech acquires a dynamic of its own. Other senses also develop such as a secret sense of hearing. Man evolves and becomes capable of sensing and hearing the various differing frequencies. He develops that is the potential of distinguishing sub-frequencies from hyper-frequencies, which are emitted from the Fifth dimension. His olfactory perceptive ability is heightened. Through it man becomes capable of perceiving another person's frequency as well as the degree of toxicity issuing from his emotions and thoughtforms.

In each and every journey the geneticists keep emphasizing that the future is not predetermined and that faith and focus are extremely essential to have our future re-planned from scratch. The rhombi that become activated on our bodies all get aligned with the divine cell of our genitors.

The second rhombus that regards the astral body covers one part of the thyroid chakra and ends at the solar plex.

Maria Zavou

ALIGNMENT OF THE HEART

The heart is the place where the soul resides and where the disc of conscience is located. Due to the effects and influences that the lower personality has on it, the psyche loses the memory concerning its origin and descent. It becomes benumbed and its brightness fades, it darkens, (which means that the disc of the heart chakra does not bear its light any more). On this disc are recorded each man's plan and mission on Earth.

The geneticists study the archive as well as the plan that concern the duration of our lives. Next, they insert a new disc and place it on top of the old one. This disc contains a new, different plan. It alters the old recordings by creating new opportunities and by negating the karmic diseases and all the hurtful and traumatic experiences as well as the toxic behaviour and attitude that lead us to conflicts. Thus, we are liberated of a future that was predetermined.

The rotation of the discs stops at specific nodal points. These points regard events that we need to analyse profoundly and comprehend since they constitute important life lessons. The nodal points are removed only when the time comes for new opportunities to be offered to us. Then the discs start rotating again according to and in compliance with our new life scenario.

In this alignment the heart becomes the sole regulator of all the energy centres. The new scenario of our life includes the future, whereas the old one is erased. In case we face some difficulties to confront and overcome a specific weakness, then some events start taking place that begin pressuring us, the ultimate purpose being that we should change our personality, our behaviour and awaken the ability to distinguish between rewarding and aversive events. When again at times we completely refuse to understand a mistaken choice we have made, the discs stop rotating. A lot of help is given to us then. The genitors ask us to make a twenty percent effort while they, with their support and their guidance, contribute to the procedure of our change, by supplying the remaining eighty percent.

The positive changes start to manifest themselves in our surrounding environment, in our interpersonal relationships and in our workplace.

All the old blockings recede, and man becomes detached from his everyday worries and starts handling his life in a more positive manner. As a result he starts attracting more positive people in his life, living happier moments and becoming luckier. The new disc creates a better and more positive future that keeps improving and upgrading, as we are capable of comprehending how and why our previous behaviour and attitude to life always led us to problems and dead ends. What we simply have to do is sit back and allow our energy body to take the reigns, since it is the sole part of us that bears within it the new luminous personality, which keeps mutating and clearing any toxic recordings. When we mentally activate the key-discs that are entered on our new heart disc, then we assist it to rotate interminably without blocking.

The second disc that is placed in the heart is placed on top of the other two. It is the light-emitting disc that regulates the rest functioning as the prime co-ordinator.

This latter disc emits over a very wide range awakening the archives of other human beings as well. In that way, the latter also manage to unconsciously enter upgrading procedures. It operates independently of the other discs' rotation. Thus, it never stops rotating. Only if the central disc of the heart chakra is jammed or blocked do the other discs stop rotating, since it constitutes the main regulator. It is then that we have to focus on the event that has charged us emotionally and seek help from our patrons and our Higher Self, by activating the keys.

The journeys, the contact with the illuminated masters and the Archangelic orders enrich our knowledge. With every journey the vibrations are upgraded and our plans are improved. During the karmic removal procedures we feel the release from our karmic load. Our alignments though help us perceive the essence of the matter, realising what exactly we have to change. We enter a new type of consciousness, which brings us in direct confrontation with the old one that had encased our heart in toxins.

Originally, the personality reacts because it cannot accept this newly acquired knowledge. With the alignment of the heart though, the illusions that produce toxins and create problems to personal relationships disappear. We change behaviour and instantly our relationships become better.

When this centre opens up completely, the ying-yang energies balance immediately. If these energies are not balanced, an internal strife commences that create cyclothymia. The whole structure changes, because the geneticists study our archives and after seeing the positive attributes we have gathered they create new scenarios.

Fear and anger are the most fundamental toxic emotions that possess the ability to stop the heart's central disc. But new neurons are channelled into that centre that operate in an equilibratory and awakening manner and that activate various talents, charismata and gifts. They also develop vibrations and a new plan that contains our mission. In addition the creative cells that are channelled into us develop a certain type of grounding, and offer us success and affluence.

The heart is the channel that will align us with the Fifth dimension during the final departure.

ALIGNMENT

SOLAR PLEXUS - GENITAL CENTRE

The three centres, namely a part of the solar plexus, the abdomen and the genital area represent the karmic emotional body that belongs to the astral carrier. The formation of the rhombus there begins at the solar plex and ends at the genital centre. Within the solar plexus and the abdomen reside the archives of the subconscious. This regards an etheric disc that contains all the material concerning karmic imprints. In it one can find the entire lower personality, which is represented by the primeval power known as instinct. The discs of these three centres remain inactive after the karmic removals have been conducted, whereas during the mutational and the aligning procedures the discs are cancelled. The outcome of these cancellations passes through special channels stretching down until it reaches the Earth's incineration core. In that manner cancellation from the cellular memory of the planet is also realised meaning that no commitment obliges the souls to reincarnate any longer.

The solar plexus and the abdominal centres are of the most difficult to be mutated.

The discs that exist in those centres convey and emit toxic behaviour that has been recorded on them from previous incarnations; behaviour which we tend to repeat and re-exhibit as we continue to reincarnate. Our personality and the attachments with the astral levels make us protagonists in a movie played over and over again. However, the masters of the Fifth dimension take it upon themselves to teach us some ways to handle the situation. The way to cope with toxic behaviour is directly related to how detached we are from it and to diplomacy. They teach and show us how to deal with it while at the same time they keep projecting intensely all our weaknesses.

The abdominal area is the command centre of our animalistic behaviour. During the alignment procedure the geneticists remove that disc, but in the cellular structure of the astral body recordings of this type of behaviour remain. In order to erase them a lot of work needs to be done.

When the new key-discs are inserted into the etheric ones of the solar plexus and the abdomen, then a series of positive chained events start unfolding in our lives that bring about development in all fields.

The geneticists channel mutational and regulatory neurotransmitters in both these centres so as to help the behavioural adjustments of the lower personality. In the abdomen an extra light-emitting disc is also inserted that emits mutational vibrations to the corresponding centres of all the other humans. The old disc that contains the recordings is destroyed. Creativity develops and affluence is provided.

A new disc is also inserted into the genital centre which cooperates with the two key-discs in stabilising the energy axon responsible for balance (spinal cord). Furthermore, the geneticists seal the genetic transfers that are responsible for toxic behaviour or any ancestral diseases, thus, liberating the new generations of these poisons.

Within the genital centre another light-emitting disc is inserted which possesses the following particularity: It prepares women's uteruses that will become portals through which the descent of the crystal children will be realised. The key-discs that are placed in the genital chakra before the light-emitting disc also activate the power of kundalini in order to reinforce creation and bring about enlightenment. The genital energy centre is related to affluence and the process of creation, but it is also often heavily burdened with vices, toxicities and debased instincts.

Through the key-discs kundalini is upgraded which in turn brings about and enhances balance to all the energy centres and conveys affluence to all levels.

Generally speaking, after the alignments of these three energy centres is complete we acquire inner freedom, self-respect, and we place ourselves in the position to take control of our lives, which from then on we lead and handle dynamically.

Issues concerning self-respect and individual freedom are dealt with and taken care of, while any "blinders" that must have been present until then are removed. Creativity is enhanced and various acts that help to develop us materialise as a consequence, opening up to us the path to abundance and well-being.

Because of the personal changes in us, our immediate surroundings change as well. One of the most important issues that evolve concerns our amorous and friendly relationships. This happens because we develop the ability to distinguish. In that way when one toxic relationship cycle ends we realise it and we move forward without resentfulness.

Were the alignments never to take place, then the etheric body, after its dissolution and after man's death, would transfer the cellular etheric information to the Earth's archive, in view of the soul's return to Earth. However, by carrying out the alignments we actually state that we now rely on our own powers and the help provided by the illuminant guides.

The keys placed in the centres keep working when the students alter their perception, attain realisation and adopt a different stance and attitude to life, otherwise they stop and become motionless. The development of their frequencies renders them invisible to the beings of low frequencies and toxic behaviour.

GENERAL ALIGNMENT

EXPERIENTIAL JOURNEY TO PLANET POSEIDON

We are standing at the station. The Atlantean Alvatar welcomes us accompanied by five other masters. He is one of the sovereigns of Poseidon. In their hands they all carry multi-faceted crystals with which they create a crystal disk around our energy bodies. This constitutes a network of protection of the entities of Poseidon, which helps the energy body adjust to the atmosphere and the planet's various characteristics.

Later on the navigating officers lead the group to the familiar gate. Gazing at Nephelon galaxy, we see planet Poseidon on the right, on the left the Emerald planet and on its right the Red planet. Above them, is the Golden planet which sends out its rays through its two satellites. These rays reach the hearts of our Higher Selves after of course they pass through the three first chakras. Then they are recycled in the centres of the energy body and through the energy cord they permeate the physical body. These rays are responsible for aligning, syntonising and healing.

We reach planet Poseidon.

At various parts of the planet we can discern a substance that amazes us greatly. It is silverfish-white, it resembles zinc and it constitutes the liquid element of the planet. It can be found in huge developmental tanks through which the souls arriving on Earth on a mission are activated and rendered syntonic. The souls that are appointed such assignments are usually crystal children or some old masters that had lived in Atlantis and are now returning back to Earth for reformation. Some of those souls will never be born, but will remain in the etheric fields of the planet. From there they will come into and be in contact with some people only to transmit to them various fundamentals and knowledge they will need to guide them.

While explaining all this to us they bring us in front of a two-level crystalline building. Each level is cone-shaped. Arrivals of various entities are performed in the first cone, whereas the second receives energies transmitted from the Fifth dimension. Before we enter the building we are led in front of a crystal pyramid. There, Archangels Iesmel, Alvaar and Achatios as well as Pythagoras and other ancient masters associated with therapy and healing like Asclepios and Hippocrates greet us. In addition, Archangels Michael, and Vachiar and the great masters Ilarion and Alvatar also are present.

After that we enter some cylinders that contain the substance we saw earlier that resembles zinc. These cylinders are actually gates that deactivate and erase the various recordings of the personality from the transferred discs.

Then, we are taken to a temple whose layout is somewhat peculiar. Its central gate is crystalline and it possesses a unique frequency and fluidity.

After that we enter a hall that tapers off in a crystal pyramid. It is open and it surrounds the first cone we saw earlier. At one of the levels of this ring we can see other groups as well. We all sit on special receptor beds possessing a different and more liquid structure. Once the receptors come into contact with the energy body, all the elements contained in our discs are immediately recorded. All around us the geneticists who have taken upon themselves to help our group observe carefully as do all the other entities that have provided us with the required keys. For the final alignment everyone awaits one of the most prominent entities to arrive, Melchisedek.

In the beginning the geneticists study the discs analytically. They scrutinise them trying to understand how they had been functioning up to now and then they examine the notches present on them distinguishing between which events we had absorbed, which we had understood, and which we had never managed to successfully confront. Additionally, they study the scenarios that will be projected in the future. They examine the new disc placed in the heart centre and they document the level and the frequency to which its rotation was performed. They also take into account the situations during which and reasons for which the main disc had stopped working. All these details, which simultaneously constitute a study of each one's personal file, are projected on special screens.

The geneticists approach us next holding vials in their hands. They pour a new substance into the smaller discs. It is a runny substance that contains codes including vital information, which is recorded on the discs. It assists us in easily recognising our shortcomings and in acknowledging the lessons that we have to learn and to assimilate, in the space of time that lies ahead of us. The navigators discharge the main discs by using this new substance. Thus, each poisonous emotion and thoughtform, as well as each inclination and projection of the astral body's cellular recording will be filtered by the navigator discs. In that way, man will be able to detect and to repair or restore any possible sign of deterioration.

THE NEW GENETIC CODE

The geneticists continue by placing a crystalline rod extending from the genital chakra to the epiphysis. In the rod there are specific parts that contain genetic material.

The rod is fitted into the spinal cord of the energy body and then all the crystal discs are projected in a holographic form. Between the projected discs and the discs of the energy body a new DNA code is created. It is comprised of four single helixes and a vertical double one. It continuously revolves around its axis and around all the other centres.

The substance that is found in various nodes within the crystalline rod is released into the centres as the genetic material is rotating. It leads to an explosion of energies which channels genetic elements to all seven centres simultaneously. Afterwards, the substance sinks back into its axon and continues flowing after being merged with the substance found in all the other nodes.

The healers check anew all the materials that had been canalised as well as the operation of the disc. Following that, they remove the crystalline rod.

Archangel Vachiar approaches us. He is holding the fiery sword with both his hands and lifts it over his head. A very strong energy flow stemming from Archangel Michael descends from the roof of the building onto the sword and starts revolving around it slowly covering both it and Archangel Vachiar completely.

Michael's force energises him and he begins to shine emitting a bright ruby light. His sword functions as an antenna of the Sixth dimension. Vachiar moves it downwards pointing towards his feet.

On the screen we watch as the power of justice and redemption, from the karmic debts inherited from our parents and our ancestors, produces a pillar that penetrates the astral archives of all the levels of all the dimensions cancelling and obliterating them. Then it passes through the etheric plane of Earth burning all the information that is present in our ancestor's archives. Towards the end of its course it enters the core of our planet where all the files and the cellular memory reside and incinerates them. Then we observe as the pillar begins to morph. It transforms into a huge red sphere that covers the heart of the planet only to remind it of the support and love it has received from its brothers of the Fifth dimension. In that way a huge file full of projections that concern the evolutionary cycles of planet Earth, is released.

After all these events, Archangels and teacher-entities near us. They take their place on the right and on the left of our energy beds. They each hold two vials in their hands and from the epiphysis they channel their contents into all our centres. What they pour into us is a condensed liquid that incorporates all the attributes of the ying and the yang energies merged with those of the masters' protection. It also includes the completed new genetic code and consolidates the feminine energy from the Fifth dimension into that of our own. The feminine energy is represented by Virgin Mary.

We stand by, watching the double energies flow alongside the spinal cord. In each and every centre they create junctions, which resemble oblique rhombi, and which concern the sealing of the genetic files and the double flows that end in the epiphysis. There is a different programme for each one separately.

We watch Ilarion and Archangel Iesmel as they reorganise the neural network and improve the synapses (between the terminal button of a transmitting neuron and the dendrites of a receiving neuron). They work on the centres adding codes that will lead to their final completion. These codes will regenerate and restructure whatever damage any cellular part of our body has sustained. For any possible complication that may arise in the future they advise us to invoke the special entity pair that has the ability to activate the keys.

After the completion of this procedure, we await two more entities, Athena and Melchisedek. Athena appears first emerging through an illuminated pillar. She represents the maternal principle, until at least we receive the initiation of Virgin Mary. She projects herself on Poseidon from another planet of the Fifth dimension with a very strong vibration that is emitted from the apex of the pyramid. Second appears Melchisedek who arrives here coming from the Sixth dimension. His form is a bit condensed. He comes in order to help and to contribute towards the final alignment. He will officially put an end to our rebirths in the third dimension.

Both these very significant entities carry two vials containing chromatic frequencies. They pour their contents into the epiphysis and then they channel them to each of the seven centres. These substances merge forming the number known to symbolise infinity (number eight), and then they permeate the discs of all the centres. The flows move downwards reaching the coccyx. Melchisedek and Athena touch two crystals on us at that point sealing thus the property of the double flow. The code of the new DNA as well as all the mutational system has already been transferred into them. Simultaneously, the rebirth process is also sealed.

THE NEW FORCE OF CREATION

A poly-morphic sphere is created which begins to pulse. It is the force of creation which we once possessed, during the times we were divine children devoid of any gender specification. In the years that followed it was removed from us, and what remained in its place was kundalini which actually is a "phantom-like" substitute for it.

Alvatar holds a multi-dimensional crystal which is actually a mobile archive, a portable poly-morphic computer. It transmits information and codes to the entire neural network along the spinal cord. It also enters the regenerating and rejuvenating codes of the cellular system. These codes assist the awakening of the cellular memory (that is, the dormant part of our mental or noetic body), which constitutes an archive containing all the information and knowledge since the Atlantean period.

Now our energy cloak has changed. It has assumed a multi-dimensional chromatic frequency. It has transformed into an iridescent tunic. The energy body glows. The Golden planet creates a golden network around our energy bodies which supports, strengthens and reinforces the new substance.

Ziron and Moira and all the other masters wave goodbye to us. They officially acknowledge that we succeeded in performing the final alignment and they reward our effort and accomplishment. As far as our final entry to the galaxy is concerned, the time has already been designated. An extension will be given to those that have to fulfil a mission on Earth. This information concerns the souls of those people who have already gone through the mutational procedure.

LIGHT-EMITTING DISCS

In order for the entity-genitors to be able to transmit the mutational frequency at a wider range they have placed three discs which they have named light-emitters. These discs are not at all affected by the discs of the centres that operate for the sole purpose of upgrading humans. Instead they operate independently. They emit high frequencies that shatter the "shells" restraining and constraining human souls.

Humans around us emit a multitude of emotions and the light-emitting discs through their reflections function as receptors of these emotions.

They locate the archives of many humans and they open them up allowing them to emerge into the light and truth of real life. Additionally, they have the potential to close the openings through which man loses his vitality, keeping that life-bearing energy within the body, in the cellular disc.

Such a procedure opens up the path first for longevity and then for immortality, which meta-humans will greatly experience and enjoy. The light-emitters open paths for positive communication. As a result men start communicating with their luminous archives exchanging vital and novel information.

By raising our frequencies to a higher harmonic we raise the frequencies of those around us as well so that the path for the coming of the crystal children will be prepared. The operation of the discs shatters the blinders of illusion, the viewpoint shifts and new goals are set.

HIGH-RANGE FREQUENCIES

LONGEVITY

The first light-emitting disc is placed in the epiphysis or in the throat chakra and joins the three centres of the mental body forming a rotating rhombus.

This disc emits creative ideas through a wide range of expressions. It reinforces and clarifies the way one thinks, not only of the individual to whom it has been inserted but also of other humans as well. These guided bursts of expression manifest themselves through immediate, direct and powerful speech.

The second light-emitting disc is placed in the heart and it joins throat and abdomen forming the shape of a rhombus once again. It is the most powerful of all the other rhombi since it activates equally the archives of other souls as well.

The third light-transmitter is inserted in the genital centre and functions as a portal through which a higher order of births, namely those of the crystal children, will be realised. In that manner, and in a gradual fashion, births of souls coming from the lower parts of the astral fields will be blocked. This disc joins the solar plexus to the abdomen and forms the third rotating rhombus. All three rhombi intersect vertically with the double axon that keeps the channel reaching the sky open, while it also joins the energies of the Earth with those of the Fifth dimension.

Summing up, the light-emitting discs have the following properties:

They are regulators of vibrations and activators of power and they reinforce the immune system. They connect to the mutational discs and they function as crystals that destroy all the negative thoughtforms. In addition, they allow people to syntonise themselves with the frequencies of the dolphins.

All the light-emitting discs are tuned to one another through the operations performed by the central light-emitting disc which resides in the heart.

SUPERIOR TEACHING

Planet Earth is evolving, as the high frequency of its discs mutates its morphogenetic fields. The frequency of all the organic beings and all the physical bodies will become more ethereal because the animalistic personality of man will be obliterated.

Matter is comprised of electron molecules that bundle together via electromagnetic bonds. Now, the electrons and their interconnections keep mutating. Thus, our bodies acquire a subtler form. The cells receive different commands and are not subject to ageing and decay.

Man of a more refined matter will be named post-human. Whenever he will decide to depart Earth, the light-emitting discs will make the necessary transformations and he will be able to return home. If he desires he will be capable of flying to Earth to promote the programmes originating in the Fifth dimension (something that is not possible at the moment, because of the crude and non-refined matter we are composed of).

Even at this specific moment entities skilled in different fields descend to the etheric plane of Earth from the Fifth dimension, in order to accelerate that transformation. Science, medicine, education, the structure of our social fabric and of our family ties, religious institutions, all will change radically. After all, all that we have been experiencing as time-travellers in the Fifth dimension, and are related to cell-morphs and to the regeneration of neurotransmitters, have already begun to be projected here, on Earth, in the form of new discoveries being made in medicine.

Many people throughout the planet are becoming receptors of codes of information that are being transmitted from the light-emitting discs. This information enters the subconscious. As a result more and more people nowadays keep materialising and realising on a daily basis whatever advanced information they seem to pick up on. In that way people function as transformers, channelling to the planet the energies of change.

INITIATION OF THE FEMININE ENERGY

JOURNEY TO THE MAUVE PLANET ZANAR

VIRGIN MARY THE GREAT FEMALE ENTITY

EXPANSION OF LOVE AND SELFLESS SERVICE

ARCHANGELS HEALERS OF VIRGIN MARY

**THE GENETICISTS OF THE
INTERGALACTIC FEMININE ENERGY**

**THE PENTACLE
ITS THERAPEUTIC VIBRATIONS**

The temple of the female hierarchy

INITIATION OF THE FEMININE ENERGY

One and a half years has gone by. The laborious mutations have ended and the students have developed and ensured a direct cooperation with their Higher Self.

During the next initiation the energy body will be structured and enriched with new elements and will acquire a higher potential. It will possess novel dynamics such as those of transmuting its personality and its emotions.

What we are concerned with here is the initiation of the female principle, that of Virgin Mary, which five great Archangels Aniel, Sochran, Norael, Kantar, and Velir surround and support with their presence.

With this initiation healing of faith, love and hope is achieved. All three constitute the most powerful elements of the feminine principle and they are channelled into us through the wisdom of Virgin Mary.

The female principle emanates from the primeval force.

With this very significant initiation of the feminine energy the energy currents of the Sixth dimension are opened. Energy streams enter the astro-noetic body and depending on the degree of assimilation from individual to individual they are consolidated as behaviour. The overtones are that these currents influence personality and as a result very significant catharsis concerning interpersonal relationships ensues.

JOURNEY TO THE MAUVE PLANET ZANAR

In the group a feeling of inner joy and satisfaction predominates. The members have surmounted their trials and tribulations and have found their true self.

We experience a phase of deep relaxation. The astral body is projected in front of the physical one and is by now connected to all the centres of the Higher Self. A large part of the astral body enters the energy body in order for some additional catharsis and transformations to take place. We have received all the personal codes necessary for the transition. These codes are secret and were given to us during the previous journeys.

We enter the first departure zone that resembles a ring and as we exit the station's second gate we observe many other entities that are about to travel through their own gates to the galaxy. At number nine, which is our gate, five teachers are waiting to descend to the etheric plane of Earth.

They belong to teams of Atlantean doctors whose mission is to channel new information and knowledge that regard advanced therapies. In addition, they will take it upon themselves to teach the indigo souls and the crystal children in whose mission there is inherent the element of medical research.

Peleus and Nephele, a couple that symbolises higher love, greet us. They have been trained in converting toxic emotions into manifestations of a higher rank. They are holding two crystals in their hands, a blue iridescent one and a pink one. These have the form of five-dimensional cubes and they keep revolving endlessly, creating various shapes, numbers and colours. They create a certain energy grid, barring astral material that has been transferred to our energy body.

By using their own inter-galactic language they explain to us that today's journey is very crucial because they will balance and seal two principles that have been fighting against each other during all our incarnations. These entail the masculine and the feminine counterparts of our essence; two energy flows that will forever be joined now with the two extra cerebral lobes that our energy body already possesses.

Our destination is planet Zanar; a planet that emits a light mauve crystalline radiation. On that planet, despite all the initiations, there are certain purgatorial procedures that are performed as well. The liquid element covers most of the planet stretching over a wide range of its surface and there are many cities overlooking huge lakes filled with that liquid. We watch it flow slowly phosphorescing along the way in varying shades of pink and purple. It is extremely difficult for one to try and describe the unique combinations of these two colours that exist here. Imposing pyramids also dominating the landscape are singled out due to their chromatic pulses.

The vehicle reaches a hangar which is covered by a crystal dome. In one of the openings found in a corridor we observe as certain rays are being emitted penetrating the space around us and we attempt to syntonise with them.

In an instant, we find ourselves in the giant central pyramid, which is made out of a vibrating crystalline material, emitting musical pulses. All around us are other pyramids as well that are joined together through vaulted corridors. The Archangels Iesmel, Alvaar, Achatios, master Phelathron as well as many other genitors lead us to one of them telling us on the way that today mother Earth will be projected as a female goddess. This goddess represents us, since her enormous womb accepted to school our souls throughout the centuries. Primarily, the astral material that we carry with us on the navigator discs will be purged and burned.

The pyramid is surrounded by frequencies of various colours. All the shades of green and mauve are the colours that predominate. In the interior we can see many crystalline pillars full of some type of pulsatory liquid containing numerous small crystal floating spheres. We enter those cylinders where the astral material existing on our navigator discs is scanned and read. Then, special spheres fly over the discs deleting any previous recordings that existed ensuring, in that way, that if a new recording is imprinted on them during the initiation it will be easily traceable. Later we are taken to the centre of another great pyramid. Its apex is linked through a circumferential vortex to the Sixth dimension, to assist the projection of various deities through it. That is the place where the couple of genitors Ziron and Moira of planet Ziron is found awaiting the projection of mother Earth.

A towering throne is energetically connected with the energy column extending from the top of the pyramid, while thousands upon thousands of gems keep sparkling on it. It is surrounded by angels dressed in blinding white costumes with cerulean crisscrossed bands. They are holding crystal bases with flamboyant flowers that seem to float in them. An unearthly kind of music is played making everyone's body vibrate in anticipation of a majestic event. We observe as extremely bright vertiginous flows of energy are created. In the midst of these resplendent grounds the arrival of mother Earth is eagerly awaited.

All around us stand various female entities that had been projected as goddesses on Earth.

We recognise Isis, Demeter, Artemis and Athena. We realise that the gate over the throne has been activated to allow the projection of the great mother goddess from the Sixth dimension.

VIRGIN MARY
THE GREAT FEMALE ENTITY

We watch as an exquisite entity wearing white materialises. She is a supreme being that represents Virgin Mary and looks as if she has just emerged from a Renaissance painting. This entity is the begetter of the female goddesses. Although only a small part of its psychic presence appears before us, its brightness is unbearable. Her eyes shine like a thousand stars and when you look at them you feel like you are travelling in space. Her smile transmits an unimaginable sweetness of love. She is surrounded by the five great Archangels Anael, Sohran, Norael, Kantar and Velir. A giant circle is formed around her by numerous female entities. She holds a chalice in her hands in which a glowing cerulean fluid seems to be moving.

EXPANSION OF LOVE AND SELFLESS SERVICE

Our Higher Self leads us in front of the supreme goddess. We drink thrice from the chalice she is holding.

The vibrating fluid contains thousands of luminous spots resembling stars, which are then channelled into the entire neuro-circulatory system and into the four cerebral lobes as well.

The energy body acquires a certain glow that diffuses into the space around it. This substance constitutes a differing form of genetic material that will help us bring into harmony our masculine and feminine sides here on Earth.

The female entities that surround the goddess are characterised by a certain feature, their moving in a circular movement fashion. Through it a pulsating sound is created which enters the energy body in the form of vibrations and information. Images and feelings are conveyed through the cord into our semi-dormant consciousnesses. When this vertiginous transition is complete the great female entity waves goodbye to us and departs through a specific channel.

We are then led to stand before goddess Earth that had arrived there in the meantime. She expresses her gratitude for the christic vibration that we transfer to her functioning as transformers. She is holding a sceptre with a beautiful crystal at the end. In it shines a miniature pulsation of the sea, a blue vibration composed of thousands of crystal molecules.

She says to us: "This is my pulse, my property and with it I will record on your navigator discs all the elements and the codes that will harmonise the central discs which have already been inserted in all your centres. The codes of the discs will develop specific bases on the Earth's etheric sheath for the goddess that will succeed me".

After uttering these words, she touches with her sceptre the navigator-discs that project outwardly. Upon them are recorded layers of vibrations that will enter the planet to create bases.

The Earth deity continues: "Some of you will come to the Blue planet that I will activate when I transfer myself to the Fifth dimension".

As our communication draws to an end, she enters seven codes into the new disc of the heart chakra. These will delete all the causes that have given rise to any type of ancestral transition in our DNA ensuring that justice will be administered upon all our actions here on Earth. The Archangels of Virgin Mary embrace us telling us how much they love us, because we have projected them in our matter. They also claim that they will keep helping us in the years to come during the healing sessions performed by them.

Our earthly time is ending and the moment for departure has arrived. We find ourselves outside the vehicle, cherishing the experience and the last images of the beautifully ornate pyramids.

ARCHANGELS HEALERS OF VIRGIN MARY

THE GENETICISTS OF THE INTERGALACTIC FEMININE ENERGY

The Inter-galactic feminine energy manifests itself in the Universe through a variety of entities. Virgin Mary is the last representative of all the entities that have descended to Earth.

Her five healers are the Archangels Anael, Sochran, Norael, Kantar and Velir. They are the Archangels of love, faith, therapy, purgation, and balance.

They transfer healing vibrations into the spinal cord; energy flows that affect and have an impact on neuroses.

It has to do with cell-shapers that produce vibrations, are productive, and operate as dischargers, regulators, modificators, equilibrists, and connectors. They create close functional connections known as synapses for every four adjacent neurons, whereas in the actual physical body there is one such junction for every two adjacent neurons.

These energy flows enter the astro-noetic carrier and their overtones operate by influencing the personality. Depending though on the extent to which each individual absorbs and assimilates them we develop and exhibit different behavioural patterns.

When man allows himself to be exposed to these vibrations he improves his immune system.

The vibrations the healer Archangels emit represent the balance between soul and body. Their message to us is that only if we cherish all the little details and all the facets of our life will we enjoy health, affluence, and harmony and will we be able to attain self-confidence. The Archangels of Virgin Mary expose us to vibrations of a reinforcing and mutational type in order to help us liberate ourselves from superstition.

Unfoldment and development of love and faith heals the person who has been led astray and has been led to perdition. When that person opens up his heart to the Archangels of Virgin Mary then he finds balance and the dark side residing in him is purged.

Their help is catalytic in balancing the psychic with the material body.

THE PENTACLE
ITS THERAPEUTIC VIBRATIONS

With the opening of Virgin Mary's channel the symbols of the geneticists are immediately upgraded. Thus, when they are channelled they contain both a golden and a blue vibration, which correspond to the masculine and the feminine element within us. This means that all the channels from now on will contain a binary aspect.

The Archangels of Virgin Mary also assist therapeutically, during the final alignment of the energy centres, taking their position beside the five parts of our energy body forming in that way an upward pointing pentacle.

Archangel Anael especially through the healing process channels cells with syntonising properties responsible for implementing information change.

Sohran —the Archangel of faith- channels cells with mutating properties responsible for acquiring information and for reinforcing faith.

Archangel of love Norael, channels cells with rejuvenating and enhancing properties. He also channels codes of love and the necessary driving forces so as to ensure that we act driven by love, an act which tends to rejuvenate our physical body as well.

Finally, Archangel Kantar channels cells with purgatory properties and Velir cells responsible for bringing about balance.

THE CHRISTENING INITIATION

THE ORANGE PLANET MATLION

CO-CREATION

THE END OF THE INCARNATIONS

THE SECRET NAME

THE CHRISTENING INITIATION

THE ORANGE PLANET MATLION

The christening initiation is one of the most important initiations. Through this the true essence of our energy body is consolidated while it also establishes a permanent cooperation with the Higher Self. In addition, the cycle of rebirths is sealed and man is liberated from the confines of karmic lesson learning.

We enter the ringed propulsion system and once again we reach the station. Peleus and Nephele the couple representing love of a higher origin await us and they syntonise the connection to our Higher Selves by using polymorphic crystals.

The vehicle has a rhomboid shape and is driven by three pilots from planet Matlion. This planet has a crystalline structure of a golden-orange hue and big tanks on its surface. The structural extensions of its cells create harmonious crystal clusters on its surface that resemble flowers and trees.

The vehicle gently lands on a base in front of a building that looks like a temple which is made of golden crystals. There is a central level where the arrival of the entities takes place, while behind us there is an inconceivably tall crystal pillar. On its end a huge sphere keeps rotating syntonising and reinforcing the storage tanks throughout the city, which is called Lor.

Various entities keep arriving on Lor from other planets and they register into programmes of cellular rejuvenation and transformation of their physical structure in terms of colour, physical composition, radiance, and movement.

Iesmel and the other masters approach us glowing with joy and say to us: "We are very proud, because now you have become official residents of your motherland. During this initiation the cycle of rebirths is permanently sealed and you will be liberated from the commitment to undergo and be subjected to the perpetual cycle of karmic lesson learning. In the past, during some other period you had received the christening initiation from an entity named John the Baptist. In the years that preceded his time the sacrament of baptism was merely looked upon as a simple rite. However, Prodromos was the first who prepared the path for the escape of the souls as he opened a gate which later on was secured and consolidated by Christ.

Both these entities were crystal souls. Of course Jesus had arrived here from a higher order. On Earth, the entity that corresponds to Prodromos's psychic projection is referred to us as John the Baptist the Precursor and it is easy for you to get in tune with his vibration.

On Earth Prodromos connected the human centre of epiphysis with the central gate he had opened with his own epiphysis. In that way, he opened the thoughts of men towards their spiritual homeland. The dark entities knew this and used their own people to force John to close the portal.

Now, this entity continues the work he left unfinished, before he came to Earth, from the Fifth dimension. Through this christening initiation he has asked for the sealing of the lower gate of the astral planes".

Before we enter the room where the baptism is going to be performed we find ourselves sitting on special bases whose interiors scan our energy bodies. From five different vials they pour a liquid substance into our epiphysis, in a sequential manner. The vials correspond to the five elements of our new personality that will become operative in our energy body.

These substances diffuse through our cerebral lobes moving along the spinal cord and then branch off reaching and entering the neural network and circulatory system. They locate the five toxic causes of our old personality and there they trigger mutations altering cellular information. For each astral karmic "tentacle" that is burned into the Earth's core, a part of its recording that was stored in the planet's memory is released. The soul's transition to the Fifth dimension will be accelerated because of that. However, the time for departure is directly proportional to the amount of karmic debt that will be redeemed that corresponds to the multitude of people living on Earth. This happens because people are directly related to and connected to Earth (since they have been inhabiting it for centuries and all their lives have been recorded on the planet's huge memory capacity).

Later on we enter a huge hall in whose centre we find a huge reservoir. Perimetrically, and on its edges there are many crystal pipes, which connect to its top, wherein a golden-white liquid flows.

The entity we referred to earlier as the Precursor has already materialised.

We witness a brightly white luminous form around which all the colour frequencies create a brilliantly radiating light. It is holding a sceptre with a large hexagonal crystal on its end that shines like a small sun. It is surrounded by Hyacinth and many Archangels. Near it stands a bright female figure. It is Virgin Mary. Her essence is extremely bright. She belongs to the christic hierarchy.

CO-CREATION

The Higher Selves together with the energy bodies enter the reservoir that resembles a huge baptistery. The liquid in there is very runny and it embraces the bodies. In it flow thousands of small crystal spheres forming groups in shadings of every possible colour. There is another type of material, also possessing golden spheres, that flows into the reservoir from the cylinders that are placed on top of it. It is comprised of elements that contain hexadimensional cores of the Sixth dimension. These spheres come together forming groups that display an intelligence of their own, which becomes evident when they choose bodies by themselves and enter them. They will be absorbed, during our return, from our astral body, which will allow them to gradually reveal their multifaceted attributes.

When the substance is finally absorbed we exit the huge tank. Our bodies shine in a variety of colour vibrations. Many energy bodies are kept in conservation matrices and project their primal essence revitalising and rejuvenating their formation from scratch. After they complete their mutational program they wake up and take their place beside us. Forming a couple the energy body together with the Higher

Self can begin from now on to work on creation cooperatively. Their union will be made official during the initiation of the Sacred Marriage. This Holy couple will strengthen us here on Earth, until at least our higher psychic constituents are integrated into the energy body during our return to our motherland.

THE END OF THE INCARNATIONS

THE SECRET NAME

The initiation continues…

Each couple is led in front of the Precursor who touches with the end of his sceptre the Higher Self's heart saying: "On behalf of the christic order and the intergalactic law of Nephelon, and in the name of the christic power and guidance I baptize you and I name you……..". The name the baptised individual is given is the same as the secret name of his energy body.

Then he touches the epiphysis of the energy body sealing the Higher Self's genital centre by forming a specific shape. This shape is intersected by an extra axis that constitutes the christic code and the access code that all the groups utilise.

Carrying on with the initiation the Precursor imparts to us the following:

"I thereby forever seal the gate that leads to continuous incarnations and I open the portal for the final return and union with the Higher Self. You have descended from the Fifth dimension but you don't remember it. The time I presented myself on Earth most of you came to me, were baptised by me, and through that ritual the first awakening was realised. Some of you were completely awakened and left, the rest of you entered the incarnation cycle, but now the time has come for your final return. The personal path for each one of you has opened, and its course and direction have been specified. It will function as a channel for the souls that will be awakened around you".

"Seven more portals have been opened in all your centres which have been syntonised with the central one.

Your frequencies are being altered by the moment, gradually and radically. In that way you tend to attract different events into your life, different associates and partners from whom you will learn and to whom you will give and offer much.

You are all syntonised and will always have my blessing.

All of us have taken you under our wings. We keep monitoring your psychograph and the mutations that you have realised. The codes that were inserted into you during the christening initiation will offer you a lot of help".

"I name you citizens of Nephelon galaxy".

With these last words Prodromos ends his christenings and sits back onto his throne. He is extremely bright.

A column of light coming from the ceiling is suddenly activated and he disappears in it.

Before we leave, the planet's most noble couple Peleus and Nephele offers to each one of us a crystal key saying the following:

"With this gift you will become capable of opening the gates of your heart and your unconditional love to all levels. Thus, you will always be attuned with us, enabling us to activate this projection and assist the assimilation of love into your lives".

THE INITIATION OF MICHAEL THE ARCHANGEL

DEVELOPMENT OF POWER

THE JOURNEY TO THE RED PLANET

THE CHRISM OF THE LUMINOUS WARRIOR

THE PERSONAL WEAPON

TEACHING ON HANDLING THE WEAPON

THE INITIATION OF ARTEMIS

UPGRADING RELATIONSHIPS
AND EMOTIONS.

The pink planet. Spheres of cellular regeneration.

THE INITIATION OF MICHAEL THE ARCHANGEL

DEVELOPMENT OF POWER

During this exceptional initiation Archangel Michael administers to each trainee a very powerful symbol, a weapon. The students are taught how to use it and for what reason they should use it. Additionally, they learn how to turn it to advantage for healing purposes. Each symbol administered to each respective student nominates him as a luminous warrior.

The students reach the understanding that during this initiation they undergo the most difficult lessons of their training and simultaneously comprehend that nothing will simply be given away to them.

The weapon they receive allows them to practice the technique of detachment and to experience catharsis later on.

Detachment means to distance oneself from one's problems. Not allowing one to actually experience the intensity of one's problem, but instead enabling one to analyze and study it internally. The most significant lesson to be learnt here is to understand how big a mistake it is to want to change other people in order to solve one's own personal problems.

With the help we receive from this weapon we are able to distinguish with great clarity between the luminous part of our soul and the old personality and its toxic emotions.

We fully understand that the discrimination between concepts like love, dependence, perseverance and persistence is something one can conquer gradually. We learn that whenever we offer our love waiting for a return of our emotions we develop toxic ones instead. However, whenever we offer our love unconditionally and without expecting anything for return then the universe -which constitutes a thinking entity- supports us ensuring that we are rewarded by receiving our own offering amplified and multiplied by many times.

Because discrimination between concepts is not an easy task, there are events that will take place that might shock us. Ordeals one has to go through continuously arise so that the trainees learn to pinpoint the weaknesses of their personality and use the weapon they have received in the most equilibratory manner.

THE JOURNEY TO THE RED PLANET

The navigators inform us that we will need to travel to the Red planet for this initiation. From there we will be beamed to an intermediary planet that connects the fifth with the Sixth dimension. We sense the difficulty inherent in this transcendence. They assure us, however, that the energy body will have to be prepared for such transitions since the time for the pre-initiation of the christic path, which will be performed on one of the satellite planets of the Golden planet, is drawing near.

We are on the Red planet. Artemis, Arion and Phelathros accompany us.

Using the navigator discs, they have already inserted into our energy body plates that contain our neural system, the discs and the light-emitters on which segments of our lower personality have been recorded. There is another plate which is inserted into our energy body. This one contains codes of the abdominal centre as well as recordings of the levels of fear of each student. All these will be burned on the Red planet and our consciousness will surpass all blockings and cessations existing in the astral body. The vehicle takes us to a specific region of the city where there are many buildings and temples occupying a vast area of land. We pass through energy pillars where cleansing and syntonising procedures take place.

We are then taken to the initiation room. A multitude of masters, well-known Archangels as well as visitors from other planets are there, distinguishable mostly by their colour vibration. We also observe the psychic part of goddess Earth being projected.

We get ready to be beamed on the verge between the fifth and the Sixth dimensions, right in the upgrading projection of the Red planet.

We are transferred into a huge hall containing thousands of crystal pillars, within which energies of various shapes are revolving. We enter one of these columns together with our Higher Self. A very complex mechanism – that operates as a transformer- towers above us hanging from the ceiling. Rotations begin assisting the realization of the transition and we feel a sense of emptiness in relation to the consciousness we have back here on Earth. I watch my students lose their sense of stability in the physical environment and I worry. However, the navigators keep them in tune and stabilise them by reinforcing and supporting them continuously. We exit into another room in which everything is in a fluidic state while the light is blinding us. We cannot even see the entities as clearly as before.

We are now standing in front of a throne experiencing ever increasing rotative vibrations.

Slowly out of the blasts of light and sound Archon Michael materialises. He is huge and appears resplendent.

He holds a chalice and a fiery sword whose pointed tip is a bit out of the ordinary since it is comprised of a number of rotating points.

The substance in the chalice concerns genetic networks of defensive cells that will activate our immune system. By drinking that substance, which also bears cellular crystals of the Sixth dimension, we will acquire both strengthened and reinforced psychic and physical endurance that will help us become luminous warriors.

THE CHRISM OF THE LUMINOUS WARRIOR

The chrism begins. Both the Higher Self and the energy body stand in front of Archangel Michael who lifts his fiery sword in the air. We see a shine. A flowing power energises the Archangel's sword and Michael places it on the Higher Self and the energy body's epiphysis and heart. The last place where he places it on is the epiphysis of the Higher Self at which point a shape similar to a clepsydra is formed.

At the point where the two triangles meet and connect is where the focal point resides. Through that focal point and via an illuminated channel descends a flowing power which constitutes our connection to the Sixth dimension.

The frequency of the Archon's voice diffuses into the room. My heart is pounding because a very powerful attunement is needed in order for me to be in the position to translate. I convey to everyone the message that Archangel Michael imparts to us.

"I proclaim you warriors of light. You will be trained in the flame of the warrior. The training will be customised according to each of your special attributes as those are recorded in your psychic archives. You can enjoy my protection, but you shall undergo a harsh training program. Special officials are connected to you to administer you strength interminably. We shall not prevent any lessons that concern your training from ever occurring however harsh those may prove to be. Using the weapon given to you wisely and properly will awaken you in order to effectively confront arising events".

The entities that surround Archangel Michael are holding discs in their hands on which various weapon symbols shine; one for each student.

Archangel Michael inserts the weapon in the heart of the Higher Self and in the heart of the energy body.

THE PERSONAL WEAPON

TEACHING ON HANDLING THE WEAPON

The usefulness and the use of this weapon are relevant partly to the way we deal with our own mistakes and partly to the attacks inflicted on us by others. Each and every mistake we make we will experience both psychically and physically which in turn will assist us to ultimately realize the proper way to handle it.

We all feel a great sense of responsibility, though our personality tends to cast shadows of doubt. We face a dilemma and wonder if we will cope in the end. The entities become aware of these negative thoughts and hasten to counteract them by temporarily shutting down the channel through which they managed to reach us.

We stand in front of Archangel Michael and we are invited to drink thrice from the chalice he is holding. This liquid contains thousands of blue and red spherules which diffuse into our entire circulatory system. The majority of these globules concentrate in the abdominal and cerebral regions for the purpose of reinforcing the physical body's immune system through continuous discharge.

Hyacinth approaches us and a towering entity of the Golden planet which will administer the pre-initiation of the christic ray does so as well. Hyacinth inserts an extra light-emitting disc in the genital centre.

This specific disc is responsible for preparing the portals found in female wombs clearing the ground for upgraded births of crystal children, thus restoring occurrences of creative events in our lives once again. These events will further affect and influence other individuals around us as well allowing them to enter a creative phase or path in a variety of fields.

The entity that will administer the pre-initiation of the christic ray, studies the plate that has already been transferred into our energy body. On it are recorded all our personal fears. It continues working by placing intricate crystalline shape-transformers into the energy body, ensuring that whenever fear is projected then both strength and an increased sense of militancy would be activated. Gradually, the web of fear will be removed from the astral carrier especially as the energy body keeps penetrating into it more and more.

In the Fifth dimension we dream about the events that are unfolding in the Sixth dimension and we feel ourselves being placed into the pillar-clepsydras for our return to the Fifth dimension and the Red planet. We exit into the room from which we were initially beamed out of as if we have awoken from a dream.

Several masters welcome us saying:

"We take great pride in you for attaining this goal and for having received this chrism. We will have our eyes on you in order to keep reinforcing the positive elements of your personality rendering you capable of living up to the expectations of your task and helping you to overcome the difficulties of your very crucial and significant role as warriors of light".

There are numerous warriors of light scattered throughout the planet. They function as transformers of our energies. When we locate you, you appear like bright little stars on Earth's surface. We are capable of doing this through the help of large computer networks and we are aware of your whereabouts every single moment. With today's training the number of the warriors of light will expand even more against that of the warriors of the dark who are striving to ruin your planet.

Believe in the usefulness of your weapon and its potential and always battle using it".

Our return is expedited on account of our stay having far exceeded the specified time limits. Our physical bodies have begun to tire out.

THE INITIATION OF ARTEMIS

The initiation of Artemis is the most fascinating one, compared to all the other initiations, and it is practised on the beautiful Pink planet. There, entities are trained; entities that have undertaken to come to Earth on assignments, whose primary objective is to focus on the psychic plan of men and to contribute towards the alteration of their archives.

The centre responsible for the projections of the Pink planet is managed by Archangel Samuel and his joint staff, who also direct the disc found in man's heart centre.

With the initiation of Artemis an emotional upgrade is accomplished and a more substantial communication between human psyches is established.

The energy bodies primarily enter the spheres that are rotating in the planet's atmosphere, high above its lakes. These spheres possess the ability to scan people's emotions and attitudes that come to light during their various incarnations. Next, the energy bodies are submerged into lakes containing some kind of genetic material. These lakes are connected through ducts within which cells of emotional reformation of a higher order flow. After the initiation is complete, the lower order emotions are revised and through the prism of love they begin to mutate. The immediate result is the creation and establishment of inter-personal or amorous relationships that are founded upon healthy and sound bases.

What we took for granted and our knowledge concerning marital and friendly relationships is thwarted. Male and female roles are counterbalanced and there is no room anymore for possessiveness or for attempts like trying to gain the upper hand.

Couples with upgraded emotions will give birth to children that will be crystal and that will teach love to the world.

We are again at the station and twelve entities accompany us during the journey. They have received the first Archangelic chrism and they have connected with some members of the group offering their protection and guidance on a daily basis.

We observe an increased mobility compared to the previous journeys. They explain to us that numerous groups from other astral systems have been synchronized with one another, in the context of a synod taking place, to visit the Pink planet which is none other than Venus in its spiritual form. They travel to various levels of the numerous cities found on this planet with the intent of upgrading their emotions.

In the vehicle we also find Peleus and Nephele at the feet of whom we have sat and by whom we have been instructed during many of our journeys. Navigators of the planet escort us. They are also surrounded by numerous Archangelic navigators belonging to the order of Archangel Samuel. Their costumes are singular; embroidered with crystal-regulators that alternately increase and decrease distances, energies and coordinates.

As we travel a beautiful planet shines in front of us. It is crystalline, bathed in light it radiates in shadings of pink. Five concentric pink circles keep rotating around it while simultaneously we watch as other vehicles approach it from different angles. The codes that are responsible for unlocking the inner gates are administered and various homes that resemble round lakes come into our sight.

In the centre we find spheres of varying frequencies. There are also multi-storey buildings in whose architecture the most dominant feature is their curvature.

Several of these buildings hover above the ground because they lack the required magnetic field that would allow them to remain on the ground.

On the various levels we discern the lakes that have formed there, which contain a substance that differentiates between the genetic recording of old emotions that existed since the origin of mankind, and the genetic recording of new ones.

The vehicle lands on top of a dome where three geneticists await us. These are the Archangels Iesmel, Alvaar, and Achatios, who represent our personal tutors. This time the navigator discs we are carrying on us contain all the difficulties we have encountered during all our relationships.

We pass through several aerial corridors. On the right and on the left we see isometrically arranged spheres that emit syntonising sounds similar to the sounds of music.

We enter a hall with no ceiling, which is found in one of the many multitudinous levels of spheres and we see a huge sphere which is open on the top side. Its centre is extremely fluidic. There are other levels there as well surrounded by round ponds of differing colours. Each one of the spheres corresponds to each one of the students of the group.

Before the initiation commences we enter an adjacent level at which many female entities have just arrived. Regulators select the specific ponds found in the hall into which the liquid that corresponds to each of us will be eventually channelled.

We are accompanied by our Higher Self and our guide; the regulators activate the rotation of the spheres, creating and sending pulses to their liquid element. Suddenly, it begins to vibrate and come to life creating a fantastic image that emits a variety of colours.

The regulator-entities connect the abdominal regions with the liquid element through crystal pipes. The vibrations emitted by the rotating spheres pass through them in a wave-like fashion.

This concerns recordings taking place on the disc of the abdominal chakra that contain upgraded information as well as information concerning different and varying modes of confrontation which bear no relation to the much older recordings.

Thereafter, this substance is channelled into the entire neural network of the energy body via a central plate. It also contains advanced information that enters the cellular recordings and erases any remaining toxic aspects that hadn't been negated until now. We watch as the spheres that keep rotating above the ponds cause ripples to form in them, and are fascinated by the aesthetic aspect of the entire region.

The procedure continues. We enter a huge crystal sphere where we find many similar ones constructing buildings in a peculiar manner, without using any supporting means or any type of scaffolds. Entities of the feminine elements have arrived representing the feminine principle that exists on Earth since time immemorial. We single out a beautiful tall and spare woman that seems to dominate this level. She possesses an upgraded form because her make-up and her temperament have been filtered after her passing from Earth.

UPGRADING RELATIONSHIPS AND EMOTIONS.

That Goddess is Aphrodite, the genitor of the Pink planet. The planet is governed by a hierarchy of groups that carry out various developing programmes like the ones concerned with emotional upgrades.

Beside Aphrodite stands Artemis. Appearing very different from the descriptions we have thus far shared with you, she emits a singular vigour and looks exquisite. Close to her stands goddess Earth.

These two divine creatures had a unique communication between each other from the first moment the former had appeared in flesh and blood on Earth. We also see a third figure, a gorgeous very beautiful entity that on Earth was represented by Virgin Mary. Her eyes shine in shades of blue and pink. All the entities are vibrating simultaneously.

Our Higher Self, together with our navigators, prepares the energy body for the grand initiation that will follow. We are driven in front of Aphrodite who represents higher love and is holding a chalice in her hands. We take three small sips of the substance existing in the chalice which contains genetic frequencies. It enriches us and provides us with the potential to perceive love and sacrifice in a different way and it assists in the clarification of our emotions and our recordings. Artemis, goddess Earth, and Virgin Mary are holding three weaponry symbols.

Artemis approaches and she hands to us the first symbol which is registered on the abdominal disc. It is a symbol of love and fulfilment of goals. It bears the energy of creation and it will reinforce and strengthen the fulfilment of our creative goals.

Goddess Earth follows, she hands the key which is directly linked to the previous one. This will have an immediate impact on the toxic emotions by directly erasing them. These emotions had predominated in many of our incarnations, had profoundly influenced our personality and had been powerfully recorded in the archives of our subconscious. It will also help us acquire emotions of compassion, love, stability and balance. Simultaneously it contributes towards the co-existence of old and new energies on the planet.

Finally Virgin Mary hands the last key that will assist us in gaining a better and more profound understanding of ourselves and of others. Concerning other people this key will help us gain a certain insight which will further assist us in identifying their primary needs. This key will also form within us and develop higher emotions in order to be able to distinguish between toxic dependence and sacrifice and between possessiveness and true love.

In that way, we acquire a very significant central weapon symbol from Artemis that will help us to fulfil our dreams and aspirations and two other extra keys that will administer to the first one the respective frequencies it will need.

Additionally, they will create a field in a cellular form that will become the entrance through which the crystal souls will pass. These souls will display cellular recordings of a higher rank; recordings that concern love and sacrifice. Thus, they will be rendered capable of developing a different philosophy concerning the manifestation and upgrade of those emotions. Moreover, they will also be the architects that will set the foundations for more advanced relationships between couples.

Once the procedure of administering key-symbols is complete the entities that had been worshipped as divine beings on Earth and had represented various civilizations choose some people from the groups and hand to each one of them a papyrus. It contains information that will help them automatically develop the area of their expertise, that part of their field, which is compatible with various religious movements.

The divine entities seem therefore to support these courses of action which the chosen students will have to impart to people in accordance with their level of progress, their habits and with the historical period they are in.

Aphrodite informs us that the genetic material in the chalices will unite the two vibrating energies that each soul possesses the masculine and the feminine one. With the fusion of these two vibrations people will feel and express themselves better.

We prepare ourselves for departure casting our eyes for the last time on those female goddesses and smiling to them we wave goodbye. We enter a corridor through which we are given the opportunity to see for the last time this "fairyland" with the hovering crystal spheres and small lakes.

The vehicle turns around and sets its course for the return…

INITIATION OF THE
HOLY MARRIAGE

ATTRACTION OF SOUL MATES

THE GENETIC UNION

THE BIPOLAR COUPLE

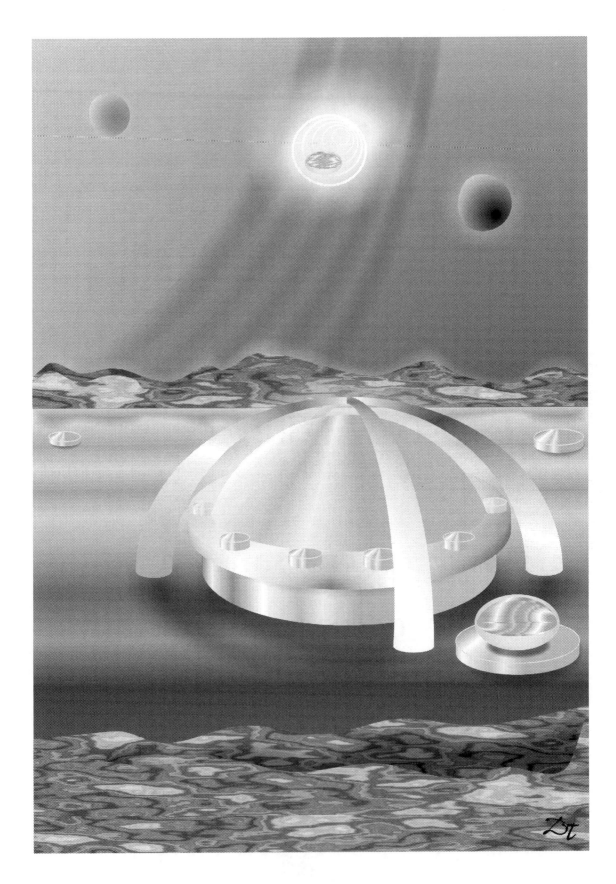

Biogenetic centre

INITIATION OF THE HOLY MARRIAGE

The Holy Marriage constitutes the most significant event on Nephelon galaxy. With this initiation the union between the Higher Self and its psychic counterpart –which is the energy body- is sealed and a holy deal is effectuated by which they will operate from now on as a couple of the third dimension.

With the Holy Marriage we totally liberate ourselves from the negative attributes of the lower personality and we allow ourselves to begin our true life. We operate on an evolutionary basis, avoiding totally poisonous relationships based on dependence, attracting people of a higher frequency and soul mates that have been preordained to enter our new plan at specific time junctions.

Together with our Higher Self we constitute from now on a bipolar couple and we experience – even here in the material world – a small portion of that bipolarity. Through this initiation many couples prepare themselves to bring to this world the first crystal children, souls devoid of karmic archives.

The trials and tribulations we undergo before this initiation are many and depend on the various levels of our consciousness.

ATTRACTION OF SOUL MATES

At the station a beloved and well-known couple greets us; Peleus and Nephele, residents of the Emerald planet, who stand for the perfect bipolar couple.

They welcome us to this grand initiation. Offering to each one of us a polyhedral crystal with a blue frequency they inform us about the fact that:

"This crystal represents the true meaning of bipolar love and you will syntonise your emotions through it. The attunement will attract near you people of the same frequency, soul mates who have been preordained to enter your plan. Thus, you will become capable of experiencing – here on Earth as well – a small part of this bipolarity. Until now you tended to choose people who were mirror images of yourselves. Thus, you were, in a way, bound to learn very harsh lessons, in order to be mindful of your subsequent actions and decisions, but toxic recordings wouldn't allow you to escape the toxicity of the illusions. Now, you can call upon the energy power of the crystal in order to attract respective companions. In addition, some of the women among you have been chosen to bring into this world the first souls of crystal children that will assist the Earth during its new evolutionary stage. The programmes concerning the arrivals of these souls will gradually and progressively be complete".

"The new species of man that will inhabit the planet, the meta-humans, will neither have karmic archives nor any parental or ancestral diseases. They will not exhibit any problematic behaviour either.

Science at the moment is very close to the discovery of unravelling the human DNA, however always remember that you are living in the past. You need first to experience all that are taking place here in the Fifth dimension – that is the future- and only after you transfer the knowledge and the experience to your dimension, functioning as transformers, will everything be realised in your dimension as well.

Do not forget that whatever you experience here you subliminally emit all over your planet through the light-emitting discs.

The information is directed towards the most appropriate minds that have already been chosen so that new research is conducted and completed and grounded".

The gate opens and we enter the vehicle.

The two navigators are wearing uniforms embroidered with festive emblems. The vehicle moves towards a huge town that lies somewhere in the midlands. That is the place where the see of the genitors Ziron and Moira is found.

From the vehicle looking down we see a crystal palace with an infinite combination of colour gradations. On the left and on the right we see two enormous pyramids with crystalline antennae so high that they seem to disappear into the sky. The sky seems to be moving looking like a living mass made up of pastel colorations and shining stars.

When we disembark we find Iesmel and Achatios and our personal teachers, who have undertaken our apprenticeship, waiting for us. Archon Alvaar is also there accompanied by five more Atlantean masters. They are holding multi-dimensional crystals, which are accumulators of information. There is a sense of expectation and joy filling the air. Our bodies that have been left behind, in the third dimension, have bliss written all over their faces. Some cry and their tears disappear twinkling slightly just before they vaporise. Explosions of colour and crystal spheres fill the air and shine all around us. Around the palace there is a central dome decorated with wavelike lines onto which a central cone is attached. It is here that arrivals of entities from the Sixth dimension are carried out, whereas on the other smaller cones, which also exist on the dome arrivals of entities coming from other planets of the galaxy are performed. These cones have a very complex conversion mechanism built into them that allows the entities of the Sixth dimension to send their energy carrier.

We are led to two crystal pyramids that lie in front of the palace. We enter the left one. In the centre we see a very bright white light. There is a very elaborate pillar on whose end a bright rotating sphere keeps shining, sending out thousands upon thousands of rays.

Each couple successively stands in front of this sphere as the latter syntonises them with its rhythm while simultaneously it sends out energy connections.

These look like lasers beamed at the energy centres and the nervous systems of each couple, forming connections that resemble slender-like golden threads. These energies penetrate every single cell of the Higher Self and the energy body. This procedure is deemed highly essential in order for the Holy Marriage to take place.

Later on, we are taken to the right pyramid in whose interior we see a rotating sphere. As it rotates it emits a wonderful vibration that we perceive as music played directly in our ears. It is the music of the spheres. These unfamiliar sounds penetrate all the cells of the Higher Self and the energy body, forming circles that unite and then break up into a feast of colours. These circles symbolise the evolutionary cycles of the energy body once its liberation has been realised.

After completing the preparation phase we start walking up the twelve crystalline stairs of the central gate.

Iesmel, Peleus and Nephele activate the codes. The gate opens and we find ourselves in the central Hall where the Marriage ceremony is held. The place is shining so bright that it almost blinds us, untuning the energy cord connections, but to prevent the worst from happening the navigators intervene using crystals to restore image and sense.

I watch ecstatically the vibrational painting on the sides of this huge room. Scenes depicting the descent of entities on Earth during various time periods are portrayed on these walls.

On the ceiling there is a huge opening through which thousands of rhombi intertwined symmetrically hang producing a wonderfully melodious vibrational type of music. Our vision becomes even clearer and we see the Archons Ziron and Moira sitting on their thrones while on the right and on the left stand the Archangels and the masters.

We observe as above the divine couple a column of light descends from the cupola and is channelled over them. Behind them there is a multi-level plane where thousands of entities of differing vibrations sit.

We recognise the tall and slender entities of the Atlantean masters of whom Alvatar is the commander in chief.

There is also a great master entity that came with Hyacinth as representative of the christic ray. He is Melchisedek who projects the same form he had assumed when he had appeared on Earth for the first time.

THE GENETIC UNION

Ziron and Moira stand up appearing deeply touched by the whole process and tell us the following:

"It gives great pleasure and relief to us that you have managed to reach this stage concerning the initiation of the Holy Marriage. Your Higher Selves have pulled off an extraordinary and miraculous feat, a self-transcendence that has led you home so that your union could be sealed after the many trials and tribulations you have suffered. Today this effort is rewarded'.

The divine couples hold crystal discs with rings of a differing chromatic vibration in their hands. Engraved codes are present in their interiors as well as secret names. The genitors take two rings in their hands each and they hand them over to the Higher Self and the energy body. Mentioning the codes and the secret names they go on to tell us:

"From now on you will be known as a bipolar couple. Now you are together again, your separation has reached its end. The reactivation of your unification has taken place and the path leading to other dimensions of the galaxy has been opened".

THE BIPOLAR COUPLE

Once the initiation rite of the Holy Marriage is complete, the two sovereigns together with Melchisedek and Hyacinth lead us into another room. In the centre an enormous pillar is rotating. There is a certain dynamic in its frequency. We sense Metatron materialising. Melchisedek is holding a chalice with a moving shining golden liquid inside. This liquid contains thousands of golden spherules. It includes a genetic substance that will constitute our syntonising window to the codes of the Sixth dimension. This concerns the christic vibration and also constitutes the final sealing of our return home. The substance diffuses to every molecule of our cellular system with alternating pulse-vibrations of golden light.

Metatron lifts a sceptre with a polyhedral crystal high above the heads of the Higher Selves and the energy bodies. He touches with it the epiphysis of each Higher Self and the epiphysis of each energy body forming simultaneously a noetic triangle. At its apex a channel of communication with the Sixth dimension is formed.

Following that, beginning from the epiphysis of both the Higher Self and of the energy body he forms two rhombi that end at the feet.

The focal point, at which they unite, forms another rhombus that also constitutes the connecting centre of the archives that belong to the heart chakra.

The point at which the two lower vertices of the two rhombi connect creates a further rhombus whose vertex points towards the starting point, which is planet Earth; while at the same time it grounds us with the Earth entity.

The rhombi empower the light-emitting disc of the heart chakra, making it emit higher frequencies that will influence other people and impel them to begin their own purgatorial processes and karmic removal rituals.

The genetic union of the rhombi portrays and formulates the structure of the divine cell that bears the principles of immortality.

Metatron disappears in a vortex created by the column's rings. Melchisedek and Hyacinth hand to each one of us a papyrus containing some complex codes explaining to us that:

"On the papyrus you are given are written each of your tasks. You will decode it using the archives' central disc you have already received in your heart chakra".

We feel that our energy body has strengthened. We feel it prevail over the lower personality now.

We return, keeping the memory of all those events inextinguishable and we feel extremely joyful for everything we have accomplished.

Temple on the Golden Planet

PRE-INITIATION OF THE CHRISTIC VIBRATION

THE GOLDEN PLANET

THE JOURNEY

BEING BEAMED TO THE GOLDEN PLANET

HYPERFREQUENCIES OF THE SIXTH DIMENSION

THE UPGRADING SUBSTANCE

THE PRIMORDIAL STRUCTURE OF THE DIVINE CELL

NEW LIFE PLAN

PRE-INITIATION OF THE CHRISTIC VIBRATION

THE GOLDEN PLANET

The first great initiation of the christic vibration takes place after two years of being subject to trials, and it is held on the Golden planet. It is the planet where the see of the great teachers and of Christ is located. Christ is preoccupied with the programs focusing on attracting souls back to their homeland. The planet is surrounded by twelve rings and two golden satellites, both on the right and on the left side, which function in an equilibratory manner and belong to the Fifth dimension. Being in command of the right satellite is master Hyacinth, representative of the solar vibration and consciousness. On the left satellite Archangel Iliel is in command, representative of both the solar and christic Word, of the grounding procedure and its application.

The Golden planet is a huge gate, a conductor through which entities can pass in order to be propelled to the Sixth dimension. It belongs to the Sixth dimension but it is projected in the fifth.

The primal seeds that restrain the lower dimensions are created in the Sixth dimension. It constitutes the centre of movement and dynamics. It is the place where the hyper-noetic Higher Selves of the Higher Selves, who move between and function in both the sixth and the Fifth dimension are found.

When the Higher Self from the Fifth dimension unites with its psychic counterpart (the energy body), it is also the time when this higher divine entity is activated. The gate towards the Sixth dimension opens after the initiation of the Holy Marriage is held.

THE JOURNEY

June 2007. The first groups are gathering in the hall getting prepared for the journey.

The faces of all the members of the group beam with and reflect joy and fulfilment. We come to the realization of the profound changes that have taken place in our life, bringing us closer to true happiness.

We are about to get transferred to Poseidon and later to the borderline between it and the Golden planet. All our energy centres will be connected to the energy centres of our Higher Self for the duration of the journey.

The journey begins and we enter the galaxy. At the station there are Archangels Iesmel and Achatios and the ruler of Poseidon Alvatar. Through a cylinder-like structure we are driven to one of the many compartments of a multi-storey crystalline building. We exit into a well-lit room replete with seats and crystal columns, which are connected to one central pillar that disappears into the ceiling. There, we notice an elaborate transformer that mutates the structure of the energy body providing it with the potential to travel beyond the Fifth dimension.

Alvatar, together with the entity known as Athena attract outwardly the navigator discs that contain all the recorded hardships we have suffered. Using special crystals they delete the recordings and by utilising accumulators of knowledge they transfer different plans with fresh solutions into the discs.

An extremely beautiful entity approaches and explains to us using rhythmic sound frequencies that it is the psychic projection of goddess Earth. It is accompanied by a multitude of female entities that represent the divine feminine energy. Among them we also find an astonishingly bright silverfish-white entity that impresses us greatly. It constitutes a projected psychic counterpart of the Moon(Selene).

Mother Earth informs us that she is fully aware of what usually happens during these missions. Its cellular system has received the required information that renders it capable of identifying us through the vibrations we emit when we are on Earth. It has already begun its journeys and its soul is partly withdrawn from Earth. In addition it is in a continuous collaboration with the new entity that will enter and inspirit the planet and that will transform the level of its consciousness. Thereinafter, they implant within each one of us a new plate containing new upgrades, whose purpose is to reinforce the signal of our presence on the planet.

BEING BEAMED TO THE GOLDEN PLANET

The Higher Self announces that the time has come to be beamed to the verge of the central gate of the Golden planet. We move towards its right satellite and then we enter crystal columns that taper off into polymorphic rooms. Each one of these columns possesses nine notches that are connected with the seven chakras of the energy body and our Higher Selves.

A very intense pulse-vibration commences within the cylinder. Frequency waves start developing transforming the energy body into a carrier far brighter and more crystalline in appearance.

These bright luminous bodies together with the transformed carrier of the Higher Self pass through the central transformer and enter a channel of superfast photons of the highest grade in order to be transferred to the satellite found on the edge of the Sixth dimension. The navigators are continuously trying to keep the cord in attunement with our corporeal frame to achieve enhanced levels of clarity for the better transfer of images and of experiential experiences.

We exit the cylinders and we find ourselves in an extremely bright room that is also vibrating. We have difficulty adjusting ourselves to this different vibration while the navigators keep regulating the umbilical-like connection cords.

We spot some entities distinct for their great height and marked out for their exquisite golden appearance. They move about in bright limpidity. A couple who function as geneticists approaches us. We are impressed by their sparkling shimmery eyes, and by their vibrating outline. They have received morphic elements of the Fifth dimension, which assists us in detecting them.

Next, we are seated on special scanning bases and the geneticists connect our bodily functions with our bodies that have remained on planet Poseidon.

HYPER FREQUENCIES OF THE SIXTH DIMENSION

Hyacinth, who has given us the light-emitting disc containing the frequencies of the Sixth dimension, approaches us. The hyperfrequencies responsible for inducing a rapid upgrade in many other souls as well have already been entered into the disc. Thus, there will be a large scale influence on the archives of those people who will be ready to enter the phase of change.

THE UPGRADING SUBSTANCE

THE PRIMORDIAL STRUCTURE OF THE DIVINE CELL

After Hyacinth a snowy-white teacher, with bright, sparkling eyes of a higher intellect, appears. They dominate our visual image and infuse us with emotions of serenity and peace. We feel as if everything comes to a standstill and the only thing we desire and pray for is for this feeling never to cease.

It is Melchior, the great mutational alchemist of the frequencies of the astral carrier. He is the one who is aware of the photodialysis of the astral carrier and the conscious transition of the soul to the Fifth dimension.

He is accompanied by two entities wearing golden robes, Metatron and Melchisedek, each holding three crystal discs for each one of us. They place them into our solar plexus, and in the abdominal and genital centres.

The plexus will protect this substance by isolating the toxic emotional projections. Into the centre of each disc they channel three spherules containing genetic material. This substance has the form of spherules and is administered to and divided among the discs. Each spherule consists of thousands of spores that will transfer themselves into the cellular pool of information for the generations to come.

Hyacinth, a figure that resembles and reminds us of Christ, approaches us next. He is a projection of Christ emanating from the Sixth dimension. He is holding a golden sphere in his hands that bears the primordial structures present in and responsible for the birth and creation of the divine cell. He incorporates that substance into the light-emitting disc and immediately generates a channel that connects the sixth with the third and the fourth dimensions. It is through this channel that empowering energy will be transferred to Earth. This energy will be transformed as it passes through a star of our own galaxy.

The Higher Self glows radiantly surrounded by a golden light while we watch in amazement as it unites itself with a dormant entity that nevertheless constitutes one of its parts that had remained inactive in the realms of the Sixth dimension.

In that manner it becomes the recipient of greater empowerment and wisdom. At the same time though our own energy body is equally upgraded acquiring thus better and improved mastery over the body of the personality.

The navigators prepare themselves for return. We enter once more the crystal cylinders and find ourselves being projected again into the cylinders found on planet Poseidon. We are integrated with our energy bodies and we begin to have a well-defined picture of the Great Hall of planet Poseidon. Next, we are brought in front of a group of twelve entities that constitute a hierarchy of their own. It is comprised of couples that also constitute the primal geneticists that had arrived on Earth during the Atlantean age.

NEW LIFE PLAN

The twelve entities offer to each one of us a silver plaque, informing us that on it are recorded our future assignments and our new life plans. All the events to happen have been imprinted and encoded and will be realised until the end of our lives here on Earth.

They go on to analyse the significant usefulness of the genetic spores we are carrying within us. A large proportion of these spores have already been embedded with the means by which the ultimate transmutation of the astral carrier will be achieved, in order to ensure the prevalence of the energy body. The weakening of the astral will lead some of us to our assumption that is the dissolution of the astral body. It is during that moment that the soul will depart through the gate that it will already have opened heading for its heavenly homeland.

During our return we come into contact with part of the etheric dimension that resembles a moving sea. Therein, live dolphin-like creatures that constitute in reality hyper-noetic entities which are connected with the dolphins that live in our seas. Certain frequencies pass through specific channels which are, on the way, converted into the sounds emitted by the earthly dolphins. These sounds not only attune but also awaken men's consciousnesses.

We return replete with a sense of nostalgic wistfulness for the serene seas we left behind while our ears vibrate with the dolphin-emitted sounds. We are back on Earth, at the starting point, trying to come around after experiencing this very strong and intense initiation. This is not the end however, and everybody is aware of that. The journeys will continue and further equally or more fulfilling experiences and knowledge to be acquired await us.

We shall never forget that we are time-travellers. Until we ultimately reach our homeland we will continue to travel to it bringing each time a reminder of it back here with us.

CHRISTIC SOLAR VIBRATION

WAYS THROUGH WHICH DIVINE SOULS ARE BORN ON EARTH

EMPOWERMENT OF PLANET EARTH

THE CHRISTIC – LUNAR PATH

THE BIRTH OF CHRIST

THE CRYSTAL SOULS FROM THE FIFTH DIMENSION

THE CONCEPTION

GENETIC ELEMENTS OF A HIGHER DEGREE

THE DIVINE SEEDS

THE DIVINE GODDESS

A SUPERIOR BEING DEVOID OF KARMA

THE PREGNANCY

THE THREE MAGI

INITIATES – ALCHEMISTS – ASTRONOMERS
THE STAR – A BRIGHT SHUTTLE

THE GUIDING CHANNEL

JESUS

A PSYCHIC ARCHIVE WITH A MISSION

THE PROCEDURE FOR THE ASCENSION

THE SECOND COMING OF
THE DIVINE ENTITIES

Pyramid of initiatory ceremonies

CHRISTIC SOLAR VIBRATION

WAYS TROUGH WHICH DIVINE SOULS ARE BORN ON EARTH

EMPOWERMENT OF PLANET EARTH

The soul of the planet is preparing itself for its passage to the Fifth dimension. From the Golden planet, in which the christic hierarchy is based, certain powers or forces are directed towards the Earth. Thus, in conjunction with the activation of a multitude of souls nearing their final homecoming, Earth's soul will also be assisted in fulfilling its departure. An ever increasing number of people are concentrating their thoughts either as groups or individually for the planet's well-being. However, little are they aware of the fact that these thoughts are usually coloured by the personality's desires as well. Such a collective form of energy is also picked up by the entities residing in the darker regions of the etheric plane. Provided, therefore, that the transferred vibration isn't exactly pertinent to the same high frequency (which is very likely), they convert it and they direct it towards their own benefit and empowerment.

Consequently, what goddess Earth actually needs is to be strengthened by vibrations it should receive from its homeland and its "soul-mates", that is, the planets and the stars of the Fifth dimension.

In order for these vibrations to reach Earth, certain transformers are required, meaning, not only celestial bodies of our galaxy, but people as well that will function as the ultimate recipients and intermediaries assisting the passage of these energies. One way through which these energies could be transferred, is through our groups during our journeys to the galaxy. For this to be achieved, the transformations and conversions that will ensue will have to be and will be multiple.

The astral body does not possess the necessary equivalent frequencies that will render it capable of passing through to the Fifth dimension. Its entrance is only allowed and simultaneously restricted to the astral realms of the fourth dimension, meaning that we cannot travel by using the astral carrier. Hence, our Higher Self unites with the astral body and forms a new type of medium that possesses the structures and morphology required by the Fifth dimension. It will also though contain elements of the fourth dimension that mainly concern the transfer of astral material for catharsis, and cleansing. This is the carrier that we refer to as the energy body. It constitutes the bodily frame that unites superior elements and combines them with knowledge of the psyche.

There is a specific type of umbilical-like cord that joins the physical body, the astral carrier, the energy body and the Higher Self, all at the same time, during these journeys.

As we enter the galaxy, certain energies are transferred originating from the golden planet, which belongs to the realms of the Sixth dimension. Channels of energy emanating from the christic solar hierarchy undergo transformation as they reach the two satellites found on the right and on the left of the Golden planet. That is where the borderline between the sixth and the Fifth dimension is also located.

Later on, these energies are filtered into the carrier of the Higher Self. Through the umbilical-like cord they are filtered again and modified by the energy body. Then, they travel through the cords to our solar system. They are transformed as they pass through any celestial body (that is, any one of the known planets of our solar system) and they enter the etheric plane of Earth to be transformed once again by its aura which lies between the etheric and the astral dimension.

In continuation, these energies permeate the astral and the etheric carrier by flowing through the umbilical-like cords.

Their final transformation occurs as these energies penetrate and permeate the material body. It is exactly then that they are unified with the rays emanating from the hearts of all the students forming the group. They are transformed and at the same time emitted in the form of a powerful ray of love and transmutation which special entities direct towards the heart of planet Earth.

Finally, we come into contact and align ourselves with the inner vibrations of Earth which progressively accentuate and increase in intensity mainly due to the transformational procedure the planet is experiencing at present. We attune ourselves with it in a way that allows the christic vibration of love to be recorded in its archives, which will consequently relieve it and ease the departure of its soul.

In that manner, the energy is transferred to Earth directly from the Sixth dimension circumventing the fourth in which toxic thoughtforms and entities dwell. Thus, Earth's salvation is unaffected and remains untouched by our desires and by any personal or non reasons whatsoever that are concerned with and are directly linked to our own limited perception.

THE CHRISTIC – LUNAR PATH

Since the beginning of the history of the planet there have always been two different approaches to learning and each one has had its own unique guiding system.

These differing lines have been channelled towards planet Earth by superior masters. Teachers residing here on Earth have always syntonised themselves with them and have always guided and still guide men that seek self-knowledge.

One of these lines is the solar one which specifically began its descending route and guiding function since the age of the Lemurians.

It was through this line that Jesus Christ himself had received guidance as well. That is the reason why, in continuation to that effect, it has also been named as Christic line. It constitutes a guiding channel which mainly operates through love and freedom.

The second line of guidance is the lunar one.

With this line the evolutionary path is subjected to conditions governed by strict rules, psychic tension and psychic pressure, conditions of constant and close monitoring and surveillance and periods of hard training through teaching.

The purity of these lines of learning and knowledge has deteriorated and has been spoilt through the ages mainly due to the lower personalities of specific people who have expressed themselves either violently, or through fear or have threatened and have sacrificed multiple human lives and have caused genocides all in the name of love. Not to mention that the clergy of various religions have become involved in this "game".

In detail the christic pathway:

Coordinates the vibrations and the energies from top to bottom.

Operates spontaneously abiding by the Law of Free Will.

Is characterised by action and an exploratory disposition.

Teaches the anamnesis of our heavenly home and the ephemerality of

palingenesis.

Accepts an a priori presence of a higher or "divine" self for every individual.

Doesn't accept occultism but does accept the enlightment of all people through open teaching.

Defines love as falling in love and as justice and friendship.

Uses dialectics to persuade and utilises mental codes, and,

Invokes powers of superior dimensions.

In the end, the solar pathway stipulates that any individual can put an end to their karma and return to their heavenly home.

THE BIRTH OF CHRIST

THE CRYSTAL SOULS FROM THE FIFTH DIMENSION

Great entities have always been born on Earth at various crucial junctures of its evolution. They have changed and shaped history, created religions and promoted civilisation.

The ancient Hellenic civilisation demonstrates a pantheon of wise men that have left their mark and have influenced many other nations existing on this planet.

During the higher type of communication I had had, I received the knowledge concerning the distinctiveness of Jesus Christ's birth which I will attempt to impart to you and explain and analyse in simple terms. Souls that have been preassigned specific missions are often sent from the Fifth dimension here to Earth during various periods with the sole purpose of paving the way for the arrival of a higher entity. These souls are named as Precursors.

A very significant teacher-soul with a crucial and very specific mission was the soul of John the Baptist the Precursor, who created a gate, a portal to prepare the coming of Christ.

The gate he created was a channel reaching the Fifth dimension. Through the holy religious practice of baptism he managed to join man's energy centres with this central channel. The activation channel created began from the first energy centre (the genital one) and upgraded all the centres up to the seventh (epiphysis) that is located at the top of the head.

In that way John the Baptist connected his channel with the ones that were activated within those that had been baptised.

That is the main reason why his adversaries decapitated him. What they wanted actually is to destroy and disrupt this channel that was connected to the psychic archive of all people which he managed to specifically activate by practicing the holy ritual.

Christ is a divine entity that had been chosen by the supreme hierarchy of the Golden planet to be sent to Earth. The Golden planet of Nephelon galaxy belongs to the Sixth dimension and it simultaneously constitutes a central channel gate towards the seventh dimension. The Sixth dimension is determined by the seminal birth of action. That is the place where all the ideas are born, where ideas that are realised in the Fifth dimension spring from.

THE CONCEPTION

GENETIC ELEMENTS OF A HIGHER DEGREE

THE DIVINE SEEDS

Had not Christ been "split in half" he would never have been able to arrive in our dimension as a soul. Because all the entities residing in the fifth and the Sixth dimensions are bipolar, meaning that the Higher Self and the soul are combined into one forming the divine couple. Such a couple was also formed by Christ and his bipolar, the great goddess that projected a part of its DNA in the birth of Virgin Mary.

This specific divine couple united and created a divine seed of a higher degree.

This primal seed had to be enriched with genetic elements of the Fifth dimension. For that reason it was sent to the Emerald planet which constitutes the centre of genetic mutations. There, the genitors Ziron and Moira assisted by geneticists added to it genetic material of the Fifth dimension.

This newly formulated seminal cell was subdivided into two parts (spores and embryos) that were then placed into specially constructed matrices (vessels or containers made of organic crystal) so that they could be enriched with other cellular elements.

Later, they inserted into it various other archives containing additional information. Once the spores took on the physical form and structure of the bodies of the Fifth dimension the geneticists gave feminine characteristics to one of its parts and sent it to Earth to be born as Virgin Mary. This particular soul had well buried within its archives the mission it was bound to fulfil here on Earth.

THE DIVINE GODDESS

A SUPERIOR BEING
DEVOID OF KARMA

THE PREGNANCY

What had to be done, before the soul of Virgin Mary entered an earthly womb in order to be born, was to form and prepare respectively the archives and the gate-womb of her mother. This condition had to be met since the superior entity referred to as Virgin Mary was totally devoid of any karmic burden.

For this to be achieved though, the astral body of her mother Anna was transferred to an intermediary nursing place located between the fourth and the Fifth dimensions. There, they gradually disposed of all the karmic imprints found in her psychic archives and they went on to channel cellular material that consisted of various archives of knowledge. These where placed into her astral womb in the form of spherules to assure that the embryo would receive nourishment containing superior genetic material.

When the embryo grew and was on the point of emerging out of its mother's uterus, a crystal soul arriving from the Fifth dimension entered it. That soul was destined to become the Great Mother and leave its mark on our world as Virgin Mary blessed by the Archangels.

Its other counterpart that was to be born as Jesus remained in the Fifth dimension on the Emerald planet waiting for the exact moment of its birth.

Around that time, there existed a secret community known as the community of the Esseans of whom a very significant member was also John the Baptist. This community had detached itself from the existing Priesthood of Rabbis of those times and its members had carefully studied ancient Hellenic and Egyptian philosophy and alchemy and were also aware of a variety of therapeutic methods. They had already cured numerous Romans and enjoyed being in their favour. They possessed the holy marks of Esoterism and knew how to commune with the Archangelic spheres and the great teachers that had ascended to heavens in the past.

Some of the members of the community were also very strong channels of communication. They received information from the Fifth dimension and were aware of the events that were destined to make history.

When Virgin Mary had reached the age of marriage, members of that community decided on appointing Joseph, another member of theirs, as her future spouse. Joseph had been informed and was aware of the mission. The directives he was given were very specific. He was not to engage into physical contact with her until the entity they were awaiting was born. Thus, when their marriage became official Mary became pregnant though still being actually a virgin.

The moment they imparted that information to me through a specific channel, I was astonished. I couldn't believe that it was actually anatomically possible for Mary to be a real virgin. What I thought up to that time was that the term 'virgin" was used to symbolise the purity of her soul.

I was also informed that such births, the result of immaculate conceptions were neither new, nor unique.

At specific intervals the wombs of certain women that were devoid of karmic burden were chosen to each bear an embryo of superior genetic elements, assisting thus the descent of great leaders to Earth.

All these births had occurred without any actual physical contact ever taking place. Gestation was formulated and monitored within special zones that constituted specifically designed nursing places located between the fifth and the fourth dimensions. There, they would implant the divine embryo.

Virgin Mary was transferred to that zone, as was her mother, by means of her astral and psychic bodies. The astral one was her personality while the psychic (energy body) one constituted the essence of her origin. In that nursing place located on the borderline between fifth and fourth dimensions she was informed of her mission as well as of who the embryo she would bear within her womb was.

Archangel Gabriel who is responsible for the descent of the souls gave her crucial directions and valuable information.

It is possible that Virgin Mary had a blurry understanding or a distorted idea concerning the whole procedure when she entered her physical frame. The body of her personality (the astral one) oftentimes limited clear consciousness. However, she had been properly trained and received extensive support by the members of the community of the Esseans.

When the time of birth approached they were given an exact focal point where contact would be made, which was Bethlehem. The synchronistic event of a census taking place led the initiated couple of Mary and Joseph to this town. The exact focal point however lied just outside Bethlehem so that not many people would bear witness to the Nativity of Jesus. Thus, only a few shepherds were present, while the wife of one of them, (acting as a midwife), practically helped the delivery of the baby, which was born without any complications. All around Mary there were constantly healer Archangels that kept transmitting energy and love.

THE THREE MAGI

INITIATES – ALCHEMISTS – ASTRONOMERS

THE STAR – A BRIGHT SHUTTLE

THE GUIDING CHANNEL

The event of the Nativity of Christ was known by the three Magi who were initiates, alchemists and astronomers and who had followed the coordinates and had pinpointed the exact location based on astronomical maps. A great planetary synod and a specific star that had stood exactly above the point of birth as if marking the location had led them there.

It wasn't actually a star though, but an extremely bright vehicle of the Fifth dimension that would also assist the channelling of the soul into the embryo. That soul was composed partly of the essence of Christ and partly of the Higher Self of Mary. A highly protected and extremely bright channel, surrounded by luminous entities that acted as coordinators, issued from the vehicle. The soul's energy body gained access into the channel and entered the infant the moment it was exiting its mother's womb.

The channel that gave the impression of and resembled the brightness of the light emanating from a very powerful floodlight remained like that until dawn, focusing on the exact location where the baby was born. This is the light that the three magi spotted. The same magi, who afterwards also proceeded into ritualistically initiating the newborn infant. At present those three wise men are with Jesus in the christic hierarchy located on the Golden planet in the Sixth dimension.

The shuttle didn't leave Earth immediately; instead it remained hidden during the entire duration of Jesus' life on this planet. It operated mainly as a transformer, preserving and maintaining the channel that kept into contact the entity of Christ with the Golden planet that was his father and his true genitor.

In that way Jesus received constant continuous guidance through that brightly shining vehicle.

JESUS

A PSYCHIC ARCHIVE WITH A MISSION

Jesus was fully conscious of and aware of his mission from the moment that the divine spark was activated within him. That occurred at the time of his initiation from John the Baptist who knew about the vehicle and the role that the superior entity he had before him was about to play on Earth.

Jesus constituted a crystal soul of a much higher degree. He possessed no lower personality archive in him and was totally devoid of any karmic imprints.

In the superior archive of his heart, which was constructed and structured with love, he would filter out influences and imperfections that existed in his astral carrier like human pain, anguish and pathos. The central structure of his cells was constructed, defined and characterised by love.

We was trained by the Esseans and indulged in studying ancient Hellenic philosophy. He felt a bond with the Hellenics as if he was related to them. All the other elements he received from Ziron and Moira of the Fifth dimension, who actually were and are Zeus and Hera.

During the time of his teachings human society was characterised by, governed by and had an austere patriarchal form, structure and hierarchy while the role of women was degraded and considered secondary and more subordinate to that of man.

He preached the importance and the value of both sexes and apart from male disciples there was a group of females who remained faithful to his teachings.

Mary Magdalene stood out for her sharpness, her clarity of thought as well as for the purity of her soul and spirit.

References that have been made throughout the ages concerning her being a prostitute are untrue, (besides, a woman that hadn't been married in those ages was looked upon as a prostitute).

She was Jesus' soul mate and like the other female disciples of his she continued teaching, as they did as well, after he departed this planet.

Jesus knew how to affect matter and how to remove the cause of disease. He was also capable of reconnecting the umbilical-like cord of life to those that had died.

The clergy of the time played a catalytic role, after him being horribly tortured, in preserving his message of love and assisting it in becoming etched in people's mind and in leaving its mark on human history. Jesus knew the way his life was destined to end here on Earth. He was also aware that had he lead a calm, peaceful, restful and ordinary life he would never have left behind him such a powerful stigma that provided the spark and the basic rudiments for the beginning of a great religion.

Both his male and female disciples went through programmes of karmic removal in order to cleanse themselves and prepare to receive superior enlightment after his departure.

Their astral bodies were firstly transferred to the borderline between the fourth and the Fifth dimensions and from there to the special nursing place where the karmic removals occurred and the program of their entire plan was transformed. Their subsequent mission was recorded onto this newly formed plan.

They united themselves with their Higher Selves of the Fifth dimension and gradually their personality started to change and mutate parallel to the training and the teachings they kept receiving through the continuous contact they had with Jesus.

Maria Zavou

THE PROCEDURE FOR
THE ASCENSION

Before Jesus' ultimate departure for the Fifth dimension took place, he activated a specific spark of power and endurance within his disciples' psychic archive that would allow them to withstand and endure the difficulties they would encounter and help them to fulfil their missions.

Some of them like John and Magdalene maintained their connection with the Esseans, who in the meantime had dispersed and usually met under complete secrecy. Others were assimilated into the local clergy and followed the religious guidelines defined and ordained by them and they altered and came up with other altered versions and differentiated scripts that deviated from the true and original texts containing the teachings of Jesus.

The moment Jesus abandoned and left his physical form it decomposed within the time frame of three days. As a result no body was left behind for his disciples to find when they visited his tomb.

The decomposition or one could say the disintegration of the material frame has remained known as Ascension which constitutes the way by which entities containing divine DNA actually depart.

During the Ascension the molecules that composed his material form broke down and were transformed into energy mass that entered his astral carrier.

However, he had to stay a few days on Earth in that structure for some final appearances to his disciples.

Thus, they were able to see him in his astral form and were given some final guidelines by him.

Following that he was absorbed by the channel transmitted by the bright vehicle situated above and was transferred there where the dematerialization of the astral elements that were present in his body took place, whereas all the upgraded archives were transferred into the soul body, the christic one that constitutes a far more superior luminous medium.

The astral elements that were removed were directly committed to the heart of the planet sealing thus the reminiscence of his presence on Earth.

In the Fifth dimension, Jesus is a spiritual master of guidance and is in immediate and constant cooperation with Christ, his genitor, who directs the evolutionary programmes conducting massive censuses of the souls that are about to return to their heavenly homes.

In the Fifth dimension Jesus also represents the christic channel and participates in the souls' evolutionary programmes.

THE SECOND COMING OF THE DIVINE ENTITIES

The message that concerns the second coming of Christ was imparted to me during a moment of higher communication in 1996. According to that message a second coming of Christ in his physical form here in the third dimension would not be meaningful since the spiritual path that had been opened with his first coming still remains active here on Earth.

His second coming has already occurred in the Sixth dimension where he continues to operate since the earthly year 1996. That means that all the spiritual ramifications and extensions of the entity called Christ that had remained dormant in the higher dimensions (ninth, eighth, and seventh), converged and merged into the sixth where he now, as the divine genitor, presides over the council of the great wise men.

Due to the impending psychic transition of planet Earth to the Fifth dimension a massive programme concerning a census of all the souls that will be awakened and returned to their heavenly homes on a grand scale has begun. These souls will "conquer" physical death and attain immortality. This programme of documentation is led by the entity called Christ. It is what we refer to as the Judgement Day. The Judgement of the souls about which Jesus had spoken and which, as it has been recorded in the past, will come into effect with the second coming of Christ.

Many syntonising channels exist that lead to the heavenly source. The christic channel operates in the same fashion that the solar path operated as well. It constitutes a channel through which souls tend to ascend the evolutionary ladder through their choices and through exercising the power of Free Will. At this moment many souls are mutating either consciously or unconsciously to whichever type of religious line they are focusing on and are aligning themselves with the channels through which they choose to return.

Through the compilation of this massive census, Christ bestows upon us the seal of immortality and grants us access for our return home.

His second coming will entail the opening of a huge gate towards planet Earth which will remain open until the earthly year 2020. Within this specific time frame many human souls will hear the calling. Then the gates of return will close and a new evolutionary cycle for Earth will commence.

This does not mean that all those that will have aligned themselves with the return will have departed by the year 2020. They will simply have focused onto the channel and will activate it at exactly the moment they will choose to leave planet Earth.

The mauve planet Zanar

AWAKENED SOULS

MEANS OF DEPARTURE

ASCENSION OF THE SOUL

BIRTHS OF INDIGO CHILDREN

BIRTHS OF CRYSTAL CHILDREN

Hall used specifically to perform initiations

AWAKENED SOULS

MEANS OF DEPARTURE

Souls leaving for the fourth dimension follow a strict departure routine. After physical death occurs the soul is transferred into its astral carrier that constitutes the body of its emotions and its personality. It is surrounded by the ethereal carrier which in turn is connected with an umbilical-like cord to the body that is now entering the decomposition process.

The disintegration and decay of the material frame's cellular structure compels the etheric body to dissolve the moment the umbilical-like cord is detached. The time needed for this procedure ranges from three to nine days, whereas for some other souls that struggle to remain in that condition, it lasts up to forty days.

There have been instances during which the soul remains attached to the third dimension. It is then that it becomes grounded or trapped between two worlds but without possessing an etheric body.

Thus, during its departure the soul maintains only its astral carrier and is absorbed by a vortex that corresponds to one of its energy centres. Depending on the centre through which the soul departs (either higher or lower) the astral level, in which it will continue experiencing the relevant emotions until it realises it has actually detached itself from the material world, is defined.

If the level of consciousness is evolved enough then the soul enters a schooling process to prepare itself for its next reincarnation.

Souls that have developed their animalistic, bestial side to a great degree are usually prone to experience the darkness of the astral levels. There, they have no alternative choice and are rapidly absorbed to be reborn again only to be given better chances for evolution.

However, the entities residing in the Fifth dimension have already dissolved the lower part of the astral level as well as the biggest part of the middle level of that plane. They have only left the higher astral levels of consciousness intact where the souls receive proper training for their subsequent births. These souls are either destined for an incarnation as indigo children or are simply transferred to the Fifth dimension to attend specially designed programmes.

From the Fifth dimension they prepare to be incarnated as crystal children, the first expedition of whom is already being carried out here on Earth.

There are souls in which the bestial nature has prevailed and have remained on Earth. As far as these souls are concerned, they will undergo dissolution of all their psychic components. Next, they will be reformed by the divine spark of a Higher Self that will also unite with them to continue their evolution moving towards the higher astral planes.

This is what constitutes actual death. They will posses no psychic individuality because they will not be in the position to keep any of their memories. In that way unconsciously and unknowingly they will start their lives over.

Some other souls that bear no bases, no indicator, no reference point, as regards their position on Earth, upon which the process of reformation could rely on will be totally and utterly dissolved. The same holds true for the souls that reside in the lower astral levels and have not yet been destroyed.

Resultingly, the form of planet Earth will change and differ. Meta-humans will be totally liberated from their animalistic nature. Whatever has to do with bestial manifestation in nature either animate or inanimate (like minerals or vegetable matter), will cease to exist on the planet.

From the animal kingdom only a few species will be spared and continue to exist. Species that will have evolved and been mutated to serve specific purposes.

Earth is approaching the end of its last cycle. When this cycle is concluded it will depart for the Fifth dimension.

Whatever souls continue to exist on the planet (that will never cease reforming) will pass away in three different ways.

The first has already been mentioned and concerns the thousands of souls that will be transferred to the higher astral levels. The other concerns the souls that have detached their karmic connections from the astral levels and instead constitute awakened spirits. When these latter souls leave their physical form behind, their etheric together with their astral body (which in the meantime will have already been detached from its lower personality), will burn up in the space of a few hours or days. The essence of its soul will enter then the already formulated immortal body we call energy body.

This body will enter a specific escape channel with which it is compatible and will eventually be transferred to some of the planets of the Fifth dimension. There, the soul will continue its schooling in an area of its own interest. It will no longer be obliged to be reborn, except for the case that it wishes to return to the third dimension to complete a specific mission.

There are two ways for the soul to reach the third dimension when it departs the fifth. The first one is to be reborn. During this event the soul does not bear any type of karmic burden. The second way is to possess the body of an adult after of course the latter's soul has consented to it. In that situation both souls share the same body, but the superior entity of the Fifth dimension is the one that dominates. There is always, however, the possibility for the elder soul to depart the chosen material frame and cross the threshold for better and more advanced levels of evolution in the astral fields.

At present, teacher entities descend into the etheric dimension and from there they guide the souls creating respective evolutionary stages in those realms for them.

However, after the new Atlantean soul enters the planet the delegations that the great masters will be forming part of, will be directly sent to Earth. A body coming from the upgraded astral dimension will be formulated and the teacher entities will have the potential to condense it and use it in order to appear to humans and teach them in person.

That is the time humanity will witness the Gods walking on Earth once again.

ASCENSION OF THE SOUL

The souls that have went through conscious mutational programmes concerning their astral and material carrier will be rendered capable of dissolving their physical form by removing or breaking down the connections between the molecules. Resultingly, the weakened astral, together with the etheric body will be burned and the souls will be able to depart in their energy bodies being completely aware and conscious of the whole process.

This procedure is called ascension, which for the Meta-humans will be very natural to perform.

Instances of Ascension that have taken place and have been recorded in the past concern only the prophet Elijah and Jesus Christ. The ascension constituted a very natural way to exit the body for these souls due to the fact that they had arrived from the Fifth dimension. The phenomenon of ascension will be finalised in and for the Meta-humans.

The crystal children will easily practice this procedure because their astral carrier will no longer have access to the astral levels that will have been destroyed.

They will exist but only as a reservoir used for cleansing and purifying interstellar matter for the descending entities to borrow in order to create a specific carrier. They will be able to form this "vehicle" in the way that meets their desires and fits their needs and will be able to change it again whenever they see it proper to do so at will.

This whole evolutionary plan concerning a big census and registration and the transfer of souls on a grand scale is already being put into effect by the entity of Christ in the Sixth dimension.

There are many people who are aware of it and others who disregard or ignore it. When at a certain time I had expressed my concerns regarding the continuation of life on our planet, they answered the following:

"You will be among the lucky few that will witness first hand these oncoming events unfolding. You will know it when you become part of this plan as well."

Now! I understand!

BIRTHS OF INDIGO CHILDREN

The evolutionary pyramid of souls consists of the lower, the middle, and the higher levels. The middle level of consciousness is the one where the soul begins to form an evolutionary plan whereas the higher level is the one in which the soul has already covered a certain part of its course and is preparing for its final incarnation either on Earth or visiting other parallel worlds.

Before their final incarnation occurs the souls are trained by teachers and by their Higher Selves and form a specific course of action and plan that will become activated the moment they are born on Earth (as Indigo children).

Vagueness and confusion has been looming in the air, mainly due to the information provided by the mass media, concerning the births of these children. The way they are born, where they come from and what the differences are between them and the crystal children are issues that appear to be obscure and ambiguous.

Births of indigo children have been documented on Earth at various historical periods. However, births of such children on a grand scale and to a massive extent have been realised from 1985 up to the present time. Being more specific since 1996 eighty per cent of births concerned indigo children. An indigo soul is one that after having gained knowledge through numerous incarnations has reached the ultimate level of consciousness.

Indigo children are charismatic and gifted and come to Earth with the aim to advance and develop those domains that are in need of change. Thus, an ever increasing number of instances concerning political, social, religious ferment regarding their basic structures and foundations have been and are being observed throughout the world.

Moreover, they possess a DNA structure that is commensurate to and resistant to the changes that are to take place on planet Earth, such as nutritional and climatic changes and geological unrest.

They tend to choose as their parents people who have already progressed, and evolved much in terms of their psychic development. In that way they maintain certain karmic bonds with their parents and share some issues that need to be resolved in order to facilitate the opening of the gate through which their final return to their heavenly homes will be accomplished. What should be noted is that their karmic burden is so minimal when compared against the karmic burden and debts which other souls are carrying and have to pay.

Indigo children develop gifts like a higher type of intelligence, insight, second sight as well as certain healing properties.

They cooperate wonderfully and efficiently with their Higher Self, creating a personal code of communication with it.

In that manner they receive guidance which further assists them in making the right choices that will allow them to carry out and fulfil their plan. They are restless personalities and their views tend to perplex their immediate environment and cause uneasiness. They can easily see through people and sense their true intentions. They tend to be independent and they tend to quickly acquire personal freedom as they follow the course of their plan unaffected and uninfluenced by anything.

If they continue to remain with their family even though they have reached adulthood it is only because it serves some specific purpose that will play a vital reinforcing role for them later on in their lives.

Indigo children constitute the gates for the descending souls of the crystal children, who constitute a higher stage of psychic development and evolution.

Births of crystal children have begun since 2000. The second and the third descent of such souls will pass through the uteruses of crystal women that form a part of the second expedition.

BIRTHS OF CRYSTAL CHILDREN

The first expedition of crystal children to Earth arriving here from the Fifth dimension is already taking place in this day and age.

The crystal children that are born at the moment come to Earth on their own accord, mainly because they have already fulfilled their own course in the realms of the fourth dimension which also entailed lessons concerning karmic imprints.

They can be born from wombs (gates) of women that have been relieved of their karmic causes. Thus, they are no longer to resolve any issues of karmic concern with their parents and their path will not be obstructed by parental emotional weaknesses.

The women whose wombs will carry and nurture such children are indigo souls. However, because these women have yet to resolve and finalise some remaining karmic issues they will have to be subjected to karmic removal and purification processes (both psychic and spiritual) in order to facilitate the passage of crystal souls through their wombs. If again the prospective mother is neither in her last incarnation nor awakened, that is, is not an indigo soul, then she will be subjected to mutational processes like those concerned with karmic removal and purification. Having reached an agreement with her Higher Self she enters groups in which trained entities lead her to the Fifth dimension. There, a lengthy preparation procedure commences which constitutes a transgression of what up to now has been taken for granted and has been documented as proper in the line of the gradual evolution of souls.

The first assigned mission of crystal children to arrive on Earth concerns souls that have already concluded their schooling and have passed from the endmost levels of the astral dimension into the fifth.

These souls are preparing themselves, just as some groups here on Earth have. However, they are conscious in what they are doing. They are fully aware of and have been effectively experiencing the whole procedure.

Before the passage through the gate into the Fifth dimension actually occurs, they are being prepared by teachers of the fifth who can and do pass through the gate into the astral plane.

Next, and after they have concluded the construction of a proper carrier (analogous to the energy body we develop here on Earth), they begin travels –flights- and undergo special mutational programmes in order to fully prepare for their final crossing into the Fifth dimension. When all the upgrading procedures have been concluded they burn their astral carrier which is then committed into the Earth's great melting pot.

This constitutes a type of death and the souls seem to be aware of the processes entailed when practiced.

The entire psychic archive of knowledge is transferred by them into the energy body next, and being accompanied by the Higher Self they reach the station located on a level that separates the astral plane from the Fifth dimension. There, they are surrounded and accompanied by teachers that have been specifically chosen to guide them as they pass through the gates that lead them onwards to the various levels of the galaxy of the Fifth dimension. There, they choose a specific planet whereupon they will prepare themselves as crystal souls before their time comes to be born on our planet as crystal children.

All these delegations share similar characteristics to those that had been sent to Lemurian and Atlantean races in the past, whose primary focus was to pass on –through mutations- the divine spark to those people who were driven and governed by their bestial nature alone.

Thus, the first crystal children are awakened souls possessing specific personalities, plans and missions. Since infancy they send out peacefulness, tranquillity, sweetness, and are distinguished for their high intelligence. They also possess the ability to enter the core of other people's souls activating their plan or their mission.

Their gifts and their talents are far more than those of indigo children. Early on in their lives they create and establish codes of communication with their parents and their immediate environment.

They possess the ability to "scan" the personalities of people and detect possible flaws or impairments present on a psychic and physical level. In their body they tend to bear seeds of a mutated DNA that renders them impervious to illnesses and various viroses.

In addition, they are neither stigmatised by any form of karmic disease nor do they inherit ancestral characteristics or tendencies. They are destined to genetically prepare the arrival of the second delegation of crystal children. Moreover, they all possess three light-emitting etheric discs.

The first one is located at the epiphysis. It is from this point that crystal children receive direct instructions from the entities of the Fifth dimension.

There is an impressive team of teachers that corresponds to each crystal child. These wise men are in a constant connection with the children's archives which they possess the potential to improve or alter just in order to promote their mission. The disc contains codes that operate at specific intervals awakening other people's intellect as well. The crystal souls are recipients of a continuous stream of vibrations emanating from these teachers that keep empowering them and protecting them.

The second disc containing codes as well is embedded into and integrated with the psychic archives wherein the entire plan as it is outlined in their assignment has been recorded. This disc has been energetically placed into the heart chakra and also functions as the central regulator of the other two. It covers an extremely wide range and due to the specific frequencies it emits it is capable of mutating and upgrading the psychic archives of other people as well.

In that manner, all those receiving these frequencies begin to awaken from the lethargy of virtual and illusionary reality and are relieved of their karmic bonds.

The third disc has been placed into the genital centre and is considered to be of crucial importance because it will prepare the gates (wombs), paving the way for the descent of the second delegation of crystal souls.

The births of the crystal souls comprising this second expedition are the ones that will pave the way for the Meta-humans that will in turn comprise the third delegation of souls arriving from the Fifth dimension.

The Meta-humans of the third expedition will posses a much more subtle material carrier (body) and will feed off solar energy. Both genders, male and female will be integrated and incorporated within that carrier, but in a different form. Some of these entities are chosen per couple to create a novel life form in their own image and in their likeness in specially constructed artificial wombs.

For the creation of these novel beings one part of etheric matter and one part of astral matter will be used. The remaining eighty percent will be gathered from the primeval matter forming the early stages of the Fifth dimension.

They will give the creatures the shape and colour they desire and the genetic transition will be completed by comprising an admixture from their own DNA.

Life-at least in form we now know it- will undergo a radical change on planet Earth. The form of matter will mutate and adjust to meet the needs of the Meta-humans. Senescence and the sufferings of old age will cease to exist as will illnesses and everybody will be aware of and possess the codes of immortality. They will come and go whenever they wish either heading towards other dimensions or to parallel universes. The portals leading to other dimensions will always be open and easily accessible by them.

Highly evolved souls of such an extent have visited Earth in the past mutating and guiding men during every cycle of the planet's evolutionary course. Jesus also constituted a crystal soul of a higher degree. He was also projected through a womb-gate relieved of karmic causes. The Higher Self of Jesus was Christ who guided him from the realms of the Sixth dimension.

Large portions of the Fifth dimension are already entering our planet arriving together with crystal souls. The indigo children (many of whom have already reached adulthood) as well as the crystal children can feel and sense these dimensional currents that keep shifting and which mainly concern new configurations of the third, fourth and Fifth dimensions. The ever increasing births of crystal souls will mark and herald the new evolutionary cycle and the new evolutionary course The New Earth will embark on.

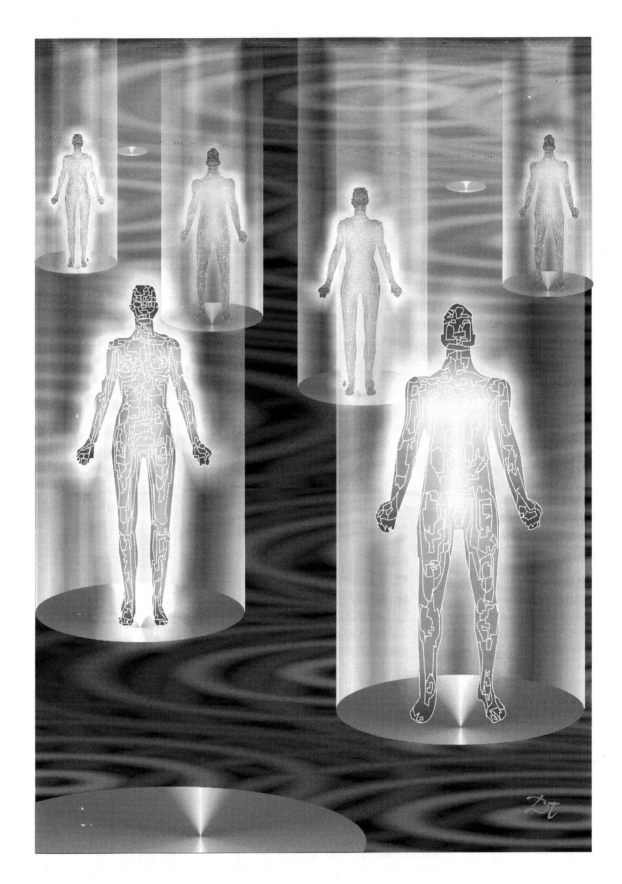

Luminous energy bodies

ELOHIM NEPHELIM

THE TWO ARCHANGELIC RACES

TIME-TRAVELLERS

TRAVELS INTO THE FUTURE

DELEGATIONS OF TEACHERS SENT TO EARTH

ENERGY SPHERES

ACTIVATION OF THE PRIMEVAL FORCE

GIFTS – SOUND-PULSES

EPILOGUE

DEDICATION

ELOHIM NEPHELIM

THE TWO ARCHANGELIC RACES

The angelic forces are subdivided into three spheres or triads or choirs. The first two transform divine thought which in turn is shaped by the order of the "Arches" (or Principalities) that also function as supervisor angels and regulators.

The third sphere consists of three orders and it supervises the fifth, the fourth and the third dimensions. The forces from which it is composed are the principalities, the Archangels and the angels.

Again every order of the hierarchy consists of two races.

Archangel Michael together with other great Archangels like Gabriel, Samuel, Uriel, Raphael, Zakchiel and others are in command of these races, which are also called overseers and regulators.

As regards the third choir or sphere the principalities, or arche, superintend the Archangels and the angels.

The Archangels consist of two races the Elohim and the Nephelim. El means powerful. The Elohim are great Archangelic orders which are governed by Archangel Michael. They fulfil the principles of creation by keeping the structure of the galaxy coherent. They provide the motion needed for the flow of life and they represent the Will of the Divine Principle.

The Elohim direct the ideas of the Divine Entity and the divine commands whereas the Nephelim constitute the action. The Elohim conceive the ideas of the Universe filter them and project them, whereas the Nephelim materialise them. The Elohim unite with the genius of Divine thought by means of an intricate and extremely sensitive and delicate but very crucial network.

The Elohim live in the realms of the Sixth dimension, whereas the Nephelim reside in the fifth. The latter receive commands from the Elohim that tend to promote their powerful ideas in order to be realised by them.

The strong presence of the Nephelim on Earth begins during the age of the Lemurians. They had been instructed to assist humans, to teach them high arts and initiate them into various technological forms.

Thus, they appeared in many forms during the emergence of and the first steps of the early civilisations. They partook in the early mutations of the human race that had taken place then, and they cooperated with the divine couples of genitors that had descended to Earth from the Fifth dimension. However, their molecular structure bore no resemblance to that of the divine couples.

The mutations the human race was subjected to were realised through transference and the delivery of babies deriving from the divine kingdoms. The fairies and various types of elementals were either integrated into human DNA or simply remained in our dimension. Some of the people living on Earth nowadays have derived from these species.

The couples of the divine entities that had arrived on Earth mated with the mutated daughters of man. These women bore a better strand of DNA because they had undergone mutational programmes. Consequently, heroes and demigods were given birth to.

The role of the Nephelim was to guide man and support him with their knowledge. Some of them however, not feeling satisfied, probably, deviated from their mission and aspired to imitate the genitors. They took in astral matter and they mated with an evolved species of women. However, their genetic material was quite different and as a result these unions were rendered incompatible. The Nephelim were devoid of a masculine and feminine divine spark. Thus, the offspring that were produced by these unions were monstrous. Giants were born, reptilians and serpent-like creatures. Turmoil and mayhem was experienced as a result in the mutational programmes.

Maria Zavou

A long-term battle began by Archangel Michael and his orders against the arrogant Nephelim whom they vanquished in the end. They cast them into the lower realms of the astral kingdom where they locked them up and sealed the gates behind them whereas all the monstrous creatures walking the Earth were imprisoned in the bowels of the Earth and all the exits leading to the outside worlds were sealed isolating them forever from it.

Those who were responsible for the mayhem, and were consequently exiled to the astral fields, were given the freedom to choose, to change their heart, so as to be allowed to return to their brothers, the Nephelim living in the Fifth dimension.

Some of them accomplished this and were upgraded and allowed to return, altering thus and deleting their negative convictions.

The rest envy people for possessing such a genetic material and for their evolution.

Others have the power bestowed upon them, mainly because of a certain degree of freedom that had been given to them, to influence people and infect them psychically and spiritually absorbing vital energy from those that generate and emit toxic emotions.

The Nephelim taught men and inspired, motivated and encouraged them to make discoveries like tools and led them to technocratic ways of development. Thus, man proceeded in creating a wide range of elaborate buildings, like the pyramids constructed in ancient Egypt.

The Elohim imparted spiritual knowledge and provided general guidance, leading to the writing of laws, and the practice of liturgy, rituals and religious belief.

Much of what had been imparted to them during various crucial historic junctures were altered by some people mainly to fulfil their personal ambitions or satisfy their personal interests. Some secrets, such as those containing the codes that permit the opening of the gates or those revealing the ways leading to mutations or even to immortality were given to a select group of wise men forming a powerful hierarchy that resides at an intermediary place on the etheric plane of Earth called Shambhala. This place can be reached and is approachable only by the grand masters who in turn only after very thorough examination and inspection forward to us their secrets.

After the genitor-gods departed from Earth, the gates that led to Shambhala were permanently closed to men, because they were considered to be unqualified and unprepared to manage and handle its secrets.

Now, the genitors are in command of the grand plan for humanity and Earth. They are reopening the gates and are again administering access codes. The plan is beginning to materialise from scratch and is now being placed on a new basis.

Both the Elohim and the Nephelim have now descended to the etheric plane of Earth and are collaborating with other Archangelic orders.

We, the people who comprise the various groups constitute also the keys, and cooperate with these forces functioning as transformers and guides.

TIME-TRAVELLERS

When the so-called "Gods" had visited the Earth with the sole intent of implanting seeds of life, they created various species of mutated people. The demigods belonged to these races.

The intervention of some of those so called "Gods" on Earth's magnetic field caused a breach and affected the flow of interstellar matter which during that time was under control. The amorphous interstellar matter began to formulate illusionary worlds mainly driven by the projected toxinoses of man's bestial attitude whenever he expressed himself through it.

That was exactly the time when the "Gods" departed, but they were never able to close that breach especially before it became a haven for the draconoids and the many other entities that had sustained and suffered denaturation.

This deterioration began the moment their lower emotions connected to the new astral fields that were under formation. From that moment they were doomed, along with some pioneers, and condemned to endure and be subjected to a long period of ongoing incarnations in order to be taught through pain and suffering and through the continuous conflict between light and darkness the truth concerning their existence. This denaturation occurred during the age of the Lemurian and Atlantean races.

After the closure of many cycles of life and evolution the planet has reached an extremely critical point during which drastic measures have to be taken to ensure its safety and salvation.

Therefore, with the sole intent of repairing this psychic breach the planet has sustained, time-travellers are being sent to Earth by higher dimensions at exactly the appropriate time junctions.

During our era what happened was that a percentage of time-travellers that had been scattered all over the planet were initially awakened. Their memory was inactive until they were connected with the entities of the Fifth dimension. In the beginning they started receiving various images and were placed into a certain schooling or training programme that would render them capable of handling and controlling their lower personality. Next, they were informed about their role, were handed the plan they had to accomplish and they set off functioning as transformers to open certain channel-gates that would allow and enable the forces of the Fifth dimension to reach the etheric plane of Earth. They connected the planet's energy centres (by means of a psychic umbilical-like cord) with the gates of the Fifth dimension to assist the gradual closure and repair of the breach.

In that way the lower astral levels were dissolved and the draconians living there perished imprisoning thousands of souls.

However, in order to restore the equilibrium, the same conditions that prevailed during the times that the Lemurian and Atlantean races flourished, thrived and evolved, had to be recreated.

Consequently, they connected the planet's psychic archives to Poseidon of the Fifth dimension (which actually stands for the future of the Atlantean age) and to other planets as well that had already completed their course. This connection gave rise to a huge energy explosion which happened in 1996. Since then, Earth has been subjected to various cleansing and purifying procedures until its final return is accomplished.

TRAVELS INTO THE FUTURE

In order for the first delegation of time-travellers to receive its orders, it connected to specifically chosen masters that had descended through special channels (time-channels) leading them from the Fifth dimension to the etheric plane of Earth.

The energy bodies were returned to the time-travellers that had opened the initial gates. These contained all the details and particularities concerning their origin. After they "clothed" themselves with them they connected through an umbilical-like cord to their divine counterpart, their other half dwelling in the Fifth dimension.

Possessing now their energy bodies they performed some alterations to their astral body detaching and removing all the "tentacles" that would suck and absorb both their vital energy and their psychic one out of them.

They began awakening other souls preaching how to achieve a central focus onto their Higher Selves and on showing the ways to connect with them.

They were further guided and directed to open all the central gates of their heavenly home in order to allow the remainder of the inactive gates existing in every country on this planet to connect with them.

As an immediate consequence astral battles ensued that were incited and instigated by the draconians and the dark entities, which had sensed their imminent destruction and annihilation.

Furthermore, an ever increasing number of time-travellers began to be awakened and the dispatch of evolved souls (indigo children) to Earth frequented as well. Many indigo souls were directed either consciously or unconsciously to become pioneering time-travellers. Specific codes were given and navigators, who were aware of the route between dimensions, were assigned to some of these early time-travellers with the sole purpose of assisting them.

Travels to the future dimensions were responsible for allowing the time-travellers to reach their true home. However, to be in the condition to operate properly as transformers and carriers of vibrations of the Fifth dimension they had to be relieved of their karmic burden that connected them to the draconians dwelling in the astral levels.

After removing the karmic cords they focused and aligned their energy centres with the channels of the Fifth dimension. Thus, their energy bodies were fully awakened through consecutive journeys and initiations.

New genetic material was channelled into their energy bodies and light-emitting discs were placed into their energy centres. These helped them refine and later on discard of and totally obliterate their lower personality. Additionally their range of influence on other people and their souls was to be enhanced and amplified since it was imperative that thousands more souls were awakened and relieved of their obligations, absolved of their commitments, and relieved from karmic bondage.

Both a subliminal and conscious mutation of all human souls began in that manner. Although these souls might not succeed in returning to their motherland in this lifetime they will at least be prepared for their ultimate homecoming.

DELEGATIONS OF TEACHERS SENT TO EARTH

There is an ongoing influx of delegations of teachers that is taking place at this specific time frame. Some remain in the etheric planes while others are born, or are preparing to be given birth to, by passing through pre-activated gates. The missions are multiple. Apart from the indigo souls the first delegation of crystal children is on the point of descending. These children are time-travellers that are and will be fully aware, since childhood, of their mission and the role they will eventually play.

Hellas' central gate has been activated after the symbolic initiation of the Olympic Games had taken place. Since then it has connected with all the other secondary gates that are found spread across the country. In addition, from Hellas certain channels have been connected both to the etheric plane of Earth and to other gates existing in other countries in order to assist the initiation of a massive mutation lasting up to the soul's final departure from the planet.

After undergoing long periods of continuous ferment and change Earth has already entered a phase that simultaneously marks the beginning of a grand new evolutionary cycle considered to constitute the post-Atlantean era.

Unfortunately, however, there are souls that have deteriorated and haven't managed to acquire the divine spark. Souls that keep vibrating in the form of astral shells and keep walking among us resembling the living dead. Nonetheless, the world of the astral dimensions and the dark entities is being dissolved on a daily basis. Due to the fact that some of these so-called shells seem to possess within them a rudimentary luminous constituent, they are bound to undergo dissolution and reconstitution processes only to salvage and retrieve these luminous elements. The rest of the souls that have totally converted to the dark side and function as its transformers, like the draconians, will be disintegrated gradually, parallel to the dissolution of the astral levels.

ENERGY SPHERES

The Fifth dimension has been extending to our dimension as well and the presence of a great deal of forces coming from other dimensions to Earth is even more frequent at this time in human history.

The energy spheres that have appeared invariably and are still showing up very vividly here and there in my house and in the places where my students live are spiritual beings that in order to manifest themselves need to condense their material constitution in advance.

Their presence is strong during our transcendental journeys and the sessions during which alternative therapies are performed. They visit Earth to offer their help concerning the impending changes that will influence both it and the people who live on it.

When man starts developing his psychic talents and gifts he may discern these luminous shapes appearing around us with a naked eye and see them exactly as they naturally are. They can be photographed by means of a digital camera as well.

Some of these spiritual entities are Higher Selves; others are Archangelic or angelic presences while others are entities of teachers.

The presences of the higher Selves as well as those of the masters are usually projected in the form of luminous rhombi maintaining perfect analogies, whereas those of the Archangels assume a spherical shape. These spheres do not constitute perfect circles, and if one is perceptive enough and observes their inner structure he/she will see that it is composed of condensed cells that in turn create nuclei in a variety of colour frequencies. People photograph them some times as spheres and some other times as if having assumed a more human form.

ACTIVATION OF THE PRIMEVAL FORCE

GIFTS – SOUND-PULSES

When the programmes concerned with transubstantiation and mutation are over, the new discs present in the energy centres of the students will contain an infinite amount of condensed knowledge. Once the keys are evoked the codes contained in them will release upgrading divine cells. The latter will work in an attuning, transferrential, and healing manner in order to bring about awakening, transmutation, miracles and the wondrous in life.

The gifts presented by the geneticists during the initiations are innumerable and they tend to activate the evolutionary archives within every individual. The gifts are vibrations of various forms the properties of which are channelled effortlessly and unhurriedly by means of sound-vibrations offering abundant help. They possess the delicate ability to discern and discriminate which enables the students to approach their divine self and expand their potentials and abilities rendering them capable of succeeding in everything.

During master Metatron's initiation certain cubes are administered that include thousands of nerve cells in turn containing new directives. Plaques with codes were also given offering new ways for creation and completion.

When karmic removals take place, goddess Earth channels its vibrations through a specific symbol (a necklace with two dolphins), which heralds the entrance of the new Atlantean soul into our planet. With this gift, advanced discoveries will be activated during this new era and the coded frequency of sounds produced by dolphins will also be deciphered. In addition, information concerning the race of Poseidon will come to light and the diode permitting superior entities coming form planet Poseidon to enter Earth will be opened.

Irian, a very significant entity that deals with catharsis and cleansing, places a mauve sphere into the archives of our plans right in the heart centre. Its vibration assists us to cope with adverse conditions and unfavourable events strengthening at the same time people's defences.

Saint Cyprian, using his crystal crucifix, cancels out the difficulties, and prints novel solutions into the new plan. The crucifix functions as a deterrent and usually pinpoints the exact areas where sinister motives and cause are usually found.

Alvatar, Ilarion and Iotheos using special crystals create an exact replica of the energy body's nervous system and place in it special gift-plaques containing upgraded cells and novel directives.

In that manner, the immune and cell systems are revitalised.

Athena, Arion and Aethra place crystal plates that are set to release therapeutic nanospherules. These induce a reprogramming of the cells, deleting memory concerned with possible organic problems that might exist. They regard novel recordings that cancel the old toxic ones and contribute to a deeper understanding of problems and the sound decoding of images that are projected into our daily round.

As far as the mutation of the epiphysis is concerned, Hyacinth places a lazuline disc of perspicuity and superior wisdom that awakens the noetic archives of those men who possess the knowledge to bring into effect the advanced programmes of returning the various souls to their heavenly motherland. Furthermore, Magoar using a seal key channels into the epiphysis superior neurohormones to balance out the various thoughtforms and to "unlock" novel solutions and ideas.

During the mutation of the hypophisis, Selenios places a key disc that cleanses and purifies the various types of toxinoses that may exist, and also discards all the obstacles that cloud and impede communication while simultaneously it offers insight. Alvatar provides us with a key that relieves us of our primary attributes that had been constructed during the Atlantean era.

The genitors Uranus and Earth during the mutation of the centre of speech integrate a light emitting disc, with an independent rotation, into it, that has the ability to alter speech. In addition, the keys held by Archangel Vachiar reinforce the dynamics of expression and strengthen the students' defence against the imposition of adverse transmissions. The light-emitting disc of Virgin Mary surrounds the dynamics of expression with a vibration of love and caring pervasiveness.

In the light-emitting disc we receive, whenever we travel to planet Uranus, is included the seminal energy of both Uranus and Earth, meaning the primordial knowledge and creative speech. This disc, which also concerns the planet's future evolution and development, carries microscopic seeds of sound-pulses which it transmits to the centres of speech of other men.

It operates independently, spreading over a wide range seeds of creation, of ideas and change, which will materialise in the future during the new Atlantean age and which will constitute and compose the foundations and bases for the meta-humans.

During the mutation of the heart centre, Phelathros administers the key that is responsible for evolving the purpose of life within the students whereas Eloim, Zochriel and Ihran position detecting cubes in this centre responsible for automatically recording all the diseases the physical body had succumbed to. Moreover, the gifts offered by Labriel produce an opening towards the solar and universal knowledge. Thus, the trainees become communicants of knowledge that concern universal dimensions.

What is more, when the mutation of the heart centre is performed on the Pink planet, the genitors provide certain keys which allow the emergence of certain points in the students' lives during which they are permitted together with their Higher Self to outline, form and create a new plan. What also should be noted here is that the vibrations of Archangel Samuel alter in a positive way the scenarios of other chosen people as well.

When the mutation of the solar plexus is performed special disc keys are inserted through which novel DNA is transferred. The key offered by goddess Earth deletes the older recordings from the planet's cellular memory, eliminating it from the five sub-dimensions (the Akashic fields, aether, fire, water, and earth). The keys given by Arion and Aethra contribute towards the better understanding of problems; assist in dealing with toxic behaviour and in general in helping discern the syntonization required for a positive development and unfoldment of the students' course.

During the mutation of the genital centre, Virgin Mary presents people with a key which attracts births of a superior type; Irian presents a key to people responsible for the opening up of creation, while Robial a light-transmitting disc key that upgrades the gates (wombs) of women. In addition, the Atlantean goddess offers a lazuline crystal which she connects to the genital disc by means of golden fibres. This latter gift is responsible for regulating the new plan as far as creation and abundance are concerned and also prepares the awakening of the kundalini power.

During the final alignment, the genitor named Alvatar inserts into all the centres microscopic silverfish-white light-transmitting discs whose vibrations activate the consciousnesses of men who are usually found working in key sectors and positions. Thus, in the next few decades powerful and significant changes will ensue on the planet and materialise in various and differing fields. The trainees will possess the potential to observe these changes because of the higher psychic constitution that exists now in their archives.

During the christening initiation, Prodromos inserts into the genital centre a disc key that seals off reincarnations and activates the required gates through which the descent of the crystal children will be realised. Simultaneously, Apollo places into the heart centre a key responsible for the rapid assimilation of the new plan and activation of the life plans of other people as well.

In the same initiation, the Atlantean goddess inserts in the hypophisis an extra key that activates a special and distinct type of lucidity to assist in better and proper discrimination between the real causes of events.

In the chrism of Archangel Michael, Athena activates Michael's weapon using a symbol key that reinforces the power of thought, perception, intelligence and distinction. Arion inserts a key that activates the students' weapons rendering them capable of dealing with their own toxic lessons, while it simultaneously empowers them by bestowing upon them the power of defending and protecting themselves. Additionally, the Archangels of justice present them with the crystal pyramid of conscience that concerns the existence of justice on all levels.

The vibrations that are transferred during the initiation of the Holy Marriage seal higher intellect and superior mentality. By using his sceptre Master Metatron during this initiation activates the crystals that the entities have already placed in all the energy centres.

Thus, in the epiphysis an apollonian opening appears, and in the hypophisis a transmutation of neurons takes place, whereas a conversion in speech manifests itself in the throat. In the heart certain gifts and talents are activated, while in the stomach a development of positive vibrations occurs. In the abdominal area arises an opening towards fulfilling and accepting missions while in the genital success and grounding are initiated.

What has to be emphasized is that through the ritual of the Holy Marriage we acquaint ourselves with knowledge that forms part of a massive archive that concerns and contains information ranging from the energy birth of the planet to its condensation in the astral and etheric dimensions.

In the initiation of Artemis, goddess Earth provides us with a union key with which the students become capable of realising the planet's past with regard to the laws and properties of the Atlantean age. Virgin Mary offers a lazuline sphere of a double vibration which activates the comprehension of other people's emotions. Moreover, Aphrodite offers plates that open up planes of higher emotions and allow our access to them. With them the trainees become henceforth capable of distinguishing between dependence and sacrifice and between possessiveness and love. Archangel Samuel also gives a polymorphic crystal responsible for the creation of love that is infused with an angelic constitution.

In the initiation of Artemis, amorous relationships are clarified. Emotions stabilise and are filtered through, while people cease to be dependent. On the other hand, through the upgrading of love people experience both psychic and mental pleasure.

The initiation of Virgin Mary is administered by all the female entities that have walked upon the Earth since the beginning of the history of the planet. Thus, every chalice bears all the fundamentals and the properties of the various female deities.

During the christic initiation both mother Earth and the Atlantean goddess offer a special disc as a gift that not only develops the creation of matter and soul but also mutates the wombs of women to prepare them to bear crystal souls. Vibrations of a higher realization, lucidity, awakening and superior wisdom, are also channelled in the form of a plate. All these are crucial elements that contribute to the creation of new turning-points in life that reinforce the ability for a smooth and creative cooperation with the Higher Self. In addition, they are conducive to the mutation of the scenarios of other people that have also been chosen, though they may be totally unaware of it. Finally, these powerful vibrations activate the union between compatible soul-mates, who are further bonded with the energy of love of a higher degree.

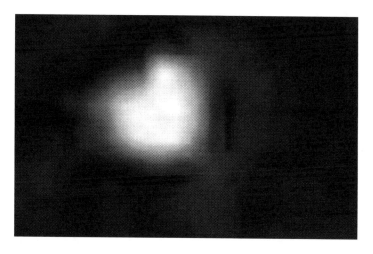

Orbit presenting a couple of entities shaping a heart

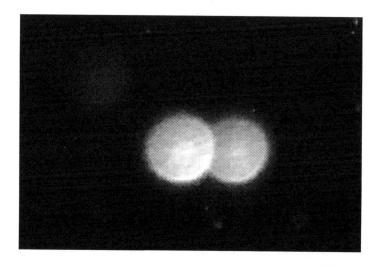

Double Vehicle

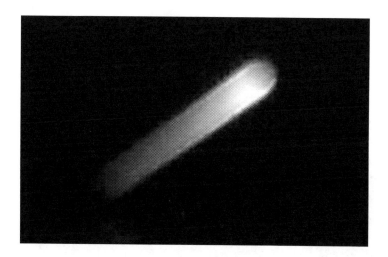

Moving Vehicle

EPILOGUE

With the writing of this book what I aspire to do is to offer people all the knowledge and the divine secrets that have been imparted to me during the higher communions I have had.

God is one and his Divine Laws are the same for all human beings. However, God does not intervene. He lets people be trained until their consciousness has expanded and they become capable of seeing the light.

During our time and age everyone can embark on this path of spiritual evolution and personal transformation and mutation, relying on their own powers.

Thus, my students having been relieved of their karmic debts and possessing a higher degree of both mentality and noesis are now capable of moving about on Earth as luminous spheres emitting the light of love and transformation.

Their vibrations activate the consciousnesses of other people, leaving behind them traces that form a path for the Meta-humans to follow and tread on.

What is portrayed in the pictures of my book is the reality of the Fifth dimension.

Each and every of my groups acquires a very clear and highly developed insight. As a result each and every trainee during the end of his apprenticeship and traineeship will possess images of and will have formed his/her own opinion concerning the wonderful planets of Nephelon galaxy.

MARIA ZAVOU

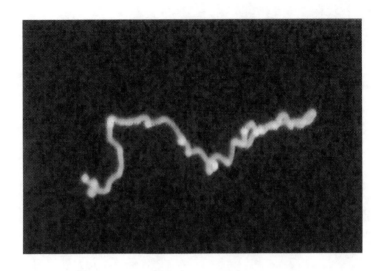

Neurotoxin

Orbit clearly presenting an angelic entity

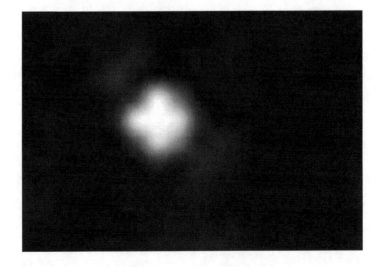

Crucifix – shaped orbit of two vehicles together

DEDICATION

With love I dedicate this book to God, whom I thank for the great gift he has offered to me.

In addition I dedicate it to my beloved students who operating as transformers of the energies deriving from the Fifth dimension have with their efforts and hard work assisted planet Earth a great deal. I wish that their light emitting discs would always activate the mission of other people and that they would spread over a wide area and distribute over a wide range the seeds of change and creation.

Finally I dedicate this book to all my readers who have appreciated the knowledge found in here and have explored it in depth and I would like to thank them for their love and response.

MARIA ZAVOU